TOPPING

TOPPING

THE AUTOBIOGRAPHY OF THE POLICE CHIEF IN THE MOORS MURDER CASE

Peter Topping
with Jean Ritchie

ANGUS
& ROBERTSON
PUBLISHERS

ANGUS & ROBERTSON PUBLISHERS

16 Golden Square, London W1R 4BN,
United Kingdom and
Unit 4, Eden Park, 31 Waterloo Road,
North Ryde, NSW, Australia 2113.

First published in the United Kingdom by
Angus & Robertson (UK) in 1989

Text copyright © Peter Topping 1989
Illustrations copyright © News Limited 1989,
unless otherwise stated

Designed by Roger King Graphic Studios, Poole.
Typeset in Great Britain by the Word Shop, Rossendale, Lancs.

Printed in Great Britain

British Library Cataloguing in Publication Data
Topping, Peter
   Topping: the police chief who discovered the
   truth about the moors murders.
   1. Northern England. Murderers: Brady, Ian,
   1938– & Hindley, Myra, 1942–
   I. Title
   364.1'523'0922

ISBN 0 207 16480 0

Contents

To Barbara, Susan and
Pamela

PART ONE

REOPENING THE MOORS MURDER FILE

1

It was a cold November day in 1986. We had driven 240 miles that morning, from Manchester, skirting London, to Rochester in Kent. After a quick lunch we drove up to the gates of Cookham Wood Prison. Now, in an interview room at the prison, I came face to face for the first time with a woman I would be seeing often over the next few months: Myra Hindley.

She was pale and slim, neatly dressed, not bearing the slightest resemblance to the defiant blonde woman in the official photographs taken twenty-one years earlier, and who had glared out from countless newspaper pages ever since. But I was not surprised by her appearance; I knew that I would be meeting a forty-four-year-old woman who had changed a great deal in her years in prison. Nor was I surprised that she greeted me politely – the prison staff had told me that she would.

But that was all they had told me to expect: they had said she would be calm, polite, but ultimately unhelpful. And that was why the meeting turned into the biggest – and most fortuitous – surprise of my whole career.

I became Head of CID (Operations) of Greater Manchester Police in early 1985. It was a busy and responsible job, and I was fully engrossed in it. Then that summer, a series of newspaper articles appeared written by a journalist who claimed that he had visited Ian Brady on several occasions, and that Brady had confessed to the murders of two youngsters, Pauline Reade and Keith Bennett. Brady was in prison for the murders of three other young people, and his partner, Myra Hindley, was also serving life for her part in those crimes.

The names of Pauline Reade and Keith Bennett had always been linked to theirs, but there was no proof that Brady and Hindley had anything to do with their disappearances – beyond the fact that Pauline and Keith both vanished at a time when Brady and Hindley were at large, and both lived in nearby areas of Manchester. That Brady was now claiming he had killed them understandably caused a stir; journalists visited the two families and the whole story, which had never been out of the headlines for long, was resurrected. The Home Office and the Director of Public Prosecutions contacted Greater Manchester Police to inquire what we were doing about this 'confession', and it was my responsibility to reply to them.

That is how I came to reopen the Moors Murders case, more than twenty years after the trial at which Brady and Hindley had been found guilty. I could have dealt with the inquiry quickly and superficially, but I realized that, at the very least, I was going to have to see Brady.

My first task was to contact Cheshire Police. The original investigation had involved five forces: Cheshire, Manchester City, Lancashire, Yorkshire and Derbyshire. Because the body of the final victim, Edward Evans, had been found in the Cheshire Police area they had been the 'host force', the one that had headed the inquiry. And it was at their headquarters in Chester that the file on the case was kept. Initially I had no intention of studying it in great detail – I just wanted to refresh my memory about the original investigation.

Like everyone else living in Manchester at the time of the Moors Murders, I had been horrified when the killings first came to light. Perhaps it affected me more than most. I came from the Gorton district, where Myra Hindley was born and grew up, and where she and Ian Brady lived during the earlier part of their killing spree. I knew Brady by sight: with his long black overcoat, dark spectacles and motorbike he was a familiar figure in the area. I was also a policeman; so I had seen my share of the rougher, tougher side of life in a big city like Manchester – but their crimes were outside the experience of even the most hardened policemen; there had been nothing like it before. And at the time of their arrest I was the father of a baby daughter, so like all parents I was deeply upset by the case.

11

But, also like everyone else , I found the whole story compelling. I remember that at a CID training course a year after the trial, one of the detectives involved in the case gave a lecture about it. We all sat there enthralled, hanging on every word.

I was particularly moved by the plight of the families of Keith Bennett and Pauline Reade, families who had never been allowed the relief, however sad, of knowing what had happened to their children. I had visited Mrs Reade as a young bobby on the beat – when a person is reported missing, the police call on the family every so often to check whether he or she has returned home; families often forget to share the news when youngsters reappear. It was a regular Sunday morning job, and I must have been one of many policemen who visited Pauline's family. Because she was older, at sixteen, than the other earlier victims of Brady and Hindley there had always been speculation that Pauline had run away from home, gone away with a boyfriend – even run away to Australia. Her grieving parents had never known any peace.

The expectations of both families had now been raised by journalists. They had been told that Brady had confessed to the murders of their children, and they were anticipating that somethimg would happen. They are decent, simple people, and in many ways forgotten people; yet they are also pestered people. Virtually every year since the Moors trial they had been upset and bothered by journalists picking over the story again.

So from the very beginning I saw the reopening of the case as a way, perhaps, to give some relief and comfort to those two families. I also knew that the Greater Manchester Police had two unsolved disappearances, possibly murders, on file, and that no matter how long ago it had all happened it was my duty to clear up those cases, if possible. There was also speculation that other killings might be laid at the door of Brady and Hindley, particularly that of a Yorkshire boy called Gilbert Dears, a borstal friend of Brady's, and I wanted to get to the bottom of that , too. Yet at the same time I had to think about the cost of reopening the case.

On 3 July 1985 the deputy head of Cheshire CID, Neville Jones, came with me to visit Brady at Gartree Prison in Leicestershire. I also took Detective Superintendent Jim Grant, who was in charge of the Operational Support Group. The prison authorities had been warned to expect us, but apart from that we thought the visit had been kept confidential.

Brady was not very keen to see us, and made this clear by refusing to leave his cell. He was in a dreadful state. I had heard reports that his mental and physical condition had deteriorated in prison, but I was not prepared for what I saw. He was emaciated, his face drawn and gaunt, his eyes bulging, and he looked extremely ill. He was up and dressed, in a sweater and trousers, but he was in a shocking physical condition. He was clearly very agitated and excited. He was also hyper-active, constantly walking about the cell, unable to sit still.

It was impossible to have a normal conversation with him. He was abusive – not to us personally, but towards the world in general, and kept sounding off about all sorts of things in a distressed and angry way. I felt he was in need of expert medical help.

He began by saying 'I don't want to see you.'

Ignoring this, I asked if he had read the newspaper article that claimed he had confessed; he said he had. I asked him if it was true to which he replied:

'I've written to my solicitor about them.'

I asked him again if it was true, but all he said was, 'Go away.'

It was obvious we weren't going to get very far with him that day. He was scornful of any suggestion that he had confessed to more murders, and swore a few more times. The prison authorities are under a statutory obligation to protect the prisoners in their charge, who have the right to refuse to see visitors, even the police. We had been with Brady only a matter of minutes, and achieved nothing. However, I was not despondent when we left; not one of us felt the door had been closed in our faces forever. As an investigator used to interviewing people I felt that, given the time to develop a relationship with Brady, I might persuade him to talk.

13

Then I had my first taste of something that was going to be a major factor in my life over the coming months. The press had been tipped off that we had visited Brady, and reporters and photographers were waiting for us as we came out. We said nothing – there was genuinely nothing to say.

But when I was asked if I was going to start searching on the Moors, I answered emphatically, 'No.' I could see no point in it. I knew just how vast and inhospitable those Moors were, and the idea of digging for bodies on them seemed ludicrous.

I went ahead and arranged through the Home Office another visit to Brady. By this time Cheshire Police had agreed that it was a Manchester case, as we were investigating the disappearance of two Manchester children, so I went with a detective chief inspector from my own force.

This time Brady refused point blank to see me. There was nothing I could do about it. It was not entirely unexpected, but it was certainly a disappointment. I knew that since his conviction other senior detectives had tried to interview him and achieved nothing, and I had been realistic about my own chances being slight. But there had been hope: and even now I didn't rule him out, as I knew that in his precarious mental state much would depend on how he was feeling at the moment when he was approached.

At this point I could have closed the case. I had ascertained that Brady denied ever making any confessions to the murders, and I had satisfied myself that I was unlikely to get anything more from him. I could easily have sent the Home Office and Department of Public Prosecutions a report setting out those facts and putting the Bennett and Reade families back in the limbo where they had been for years.

I thought about it for a long time, and in the end I felt it was my responsibility to do more. I knew that if I didn't, nobody else would – it was already more than twenty-three years since the disappearance of Pauline Reade: people were getting older and their memories were fading.

There had been a tremendous response to the news that I had visited Ian Brady. Hundreds of members of the public had written or telephoned police headquarters, most of them claiming to have seen Brady and Hindley on the Moor during the years that the murders were being committed. We had to check out all their claims, and to do that with any authority we had to know all there was to know about the original investigation, which meant reading files that filled several huge boxes.

At this stage I decided to set up a small inquiry team to work closely with me. I have always preferred small committed teams, in which every member knows what is going on, to big operations with detectives being asked to carry out inquiries whose significance they do not necessarily appreciate. I chose two men with whom I had not worked closely before, but whose reputations made me believe they would be perfect for the job – and I was right. Detective Inspector Geoffrey Knupfer and Detective Sergeant Gordon Mutch were both experienced detectives working in the Serious Crimes squad, dealing with murder and other major offences. I knew that they were both good at paperwork, skilled at investigation, sensitive and able to cope with a lengthy inquiry that might not show instant results.

Geoff, I had heard, had many fine qualities: he had been a detective sergeant for years and knew his job inside out. I knew that Gordon had worked with distinction on an internal inquiry outside the Manchester force area. I was sure that they would both be hard-working, loyal and discreet. This last quality was important: I had already had a taste of just how interesting this inquiry was to the media, and I didn't want any leaks jeopardizing it. It was no great secret that the inquiry team had been set up, but it was vital – and would become more so over the months – that the exact direction of our work remained confidential.

Our first job was to go over the original investigation in detail. Over the years a great deal had been written about the case, and a great many theories put forward. But it was all speculation and research by journalists and writers; I wanted to go back to the police investigation. I decided we should also interview as many of the policemen who had worked on the

15

original case as possible, together with the other witnesses who had given evidence at the trial.

It was as Geoff, Gordon and I began to plough our way through the files that I began to change my mind about searching on the Moors. There was not a lot in the file about the disappearances of Pauline Reade and Keith Bennett, as the original case against Brady and Hindley had been constructed round the murders of John Kilbride, Lesley Ann Downey and Edward Evans. But there were hundreds of photographs in the files – photographs taken by Brady on his visits to the Moors. I realized that, if it had been possible for detectives working on the case all those years ago to locate the areas of the graves from the photographs, it should be possible for us to do the same thing today.

I knew that part of the defence put forward at the trial had been that pictures taken near the site of Lesley Ann Downey's grave had nothing to do with her murder because they had been taken before her death – and the defence claimed this could be proved from the clothes she was wearing in the pictures. But perhaps those photographs could be a pointer to Pauline Reade's grave, since Pauline had disappeared eighteen months before Lesley Ann was killed.

At that stage we were working on the belief that all the victims had been murdered somewhere else, and then driven up to the Moors to be buried. It is rough ground for walking over at the best of times; carrying a body it would be much more difficult. So we worked on the premiss that the victims would be buried within a hundred yards of the road, just as John Kilbride and Lesley Ann Downey had been.

The more we studied the file, the more convinced we became that it might be possible to find burial sites from the photographs. But we faced a problem that the original Moors team had been spared: after twenty-three years, what would remain of a body buried up there? Lesley Ann, buried in peat, had been nearly perfectly preserved when her body was found ten months after it had been buried. One arm, exposed, had been damaged by animals, but that was all. John Kilbride, on the other hand, had been in the earth for nearly two years and his body was badly decomposed.

16

But we knew that that was because he had been buried in a stream bed, not because he had been underground longer. What we needed was expert advice.

So I went to Leeds to meet Dr Mike Green, at the time of the original investigation a very young pathologist assisting Professor Gee, who performed the post mortems. Professor Gee himself was ill, but Mike, now a Home Office pathologist working at Leeds University, was very helpful and enthusiastic. Would there, I asked him, be any chance of discovering identifiable remains of bodies buried over twenty years ago? And if so, would it be possible for trained dogs to sniff them out? His answer was optimistic. He explained that if the body had been buried in peat it could have been well preserved, and because of the degeneration of tissue into 'adiposia', a fatty substance, it would give off an odour that a dog could detect. I recalled the remarkable discovery of Lindow man, a 2500-year-old body found two years earlier, perfectly preserved in peat, just a few miles away in Wilmslow, Cheshire.

In the meantime I had asked the Home Office Research and Development branch if any new techniques had been developed in the last twenty years that would help us in the search for bodies. Unfortunately none of the techniques used nowadays in archaeology – sub-surface radar, aerial photography and so on – was thought likely to help. But dogs, it seemed, could be very useful. In 1965, when the police originally searched the Moors, there were no dogs trained in the detection of buried bodies. But since then a lot of work had been done with them. Although Greater Manchester Police did not have any dogs trained in this way, West Yorkshire Police did – and some of the areas of the Moors that I wanted to search were in West Yorkshire. So I obtained permission from them to carry out the search, and 'borrowed' their dog handler Neville Sharpe and his collie.

During the summer of 1986 Neville, dressed in plain clothes and working as unobtrusively as possible, searched the Hollin Brow Knoll and Shiny Brook areas of Saddleworth Moor. It could not be a systematic search because that would have aroused attention. He drew a blank. We also searched areas not on Saddleworth, but where Brady had been a regular visitor.

We knew from photographs that woods at Whaley Bridge in Cheshire were one of his favourite haunts; that knowledge was supported by evidence given by David Smith, Myra Hindley's brother-in-law and the man responsible for turning Brady and Hindley in to the police. And among our many letters and phone calls from the public was one very detailed siting of Brady and Hindley at Whaley Bridge.

David Smith had talked about one occasion when Brady had wandered off through the woods on his own, and I knew that the graveyard of Taxal church was thereabouts. I wondered, as others have done, if Brady had been interested in Devil worship. (People had noticed that the Ordnance Survey map reference for the part of Saddleworth Moor we were looking at contained the number 666, supposedly the Devil's number.) So I asked Neville to take his dog through the woods and the graveyard. But he drew another blank.

It was obvious that a more systematic search was needed. We felt that after this we could fairly say we had tried everything. We sensed more and more strongly that the bodies were on the Moors in the areas we had pinpointed, and that it would be wrong to give up searching for them at this stage.

In the meantime, Ian Brady had been moved from Gartree Prison to Park Lane Hospital in Liverpool, a secure mental institution for prisoners. It was what he wanted: he had argued for years that he should be in hospital, not in prison. Having seen him, I felt it was the right decision.

Shortly after he was transferred I visited Dr Malcolm McCulloch, the Medical Director of Park Lane, and Dr Hunter, who was supervising Brady's case. I explained that I was reopening the Moors case, and that there would be publicity. I asked to see Brady when he was fit enough – which at that stage he was not.

Brady had been on my mind a great deal. I had been puzzling over what made him tick, and trying to work out strategies to get him to co-operate. I wondered what effect the publicity surrounding the reopening of the search would have on him. I felt it could go either way: he might close the door on me forever, or he might feel that, as something positive was being done, it was the right time for him to confess.

Preparations for the search went ahead. We decided to tackle a two-and-a-half-mile stretch of Moor, going in from the road a hundred yards. The piece of land was divided into a number of hundred-yard sections, each of which would be searched by a dog, and then the search repeated with another dog. It was November and it was cold, but not too cold, and we hoped to get three or four weeks' searching completed before the weather closed in.

The press found out what was being planned, and the exercise received an enormous amount of coverage. I was surprised. Until then my only contact with the press, apart from the Stalker affair, had been confined to the odd press conference on a major crime inquiry. But suddenly everyone seemed to want to know about me personally. I came in for a lot of criticism – I wasn't surprised about that because I had initially thought that searching the Moors was a pointless exercise. I could not explain to the media why I was doing it now, so I simply had to ride the storm. I had of course, kept my immediate boss, Assistant Chief Constable Ralph Lees, informed all the way along, and he in turn had briefed the Chief Constable, James Anderton. I had their full support. But it was a strange experience to be attacked on all sides and to be unable to speak up in my own defence.

I had already made inquiries about the chances of persuading Myra Hindley to talk, and I had been told in no uncertain terms that I was wasting my time. She had resolutely protested her innocence all the years she had been in prison.

There had been newspaper reports that at one time, in the early part of her imprisonment in Holloway, she had had a temper tantrum and publicly shouted about the murder of Pauline Reade. The source of the reports was a woman who worked as a nurse in Holloway at that time, and who said the violent outburst was also witnessed by two other prisoners, the spies Helen Kroger and Ethel Gee. Neither could offer any corroboration – Ethel Gee is dead, and Helen Kroger and her husband are living behind the Iron Curtain, having being exchanged in 1969 for Gerald Brooke. But I did interview the nurse, Doreen Wright.

Although the outburst sounded uncharacteristic of Myra Hindley, I felt that Mrs Wright was a truthful person, not someone who was merely seeking publicity. She had been genuinely troubled by what she believed she had heard – although subsequently the details she claimed to have heard about the killing of Pauline Reade proved to be completely wrong. Still, at the time it gave me a small hope that Myra Hindley was perhaps not as impenetrable as everyone seemed to think.

Before I saw either her or Brady, I contacted the DPP to discuss the possibility of a further prosecution, if either of them did confess. I wanted to know if it was possible to offer them immunity from prosecution. My view was that they were already serving life, they were highly unlikely to be released in the foreseeable future, if ever, and that I had two grieving families to consider. I felt that Myra Hindley might be prepared to help if I could offer her immunity – Brady was unlikely to be influenced by it, because in his state of health he is never going to be released. But the DPP was unequivocal: there could be no immunity. Brady and Hindley had to be treated exactly like any other murder suspects.

So I went to see Myra Hindley empty-handed. I went without much hope, regarding the trip with Geoff Knupfer to Cookham Wood as little more than routine. But I had given quite a lot of thought to how I would approach her. At the time of the original investigation she had been questioned by a number of outstanding detectives, including Detective Chief Inspector Joe Mounsey from Lancashire Police, a brilliant interrogator. She had not cracked. She had been through a trial which had made headlines around the world, and had remained stony-faced and unhelpful even under skilled cross-examination. Brady had tripped himself up a couple of times in the witness box, but she had given nothing away. She had been in prison for twenty-one years, and it appeared to have had no effect on her. Whereas Brady's physical and mental health had broken down, she seemed to be as strong as ever. She had also, since her conviction, been interviewed by detectives to try to get her to confess. They had all come away disappointed.

I knew therefore that there would be no point in going to Cookham Wood, cautioning her, and then demanding that she tell all about the murders of Pauline Reade and Keith Bennett. That tack would get nowhere. I would probably get nowhere anyway, but I was prepared to give it a go. I decided not to caution her – I would not speak aggressively and accusingly to her, and, crucially, I would not ask her to confess. I would simply point out to her that I believed Ian Brady was responsible for the disappearances of Pauline and Keith; that I knew he was in the habit of taking Hindley on to the Moors and photographing certain places, and that therefore I would be grateful if she would help us by looking at maps and photographs to try and locate places that were of special interest to Brady.

It would be a reasonable request, put to her politely. She was on record as saying that she now believed Ian Brady was guilty of the Moors Murders (she had said it in her parole application to the Home Office in 1979). She would, I was convinced, either prevaricate or be openly unhelpful – but it would be harder for her to refuse to help than if I went in heavy-handed. So that was how I approached her when she walked into the interview room at Cookham Wood Prison on Monday 17 November 1986.

2

The Moors Murders case began, for the police, with a phone call from a public callbox on the Hattersley overspill council estate, near Manchester, at ten past six on the morning of 7 October 1965. A frightened young man stammered out a message that would start the most sensational murder investigation this century. Five minutes after the call, a police car drew up outside the phone box and the terrified young man – clutching a screwdriver and a carving knife for protection – and his equally terrified wife were driven to Hyde Police Station. There they told their story to police officers who had no idea just how important it was all going to be.

The young man was David Smith. He was seventeen. His nineteen-year-old wife, Maureen, was Myra Hindley's sister. Over the previous months David and Maureen had become very close to Myra and the man she lived with, Ian Brady – close enough to spend many hours in their company, drinking wine, going for drives up to the Moors, borrowing books and records from them. David Smith, young, naïve and impressionable, listened in awe while the older man – Brady was twenty-eight at the time of his arrest – talked about politics, religion, crime, murder. They practised with guns together on Saddleworth Moor, and stayed up into the early hours plotting bank robberies. Brady bragged about how easy it was to murder someone and get away with it.

David Smith came from a very poor background. He could not remember his mother. He had been brought up by his grandparents – calling them Mum and Dad, and not being told until years later that they weren't – with occasional visits from his father, who would arrive smelling of beer. But his father quarrelled with his grandmother, and when he was nine years old the boy was dragged away from her to live in squalid lodgings. His father was frequently not there, and the young – and deeply disturbed – boy was left to grow up on the streets. He became, inevitably perhaps, what used to be termed a 'juvenile delinquent'; by the time he was ten he was smoking, by eleven he was drinking, and at eleven years and nine months he had his first conviction, for wounding with intent. More convictions followed: at fourteen he was charged with assault causing actual bodily harm; and at fifteen with housebreaking and larceny. He was a street fighter and a thief – but he was not a murderer.

He married Maureen Hindley after getting her pregnant when he was sixteen and she eighteen. Her family were horrified. David Smith's lodgings were just a couple of streets away from the Hindley's home – and next door but one to a young girl called Pauline Reade, who was a sixteen years old.

Gorton was a poor district, and the area where the Hindleys and David Smith lived was one of the poorest. There was some heavy industrial work to be had, and in the sixties there were plenty of office and factory jobs about. But David Smith did not keep any job for long. He was known locally as trouble, whereas the Hindleys were a respectable family.

When Maureen was born Myra was four years old; she moved to live round the corner from her parents, with her grandmother. It wasn't a major family split because the two houses were very close, and Hindley divided her time between both places. The houses were two-up-two-downs with no bathrooms and out-side lavatories. Families used to bathe once a week in tin baths in the kitchen. Hindley's father, Bob, was partially crippled when he was injured at work, and was usually seen by the neighbours limping to and from the Steelworkers pub, no more than a hundred yards from their home. Her mother, Hettie, was a hard worker. Hindley's parents did not get on well, and shortly after her arrest they were divorced. But it was a normal childhood, with plenty of affection being shown to her by her Gran, Mrs Ellen Maybury, and her mother. She was also, despite the four years' difference in their age, very close to her sister, whom she called Mo or Moby.

Ian Brady's background was very different – but nowhere near as tough or as cruel as David Smith's. Brady was the illegitimate son of a Glasgow waitress, living in a rented room in the Gorbals, the city's notorious slum area. He was christened Ian Duncan Stewart. When he was still a baby his mother fostered him out to a family whom she knew, the Sloans. John and Mary Sloan had two sons and two daughters of their own, all older than Ian. They were happy to take him in, and he took the name Sloan.

Like Hindley, he had a good and loving home background. He was treated as one of the family, and never made to feel any different from Mrs Sloan's own children. His mother visited him at weekends, and when he was old enough to understand he was told that the Sloans were not his real parents. Like David

23

Smith, however, he grew into a difficult adolescent, getting into trouble with the law for housebreaking. Unlike Smith, he did not get involved in street fights or other violence. But by the time he was thirteen he was appearing before the juvenile court, and before he left school at fifteen he had two convictions. The Sloans, a law-abiding family, were baffled, but they remained supportive and he continued to live with them. On his third appearance in court, three weeks before his seventeenth birthday, there were nine charges against him, and his family were sure that he would get a custodial sentence.

But the Glasgow courts saw a way out of their predicament that would not involve filling a Scottish prison with yet another wayward teenager. They put him on probation, and they made one of the conditions of his probation that he should live with his natural mother. By this time, his mother had married an Irishman called Pat Brady and moved away from her native Glasgow to live in Manchester. So Ian Stewart/ Sloan caught a train in Glasgow and got off in Manchester with a new name: Ian Brady.

He continued to skirmish with the law, and a year after arriving to live with his mother he was sentenced to two years' borstal training, again for stealing. He was originally sent to Hatfield in Yorkshire, a borstal for above-average-intelligence offenders with relatively small criminal records. But he got into trouble there for brewing his own alcohol and getting drunk, and was transferred to the much tougher Hull borstal, where he met youths who were already on their way to becoming hardened criminals.

When he returned home to Manchester he lived with his mother and step-father again, and managed to stay out of trouble. He had had a series of dead-end jobs before, but when he was twenty-one he studied book-keeping and got a job as a clerk with a small company called Millwards that supplied chemicals, mostly to the cotton industry.

Myra Hindley, too, drifted from job to job when she left school at fifteen. She had learned shorthand and typing, so it was not difficult for her to find work. Although she had been bright at school – she was always in the top stream of Ryder Brow Secondary Modern – she had been very bad at attending, and she had the same problem at work. In fact, it was her chronic absenteeism that cost her one job.

When she was eighteen she started work as a typist at Millwards. She met Ian Brady on her first day there and, because he was one of the clerks who dictated letters to her, they were soon thrown into each other's company. Very quickly she became besotted by him. Brady looked different from most of the men she knew: he was always dressed smartly in a suit and collar and tie, and his hands did not look like the rough working hands of the men she knew from Gorton. He was good-looking, too, although he rarely smiled. But Brady, who had shown very little interest in girls up to then, ignored her, and this greatly increased her desire for him. Six months after she started work there she began to write a diary, to which she confided her longings:

23 July (1961: her nineteenth birthday) Wonder if Ian is courting. Still feel the same.
1 August Ian's taking sly looks at me.
2 August Not sure if he likes me, they say he gambles on horses.
8 August Gone off Ian a bit.
13 August Wonder what Misery will be like tomorrow?
14 August I love Ian all over again.
29 August I hope Ian loves me and will marry me some day.

It was all silly schoolgirl stuff, but it shows how deeply she was smitten by him. He cannot have failed to notice it, and it is remarkable that it took him until Christmas of that year to ask her out. Unlike him, Myra Hindley had been as interested in the opposite sex as any girl of her age, but she had only had one serious boyfriend, a lad called Ronnie Sinclair who worked for the Co-op and to whom she had been engaged. Hindley, although not pretty, was a striking-looking girl. She had been good at sport at school, and had a fit, athletic body. Her hair was dyed blonde and she wore a

25

lot of make-up, but that was the fashion in the early sixties.

When they did eventually go out together it was no conventional courtship. He took her to see films about the Nazi atrocities. He persuaded her to read the sort of books that interested him, books about torture and sadism – one of his favourite writers was the Marquis de Sade. Hindley was deeply impressed by Brady's use of long words and his intellectual arguments demolishing the existence of God and deriding religion; before long the girl who had become a devout Roman Catholic in her teens was rejecting God, denouncing marriage and cutting herself off from her friends and family. In court, less than four years later, her sister Maureen would describe the change:

> She used to go to church, liked dancing, she was quite normal, she liked the normal way of life and had many girlfriends. She liked children. She also liked swimming and reading. She stopped going to church. She said she didn't believe in it. She didn't believe in marriage. She said she hated babies and she hated people. She never used to keep her things under lock and key, but she started after she met Brady. She kept books, her tape recorder, all her tape recordings and all her clothes locked up in the wardrobe.

Although they did not know it at the time, the first involvement the police had with the Moors Murders case came more than two years before that frightened phone call from the callbox in Hattersley, when Mrs Joan Reade rang them early in the morning of 13 July 1963 to report her daughter Pauline missing. Pauline, a pretty sixteen-year-old with a wide smile, had gone on her own to a dance the previous evening – at least her worried parents believed she had been to a dance. Police enquiries soon established that, after leaving home at 7.30 p.m., in broad daylight, Pauline had vanished. She had not turned up at the dance at the Railway Workers' Social Club, nor had she spent the evening with any of her friends. There were rumours that she had run away to Australia with a fairground worker, but this didn't fit the picture of the home-loving, gentle girl who worked at the same bakery as her father, Amos. The police made extensive inquiries but were unable to come up with anything of any comfort to Mr and Mrs Reade. Joan Reade, devoted to her daughter, was unable to sleep or eat, and refused to lock her back door in case Pauline arrived home. It was twenty-four years before she knew for certain that Pauline would never come through that door again.

Four months later another youngster went missing. John Kilbride, a cheeky-faced twelve-year-old, spent the morning on Saturday, 23 November helping his elderly grandmother around the house and tidying her garden. He went home for lunch, to the council house in Smallshaw Lane, Ashton-under-Lyne, where he lived with his parents and six younger brothers and sisters.

In the afternoon he went to a local cinema with a friend, John Ryan, and afterwards the two boys went to Ashton market to earn a few pennies helping the stallholders. 'We went and fetched a trolley from the station for a man on the market. I got sixpence for this. John got about threepence or sixpence,' said John Ryan, a slight fourteen-year-old when he gave evidence against Brady and Hindley at Chester Assizes two and a half years later. 'Then we went to the man who sells carpets in the open market. There were two lads there, one from the same class as me. After I had some talk with them I decided to go home. When I set off to catch my bus John Kilbride was not with me. I last saw him beside one of the big salvage bins on the open market, near the carpet dealer's stall. There was no one with him.'

When John was not home by early evening, Sheila and Patrick Kilbride checked at the homes of relatives and friends and then called the police. A massive search was launched. Over seventy statements were taken and five hundred posters, with a big picture of gap-toothed John grinning from them, were distributed. Eight days after his disappearance, on a bitterly cold Sunday, two thousand volunteers combed every scrap of waste land and every derelict building for

27

miles around, while police dragged canals. Nothing was found. But, unlike Joan Reade, Sheila Kilbride would not have to wait half a lifetime for news of her son.

The next child to go missing was another twelve-year-old, Keith Bennett. He disappeared on his way to his grandmother's house, seven months after John went missing. Keith's mother Winnie, recently remarried to Jimmy Johnson, watched him walk along Eston Street, Longsight and into Stockport Road as she made her way to a local bingo hall. It had been arranged that Keith, the oldest of four children Mrs Johnson had at the time, would spend the night with his grandmother, as he did every alternate Tuesday.

Keith had broken his glasses at school, so his mother watched anxiously as he crossed the busy main road at the zebra crossing. The first that she knew about his disappearance was when her mother came round the following day and asked why Keith had not come to stay. They both panicked when they realized he had been at neither home. After checking at his school, Mrs Johnson called the police.

There was no trace of Keith. As part of their extensive inquiries the police brought in his stepfather for questioning four times in the next two years, they took up the floorboards in the house, and they inspected under the concrete of the backyard. Jimmy Johnson bears these officers no grudge: he appreciates that they wanted to be as thorough as they could in difficult circumstances. Despite rumours connecting their son with the Moors case, like Mr and Mrs Reade the Johnsons had to wait more than twenty years for positive news of what had happened to Keith.

The following Christmas, another child went missing. By then Myra Hindley, Granny Maybury and Ian Brady, who was now living with Hindley, had been moved from Gorton as part of a slum clearance programme, into a three-bedroomed terraced house on a huge Manchester overspill housing estate at Hattersley in Cheshire – on the way to their beloved Moors. Brady and Hindley were still working at Millwards, travelling to work in a Mini Traveller that Hindley now owned.

Three months after they moved there, Lesley Ann Downey disappeared. It was Boxing Day, 1964. The ten-year-old girl went, with her two younger brothers, from the family's council house in the Ancoats area of Manchester to a funfair ten minutes' walk away in Miles Platting. The little boys came home, Lesley Ann did not.

By ten o'clock that night, her mother Ann and Alan West, the man who would have been Lesley's step-father had she lived, and her older brother Terry had tramped the streets of Ancoats and Miles Platting in an ever-growing frenzy of anxiety. The police were called, and over the next few days the funfair was ripped apart, the showmen's caravans were searched and hundreds of people were interviewed. There was massive publicity about the case, and for weeks after she vanished there were reported sightings of Lesley Ann in Morecambe, Blackpool, Torquay, Bournemouth and even Belgium.

Her mother lost the baby she was carrying. But she, of all the children's mothers, would have the shortest wait for news of her child – just ten harrowing months, followed by a lifetime of consuming bitterness towards the killers of her daughter. But Lesley Ann Downey was not the last victim of Brady and Hindley.

It was at this time, in the early months of 1965, that Ian Brady was getting particularly friendly with David Smith. Perhaps he had tired of having only Hindley as his devoted admirer, and needed more attention and adulation. The naïve teenager certainly gave him that, turning to Brady as a father figure for advice in his constant financial crises. Smith and his wife, whose baby daughter had died, were living close to Brady and Hindley in a flat on the Hattersley estate.

What happened on the night of Wednesday, 6 October, 1965 is probably best described in David and Maureen Smith's own words, as told to the police and the court. Maureen said it was about 11.30 p.m. when her sister arrived at their flat. She and David were in bed, but she got up and let Hindley in.

Myra asked if I would give a message to my mother. She said to tell her she'd see her tomorrow. I asked her why she'd come round so late. She said she'd forgotten to come round earlier on. She asked David if he would walk her home because all the lights were out. David said he would walk her home and would only be a couple of minutes. He took the dog's stick with him. It was something he normally did.

David continues the story:

We got almost to Myra's house. I intended to leave her there, then she said, 'Ian has some miniature wine bottles, come and collect them now.'

As we got to the front door Myra stopped walking and she said, 'wait over the road, watch for the landing light to flick twice.' I didn't think this was unusual because I've had to do this before, whilst she went in to see if Ian would have me in. He's a very temperamental sort of fellow.

I waited across the road as Myra had told me to, and then the light flicked twice so I walked up and knocked on the front door. Ian opened the front door and he said in a very loud voice for him, he normally speaks so soft: 'Do you want those miniatures?' I nodded my head to say yes and he led me into the kitchen which is directly opposite the front door, and he gave me three miniature bottles of spirits and said, 'Do you want the rest?'

When I first walked into the house the door to the living room, on my right, was closed. After he'd put the bottles down Ian went into the living room and I waited in the kitchen. I waited about a minute or two and then suddenly I heard a hell of a scream; it sounded like a woman, really high-pitched. Then the screams carried on, one after another really loud. Then I heard Myra shout, 'Dave, help him,' very loud. When I ran in I just stood inside the living room and saw a young lad. He was lying with his head and shoulders on the couch and his legs were on the floor. He was facing upwards. Ian was standing over him, facing him, with his legs on either side of the young lad's legs. The lad was still screaming. He didn't look injured then, but there was only a small television light on, the big light was off. Ian had a hatchet in his hand, his right hand, he was holding it above his head and then he hit the lad on the left side of his head with the hatchet. I heard the blow, it was a terrible hard blow, it sounded horrible.

The young lad was still screaming and he half fell and half wriggled off the couch on to the floor, on to his stomach. He was still screaming. Ian went after him and stood over him and kept hacking away at the young lad with the hatchet. I don't know how many times he hit the lad, but it was a lot, about the head, the neck, and the shoulders and that.

The lad was seventeen-year-old Edward Evans from the Ardwick area of Manchester. Brady, who could not deny being involved in the killing of Evans, would tell the court later that he had picked the youth up at Manchester Central Station and persuaded him to come back to his house in Hattersley with him and Hindley. Brady said the purpose of the visit, as far as Evans was concerned, was a homosexual encounter. He would also claim that David Smith was involved in planning the evening and taking part in the killing, after the two of them had agreed to 'roll a queer' for money to pay David and Maureen's rent arrears. But if that was the plan, Edward Evans was a poor choice: he was only an engineering apprentice, and even on pay day there would be little money in his wallet. And the accusations of homosexuality against Evans, made by Brady at the trial in 1966 when the world was a lot less liberated than it is today, were particularly cruel to the youth's family and possibly without foundation.

David Smith said he felt his stomach turn as he witnessed the violent attack on Evans. He described Brady as swinging the hatchet about, one blow grazing Myra Hindley's head. 'I was shaking. I was frightened to death of moving and my stomach was twisting. There was blood all over the place, on the walls, fireplace, everywhere.'

Brady wound a piece of electric flex around Evans' neck and pulled it tight, swearing and calling him a 'dirty bastard'. Smith said he heard strange gurgling noises coming from the youth. Then Brady turned to

Hindley, who had been standing in the room all the time, and said:

'It's done. It's the messiest yet. It normally only takes one blow.'

Then all three of them, Brady, Hindley and Smith, set about cleaning up the room. At some time during the screaming seventy-seven-year-old Granny May-bury, upstairs in bed since 8 p.m., had called down to ask what the noise was, and Hindley had told her that she had dropped a tape recorder on her foot.

Because Brady had sprained his ankle in the frenzied attack, they decided that they would not take the body up to the Moors for burial that night, but would wait until the following day. Smith would bring the pram that had belonged to his dead baby daughter to enable them to move the body. In the meantime they decided to wrap up the corpse and move it to a spare room upstairs. As they struggled with the unwieldy bundle. Brady made a joke: 'Eddie's a dead weight,' he said.

'Both he and Myra thought it was bloody hilarious,' Smith told the police next day. 'I didn't see anything to laugh about.'

After Brady and Smith moved the body, with Hindley holding Gran's door closed just in case the old lady decided to wander out, they all sat around drinking tea, planning the burial. Hindley and Brady discussed another occasion when they had taken a body up to the Moors.

'Do you remember that time we were burying a body on the Moors and a policeman came up?' said Myra. 'I was in the Mini with a body in the back. It was partitioned off with a plastic sheet. Ian was digging a hole when a policeman came and asked me what the trouble was. I told him I was drying my sparking plugs and he drove off. I was praying that Ian wouldn't come back over the hill whilst he was there.'

David Smith said he went along with them – helping with the cleaning up and pretending to relish the night's work as much as they obviously did – out of sheer terror. He feared he would be Brady's next victim. When at three o'clock in the morning, they told him to go home, he ran all the way, fearful that Brady would come after him. He woke Maureen, told her what had happened, and together decided to go to the police as soon as it was daylight. That was how the terrified couple came to be in the callbox in Hattersley, armed with a screwdriver and a carving knife in case Brady found them, in the early hours of the next day.

After listening to the youth's incredible story, the police did not know what to make of it. He talked about guns, bodies buried on the Moors – it all sounded like something out of a late-night horror movie. But they certainly took him seriously, and at twenty past eight that morning Superintendent Bob Talbot of Cheshire Police knocked on the door of 16 Wardle Brook Avenue, wearing a bread deliveryman's white coat and carrying a basket of loaves. With Smith's warning about guns in mind, he had not wanted to turn up with his uniform on show.

Myra Hindley was ready to go to work, but Ian Brady with his injured ankle was in bed in the living room (he and Hindley always slept on a sofa bed downstairs) writing a note to excuse his absence to his boss at Millwards. The house was clean and tidy, and David Smith's story seemed all the more unbelievable.

But a search revealed Edward Evans' body in a locked room upstairs. Brady, who was immediately arrested, admitted that he and Evans had had a fight, but claimed that Evans' death was an accident. Hindley was also taken to the police station, but was not arrested for another five days. She was not allowed back into either her car or the house, but allowed to sleep at her aunt and uncle's home. Inside the car a slip of paper was found, containing a list of abbreviated words such as HAT, ALI and GN. The police were able to decipher these three as hatchet, alibi and gun, but some of the others baffled them.

Although loaded guns had been found at the house in Wardlebrook Avenue, there was nothing to connect Ian Brady with any murders other than that of Edward Evans until the discovery of an old exercise book. Scrawled among the names of film stars and Ian Brady's own name was one that made Cheshire Police realize the scope of the case: John Kilbride. John, the missing twelve-year-old from Ashton-under-Lyne, was on the files of the Lancashire Police, so now they too became involved in the operation. And if one missing child could be accounted for, what about others? Officers from the Manchester force soon arrived at Hyde Police Station, where Brady was being held. They had three unsolved disappearances to talk to him about: Pauline Reade, Keith Bennett and Lesley Ann Downey.

But talking to Brady was getting them nowhere. He would admit nothing, apart from his involvement in the death of Edward Evans. On 11 October, Myra Hindley was arrested and charged with being an accessory to the murder of Evans. If the detectives handling the case thought they might get more out of her, a woman, than they were out of her lover they soon learned otherwise. She resolutely said nothing, even under the fiercest interrogation.

A substantial collection of photographs, most of them scenic views but also some harmless-looking family snapshots of Myra Hindley, her dog or Ian Brady, were found at the house; many of them had been taken against a background that looked like Saddleworth Moor. David and Maureen Smith were taken up to the Moors to point out areas that Brady and Hindley had taken them to visit, but they found it difficult to remember exactly where they had been. Then came a breakthrough: Pat Hodges, an eleven-year-old girl who lived next door but one to Brady and Hindley, had been taken by them up to the Moors on several occasions. She proved to have a better memory for places than the Smiths, and was able to guide the police to the locations the couple were most fond of.

One hundred and fifty policemen were now drafted in to search the area thoroughly. Officers spent hours pouring over the photographs, trying to locate exact sites. Confirmation, when it came, was almost by accident, when a young policeman saw a bone sticking out of the peat. The search had unearthed many bones of dead sheep, but this was a human arm bone. Careful excavation unearthed the body of Lesley Ann Downey, naked and with her clothes piled at her feet. It was an appalling discovery, even though it justified the search and established beyond doubt the monumental proportions of the case.

David Smith had told the police that on the night before Edward Evans' murder, Brady and Hindley had taken two suitcases from the house. Detective Sergeant Jock Carr rang the British Transport Police and asked them to check left luggage offices. The cases were found at Central Station. Five days later Detective Chief Inspector John Tyrrell from Manchester Police searched the house in Hattersley again. In the spine of a small white prayer book, given to Myra Hindley by her aunt and uncle after her first communion, was a left luggage ticket. Suddenly the abbreviation TICK and PB from Brady's list were explained: ticket and prayer book.

The suitcases contained some horrific material: books about sexual perversion, a black wig and two coshes. There was also a tin with some photographs in it, but these were not more of Brady's scenic views of the Moors; there were pictures, all of Lesley Ann Downey naked. In some she was standing, in others lying on a bed. One was of her praying, and another was a back view with her arms spread wide.

As if that was not enough, there were two tapes. One contained some recorded radio programmes: *The Goon Show* and a programme about the rise of Adolf Hitler. It was a comment on Brady's tastes and interests, but nothing that was going to strengthen the case against him was heard until the tape reached the last track. It was to constitute perhaps the most notorious piece of evidence ever presented in a British court of law.

It starts with Ian Brady addressing the dogs (there were two living with them) brutally, telling them to get out of his way. That is followed by banging, heavy footsteps and other noises. Myra Hindley speaks, but her voice is too low to be able to tell what she says. There are more footsteps and more whispered conversation, until the air is ripped by the scream of a child.

From then on, for thirteen terrible minutes, the tape contains the sound of Lesley Ann Downey pleading for her life, screaming, struggling to breathe, retching. Her mother, distraught after identifying her daughter's body, had to listen to the tape and confirm that it was Lesley Ann's voice.

'Can I just tell you summat? I must tell you summat. Please take your hands off me a minute, please. Please – mummy – please . . . I can't tell you (grunting sounds) I can't tell you. I can't breathe. Oh . . . I can't . . . dad . . . will you take your hands off me?'

When she asks what they are going to do with her he tells her they are only taking photographs.

Myra Hindley can be heard repeatedly telling her to 'Hush' and to 'Put it in your mouth and keep it in.' At the beginning her voice is quite soothing, but she soon loses patience with the crying child. 'Shut up or I'll forget myself and hit you one. Keep it in,' she says.

Lesley Ann begs them not to undress her, and tells them she wants to go because she is going out with her mother. Brady, still trying to persuade her to put something in her mouth, says 'The longer it takes you to do this the longer it takes to get you home.'

But his persuasive tone soon evaporates and he says, 'Put it in. If you don't keep your hands down I'll slit your neck.'

When the child complains that her neck hurts, Myra Hindley tells her to 'shurrup crying'.

'Hush. Shut up. Now put it in. Pull that hand away and don't dally and just keep your mouth shut please . . . . Wait a minute, I'll put this on again. D'you get me?' She tells the little girl to 'put that in your mouth . . . packed more solid'.

The tape ends with Christmas music, a tune called 'Jolly St Nicholas' followed by the familiar 'Little Drummer Boy'.

Looking at the photographs of Lesley Ann Downey and hearing the tape, even twenty-one years later and even though we knew what to expect, came as a profound shock to Geoff Knupfer, Gordon Mutch and me. I can understand the hatred and anger the policemen on the original case must have felt towards Brady and Hindley, and admire their professionalism. They had to carry on investigating the case, despite being shocked rigid by the tape. Nobody who has ever heard it could fail to be deeply moved. It was obviously a very strong piece of evidence against them, and particularly against Myra Hindley. It put her, in the minds of those who heard it, on a par with Brady in terms of guilt. It showed just how deeply she was involved in everything that went on.

Shortly after the tape was discovered, another body was found: John Kilbride, buried on the opposite side of the A635 to Lesley Ann Downey. Detective Chief Inspector Joe Mounsey's persistence with the photographs paid off when he was able to identify from them the exact location in which to dig. The body had been buried in a stream bed, and was badly decomposed, but the clothes were clearly identifiable and there was no doubt about who it was.

Faced with the fresh evidence from the luggage office, Brady admitted to the police that he had taken pornographic pictures of Lesley Ann Downey. But he claimed that she was brought to his house by two men, and left there alive, with them. Although Myra Hindley showed some emotion when the tape was played – she cried and said she was ashamed – she quickly regained her composure and continued to state: 'I didn't do it. Ian didn't do it. I suggest you see Smith', a familiar litany to the policemen questioning her. The only other time that the police saw any emotional response from her was when they told her that her beloved dog, Puppet, had died under the anaesthetic during an attempt by a vet to determine its age by analysing its teeth (Puppet figured on quite a few of the moorland photographs, sometimes as a young puppy, so its age was crucial for dating visits by Brady and Hindley to the Moors). Unknown to anyone, the dog suffered from a kidney complaint. Its death made Myra Hindley furious, and she accused the police of being 'murderers'.

The search for bodies continued, but winter was drawing in and in November it was called off. By this time Ian Brady had been accused of three murders: Edward Evans, John Kilbride and Lesley Ann Downey. Myra Hindley had been charged with the murders of Edward Evans and Lesley Ann Downey, and with harbouring Brady after the murder of John Kilbride. David Smith's evidence and that of the tape was felt sufficient to charge her with two murders, but in the case of John Kilbride there was nothing to link her to the killing, except that she had driven Brady to the Moor (he never learned to drive). By the time the case came to trial, though, the prosecution had added the charge of murdering John Kilbride to her tally.

Before the main trial there was a committal – a rerun of the evidence in a magistrates' court to decide whether there was a case to be answered. The laws on committal proceedings have now been changed; in those days the prosecution in every case faced the ridiculous, and very expensive, prospect of presenting its case twice in full – first in the lower court and then at the trial proper. Today the time spent on committal has been restricted, the procedure simplified and press coverage usually limited. The Moors Murders committal was heard in public, with unrestricted reporting. The case had been making headlines around the world since the arrest of Brady and Hindley, and the turn-out of press and television people for the committal and then the full trial was phenomenal.

The trial was held at Chester Assizes, opening on 19 April 1966 and lasting fourteen days. The evidence was, of course, sensational, especially the tape recording, which was not heard in open court at the committal. The reliability of David Smith's evidence was called into question when it was revealed in court that he was in the pay of a newspaper – but in fact his evidence against Myra Hindley was less damning than the original statement he had given to the police, before any question of newspaper sponsorship arose.

Brady, whilst at pains not to incriminate himself, tried to help Hindley by painting her as his obedient lieutenant. When asked whose views would prevail in any discussion between them, he replied, 'Mine. She was my typist at the office. I dictated to her at the office, and this tended to wrap over.' They both tried to implicate David Smith, particularly in the killing of Lesley Ann Downey. The names of Keith Bennett and Pauline Reade were mentioned only once in court – by Brady, who made a reference to the police questioning him about them.

Brady gave evidence for eight and a half hours, Hindley for six. Neither took the oath on the Bible, preferring to affirm, in line with the atheistic views to which he had converted her. When asked about her feelings for Brady she said: 'I became very fond of him. I loved him – I still love him.'

Under questioning about the tape, she described her own attitude to Lesley Ann Downey as 'brusque and cruel', but she said it was because she was worried about anyone hearing the child screaming while Brady was trying to take pictures of her. Hindley faced a relentless barrage of questions about the tape, and about the moorland photographs. She denied knowing that any of the pictures had been taken near the graves of children. It was, by any standards, a fierce cross-examination, but she withstood it, stuck to her story and gave nothing away.

Inevitably, they were found guilty – Brady to all three murder charges, and Hindley to the murders of Edward Evans and Lesley Ann Downey. Although she was found not guilty of murdering John Kilbride she was found guilty of the lesser charge of harbouring Brady after the murder. Brady was given three life sentences, Hindley two, with seven years for harbouring.

The death penalty had been abolished during the months that they were imprisoned awaiting trial, so there was a predictable public outcry calling for its reinstatement. The couple spent one more night at Risley remand centre, where they had been held during the trial, and the following day Myra Hindley was taken to Holloway Prison and Ian Brady to Durham Jail.

In the months after the trial, five books were published about the Moors Murders. The case attracted more public interest than perhaps any other before or since. It was obviously gruesome, but it also had an added ingredient that made it fascinating: Myra Hindley. Most mass murderers operate alone, and women are very rarely associated with murder on a grand scale. Women do kill children, but usually their own; it is rare – probably unique – to find a woman involved in their random killing. Because of this interest Brady and

Hindley have never been long out of the headlines. Every switch from one jail to another, every important visitor, every clutch of anecdotes from fellow prisoners was guaranteed full coverage by the media.

Myra Hindley seemed to attract trouble. She caused a massive scandal when a governor of Holloway took her out for a walk on Hampstead Heath in 1972, and two years later she was in the dock at the Old Bailey charged with trying to escape from prison, a plot hatched with one of the prison officers who was her lesbian lover. She was given an extra twelve months, to be served at the end of her life sentence.

Over the years she has enjoyed the support of some distinguished people, perhaps the most notable being Lord Longford, who befriended her and Brady and has been outspoken on their behalf ever since. Until 1971 Brady and Hindley corresponded with each other, but by then Hindley had re-embraced the Catholic faith and repudiated his beliefs and philosophies, so she ended the correspondence.

Throughout her sentence she has protested her innocence, and has been able to convince many people around her that her role was merely that of Brady's dupe. She expressed this view at great length in a thirty-thousand-word document she wrote for the Home Secretary in 1979, depicting herself as an innocent, wronged young girl being savagely punished for crimes she had little to do with. It was a plea for parole, which was turned down. The public outrage at the mere suggestion that she might get parole was enormous.

Ian Brady, without ever admitting his guilt, has always eschewed the idea of parole. From time to time he has used the press to remind Myra Hindley of the hold he still has over her: the hold of knowing her full involvement in the murders, not just the ones of which they were convicted but also those of Pauline Reade and Keith Bennett. For instance, when Lord Longford complained that he had been 'conned' into talking to the Sunday Times about Myra Hindley, Brady wrote that Longford had indeed been conned, but not by the Sunday Times.

Interest in the case has never waned; by the mid-

1980s there was a fresh spurt of books about the case, and newspapers were finding fresh stories to write about one or other of the chief protagonists every week. It was against this background that the case was reopened.

3

At Cookham Wood Prison Myra Hindley was quiet while I talked about how I believed she could help me. Even if she was innocent of direct involvement in the deaths of Pauline Reade and Keith Bennett, I believed she had information that would be useful to the inquiry. I reminded her of the continuing public interest in the Moors case, despite the fact that it was more than twenty years since the trial, I told her what she must surely have realized: that fascination with the case would never wane until those missing bodies had been found and finally laid to rest.

I was about to start a systematic search of the Moors, I told her and I had good scientific reasons for believing that bodies buried there twenty or more years ago could still be intact – so whether she helped or not, I might well find them. I said that I would also be seeing Brady: I knew there was no love lost between them now, and I believed she might want to counter any help she thought he might give me. I was going to play a cat and mouse game between the two of them, and I knew I would have to be subtle and patient if I was to succeed.

Hindley listened very intently to everything I said. Her face was pale, and she chain smoked. She paused and thought deeply before she spoke, obviously evaluating everything she said in her well-spoken, very precise and meticulous way. She was not going to be outsmarted; she would never allow herself to be trapped verbally. If anything was to come of our meeting, it would be only when she believed it was in her interest.

I told her about the distress of the two families whose children were still missing, knowing that she had received a letter days earlier from Mrs Winnie Johnson, the mother of Keith Bennett. She told me about the letter, and I could see that it was troubling her a great deal. It was a hopeful sign: I felt that I already had my foot in the door.

The letter ran:

Dear Miss Hindley,

I am sure I am one of the last people you would have expected to receive a letter from. I am the mother of Keith Bennett, who went missing no-one knows where on June 16 1964. As a woman I am sure you can envisage the nightmare I have lived with, day and night, 24 hours a day, since then.

Not knowing whether my son is alive or dead, whether he ran away or was taken away is literally a living hell, something which you no doubt have experienced during your many, many years locked in prison. My letter to you is written out of desperation and faint hope, desperation because I know that for so many years neither you nor Ian Brady has ever admitted knowing anything about my son's disappearance, and hope that Christianity has softened your soul so much that you would never any longer knowingly condemn someone to permanent purgatory.

Please, I beg you, tell me what happened to Keith. My heart tells me you know and I am on bended knees begging you to end this torture and finally put my mind at rest. Besides asking for your pity the only other thing that I can say is that by helping me you will doubtless help yourself because all those people who have harboured so much hate against you and prevented you from being released a long time ago would have no reason left to harbour their hate. By telling me what happened to Keith you would be announcing loudly to the world that you really have turned into the caring warm person that Lord Longford speaks of.

I am a simple woman, I work in the kitchens of Christie's Hospital. It has taken me five weeks labour to write this letter because it is so important to me that it is understood by you for what it is, a plea for help. Please, Miss Hindley, help me.

Myra Hindley seemed to be genuinely moved by the letter, and said she would like to help. I had already told her I thought she should be legally represented when she spoke to me, and she agreed. So the prison authorities contacted her solicitor, Michael Fisher, and Geoff and I waited at Cookham Wood until he arrived.

It was to be the first of many meetings with him. My initial impression remained constant through all our dealings: he was young, enthusiastic and as helpful as he could be. I have learned since that he has a habit of taking on unusual cases, involving people accused of being members of the IRA and other terrorist groups. But I can judge him only on my experience in this case: he never hindered our investigation, and I feel that behind the scenes he played a very positive role in encouraging Hindley to co-operate with us.

I told them both I was not cautioning her, so that anything she said during the interview would not be admissible evidence in court. Then I went over the same ground we had covered earlier, and she began to tell me about places she had visited on the Moors with Brady. I was not taking notes, and I could not push her too hard, because I did not want to spoil our good start by now seeming aggressive.

We stayed with her until after 8 p.m. The prison authorities were very helpful, and gave me every opportunity: the staff here and at Park Lane, where Brady was held, proved to be an enormous asset throughout the long and difficult inquiry. Finally, after much discussion, Hindley agreed to look at photographs and maps of the Moors, to point out places that had been of particular interest to Brady, and we arranged to return the next day with them.

I had been warned that the press were outside, and had agreed Michael Fisher would give them a short statement saying that Myra Hindley was helping us. But as I walked to the car park I hadn't realized how many of them there would be. A whole battery of flash bulbs went off, and I was blinded for a few seconds by the intensity of the sudden light. Microphones were thrust in front of me and questions were shouted from all sides, and it was all that Geoff and I could do to get through to our car.

Looking back at the case now, I think it is impossible to overestimate the importance of that first meeting with Myra Hindley. It was from there that the success of the whole inquiry stemmed – and it could so easily have gone against us. I did not know it at the time, but she had gone beyond the point of no return. I had hoped, at best, that our visit to her would create publicity that would play on Brady's mind; in fact we achieved much more.

I believe she decided to co-operate for a combination of reasons – it certainly was not, as some newspapers insisted, because I offered her a deal, with immunity from prosecution. First, I think she was worried about Brady. He had already allegedly confessed to a journalist, she knew that his mental state was very precarious, and I feel she was concerned that he might at any moment decide to talk in detail to me. If there was any benefit to be gained – in terms of public approval – from being the one to help find the bodies, she wanted to make sure it was hers. Second, she knew we were about to search the Moors systematically concentrating on areas we had narrowed down from photographs, and she knew when I showed her where we would search that there was a chance we would find a body anyway. Third, she accepted that the case would never be out of the headlines while Pauline Reade and Keith Bennett were unaccounted for, and if she ever wanted parole – however far in the future – it was in her interests to clear the air now. She has always maintained that by co-operating she was not looking for personal advantage, and did not expect ever to get parole. But I am quite cynical about her motivation, and I believe she is hoping to be released one day. She is realistic enough to know that it won't be in the near future, but I believe she has hopes that in ten or fifteen years' time she may be free.

Fourth, there was the letter from Mrs Johnson – though I do not believe this was a very strong reason. I think if Hindley had been so moved by the plight of the families, she had had plenty of earlier opportunities to put them out of their misery. None the less, I had to

44

accept what she told me at face value; she did seem to be genuinely upset by the letter, and it is possible that she had only recently been able to face the truth of her guilt after years of shutting it out. When she talked to me about the letter she was troubled by it.

The fifth reason was the way we approached her. Being polite and unaggressive, not accusing her of anything and leaving her a way out – by allowing her to point the finger at Brady – seemed to me the best possible approach, and it caused her to lower her guard. It gave her the opportunity to let the public see she was helping us, but without implicating herself. During an interlude in our meeting when Myra Hindley was not present I remarked to Michael Fisher, 'I wasn't quite expecting that.' 'Nobody has approached her like that before,' he replied.

As we drove back to Manchester, the mood in the car was a mixture of exhaustion and elation. We knew we had achieved an enormous breakthrough, but we were frightened of counting our chickens before they hatched. Myra Hindley had said she would help us, but we had to wait until tomorrow to see if she really meant it.

It was another early start next day, and another long drive back to the prison. The newspapers were full of the story of our visit the day before and headquarters kept me in touch by radio phone with the many inquiries that came in during the day.

Myra Hindley showed particular interest in pictures of Hollin Brow Knoll and Shiny Brook, two areas of the Moors that we had already identified as top priorities. The Knoll, a rocky outcrop just a few yards from the road, was where Lesley Ann Downey's body had been found, but we were sure that many of the photographs of it had been taken before her death, and so of the possible locations for one of the other graves it was our front runner.

Shiny Brook is a stream that runs across the Moor, more or less parallel to the road but about three-quarters of a mile in. Because of the distance from the road it did not seem an ideal site for a grave, but we knew from the large number of photographs Brady had taken of it that it must have been one of his favourite places. Some of these pictures had been taken in the stream bed and others by a small waterfall that feeds the brook; many showed Myra Hindley. Going through the files we had discovered that Pat Hodges was not the only child Brady and Hindley had taken up on the Moors with them. Carol and David Waterhouse, also the children of neighbours in Hattersley, had been questioned during the original inquiry and taken up on to the Moors by the police to show them places they had visited with Brady and Hindley. But they had not been able to add anything new, so they had not had to give evidence at the trial. There were photographs of them taken at a man-made weir that filters water from Shiny Brook into a reservoir feeder stream. So that whole area was of enormous interest to us, and this was confirmed by Myra Hindley. She told us, however, that it was impossible to be sure of the locations favoured by Brady without going back to the Moor – which she said she was willing to do.

It was late when we left her again. The reception from the waiting journalists was huge, and their excitement became almost tangible when Michael Fisher told them that his client was willing to return to Saddleworth Moor. I would have liked all knowledge of a visit to have been kept secret, because press interest would make the organization a much more difficult task. But it was not my decision, anyway – Hindley would only be allowed to visit Saddleworth with the approval of the Home Secretary.

Her offer to go back to the Moors would prove to be a very significant step. The following morning's papers interpreted her planned visit as Myra Hindley returning to places where she had helped Ian Brady bury children, rather than as Myra Hindley pointing out areas that had been of great interest to Ian Brady. The public were given the impression that she had made a deeper commitment than at that time she had, and she herself realized this was what they thought. It nudged her inexorably in the direction of her eventual confession.

The following day I was urged to hold a press
conference in Manchester, since hundreds of phone

calls had been received from Britain and abroad. The hall was crowded, with about sixty or seventy press, radio and television reporters. The Deputy Chief Constable, John Stalker, and my immediate boss, Assistant Chief Constable Ralph Lees, were present, but I was the one who had to field the questions. When the reporters made it clear that they intended covering the search of the Moors we realized there would be logistical problems with all those extra cars. The A635 is narrow, dangerous and regularly shrouded in mist. So we agreed to meet them at Stalybridge Police Station, bus them to the site and allow them to take pictures; then, we hoped, they would keep their promise to leave us alone to complete the search. I genuinely believed, despite the cohorts of journalists I had encountered outside Cookham Wood and again at the press conference, that interest in the search would wane quickly and that we would be left to get on with our task. It was, looking back, a little naïve of me.

The search began the next day, 20 November, with thirty men and dogs provided by Lancashire and West Yorkshire police forces. It was a very misty morning, the first of many I would see on Saddleworth Moor; but by mid-morning the mist had cleared and the photographers were able to get their pictures.

The following day I travelled to London for a meeting at the Home Office. We talked about public interest in Hindley's proposed visit to the Moors, the interest of justice, the seriousness of the investigation, the suffering of the two families and the likelihood of a visit producing a positive result. The Home Office officials were naturally concerned about public safety, and the safety of those who would accompany her – it is well known that there are people in Manchester who would risk their lives to attack Hindley.

Another obvious problem was the media. I told them I hoped to keep any visit secret, but it was then explained that if the Home Secretary was asked a direct question about it he could not compromise himself in any way to protect its secrecy. Another suggestion was that we should treat the media responsibly, and co-operate with them to arrange sensible coverage. But I knew that, while most newspapers would have agreed to this, freelance journalists are well aware of the tremendous financial rewards for a picture of Myra Hindley – I was later told that they were offering as much as £20,000 for one clear photo of her. Hindley herself had been very anxious about this aspect of any visit: she didn't want to become the focus of a media circus. I suspect that she was concerned to keep her appearance secret – she now looks so different from the photographs taken of her at the time of the trial. The Home Office officials agreed that a prisoner taken out of jail should not be subjected to press harassment. We agreed that I would set down in writing an operational plan for carrying out the visit, taking into consideration the safety of the public, the prisoner and the people around her, and causing the minimum disruption to the public.

The search of the Moors continued. The conditions were atrocious, but at least the ground was not frozen. High moorland places have a weather system of their own: I soon discovered it was futile listening to the local weather forecast, or trying to judge by the sky a mile away down the road. A beautiful day as we set off from Manchester could deteriorate into appalling conditions on the Moor, which in the space of one day could experience every kind of climatic change from sunshine via mist to snow and back to sunshine again. When we started the search, one of the dog-handlers from Lancashire said to me, 'It's OK, boss, we're used to working in bad weather. We've seen it all up on the Lancashire Moors where we train our dogs.' Later on he confessed to me he had never experienced such conditions and had never worked in horizontal rain before! On the second day we found it had snowed, and the dogs just frolicked in the snow. I remember thinking: 'What am I doing up here?'

The area we were searching belonged to two land-owners, a farmer by the name of Crowther, whose farm buildings are not far down the road from Hollin Brow Knoll, and the local Water Authority. Mr Crowther allowed us to cut through any fences that we needed to, as long as we reinstated them to protect his animals; the Water Authority were equally helpful.

From time to time the dogs would scent something

and we would dig; but the only remains we found were those of sheep, foxes or other small animals. On one occasion they found the perfectly preserved body of a small dog which had been buried, presumably by its owner, about two feet below the ground. Experts calculated it had been there between three and five years. The find renewed my faith in the Moor's unique preserving properties, and demonstrated that, despite the cold weather, the dogs were still able to find buried remains.

By this time the strength of public and media interest was clear. Although we had bussed the journalists up there at first they were now bringing their own vehicles, and we had terrible parking problems as their cars lined the side of the road. They rented ground off Mr Crowther and brought up trailers and pantechnicons full of television equipment. All the national press were there, and the ranks of reporters were swollen by feature writers who had been sent up to research 'colour' stories.

I was warned by the Greater Manchester Police press office that if the search didn't produce rapid results, the press would 'turn' on me. I didn't believe it; as far as I was concerned I was doing a job, and I assumed they would understand that. But they were under pressure from editors who were spending a lot of money to keep them up there; they needed to justify being there. After the initial excitement the stories started to turn sour.

There was speculation that the whole search had been stage-managed to take attention away from the Stalker affair; the suspension and subsequent reinstatement of the Deputy Chief Constable had been a major news story. Experts were produced to take public issue with the expert advice I had been given: they argued that after twenty years or more there would be no identifiable remains to find; they said the watertable of the Moors meant that the landscape was constantly shifting, making it impossible to identify places from old photographs (we knew this wasn't true – we were doing it!). They clamoured about a waste of money and expertise. One or two politicians jumped on the bandwagon – I believe they were cynically exploiting the situation for their own publicity purposes.

The press office tried to help me, but it was me the reporters wanted. I was the one they were portraying as 'the man with a mission'. In the end I agreed to hold a press conference on the Moors twice a day, before we started work and after we finished; I could well have done without it. One of the accusations levelled against me was that I was courting publicity. The efforts we had made to lay on coaches on the first day of the search were thrown in my face. 'What chief superintendent lays on coaches for the press?' They sneered.

The reporters who were up there every day – the hard core of local newspapermen and national reporters based in Manchester – were intelligent and responsible. We developed an admiration for each other, born out of the conditions we were all working in: if the weather was appalling for us, it was no better for them. Some of the freelances were very grateful for the work – I was told towards the end of the inquiry that more work had been provided covering the Moors search than reporting on the coal miner's strike

But there were others who would come up for one day and then write about it dimissively, as though we were some crackpots on a doomed mission. They often got their facts wrong, which dismayed the regular reporters more than it did me. It got personal, which at first I found rather hard to take. One writer sniped at me for wearing 'a chain store anorak'. Yes, my anorak did come from a chain store: it was a Christmas present bought from Marks and Spencer by my daughters, Sue and Pam, and they were hurt by the criticism. But would I have been a better detective in the eyes of that journalist if my anorak had come from Harrods? If I had been dressed from head to toe in designer clothes, would I have been able to find Pauline Reade's body any faster? At the press conference the next day I was asked to comment on the article. When asked what I was doing, I couldn't resist the retort: 'Saving for a bespoke anorak.'

When the laughter subsided, the questions turned to more serious issues.

What concerned me was the effect that all this might

be having on my wife and daughters. They would be stopped in the street and asked about the search. They would hear me being criticized – sometimes quite openly, to their faces. But all three of them were right behind me and never faltered in their belief that what I was trying to do was right. They were concerned and anxious for me, and I know it hurt them a lot. I had been turned virtually overnight from an anonymous policeman into someone whose face and name were recognized across the land; it was not an experience I relished.

The wives and families of the rest of the Moors team also had to deal with unwarranted and ill-founded criticism of the search, which made me angry. It was not what they deserved considering the tremendous efforts they were making. None of them had any doubt about the need to search the Moor, and none of them asked to be transferred back to normal duties. The lads even had to ride criticism from their own colleagues – there were plenty of other policeman who thought we should not be up there 'wasting our time'. But if anyone hoped that the criticisms would unsettle the unity of the team they were disappointed. It strengthened us.

The Moors team was a hand-picked band of experienced detectives from the Serious Crimes squad. As soon as I considered openly searching on Saddleworth I knew that Geoff and Gordon and I would need assistance; although we were working together very well, it was a bigger task than we could handle alone. But my instincts and experience still told me to keep the team small, so that I could keep all its members fully informed about what we were doing; that is the way to engender loyalty and dedication. Initially I chose two more teams, each comprising a detective sergeant and a detective constable. Detective Sergeant Steve Southward is a quiet, deep-thinking man who never speaks hastily, but is quite prepared to make his views known when he feels it is necessary. He was teamed with DC Alan Kibble, one of the jokers in our pack – we could rely on Alan to make everyone laugh even when there wasn't a lot to laugh about; but he too was dedicated to the hard work we faced. Detective Sergeant Martin Flaherty was teamed with DC Pat Kelly. Martin is very hard-working and enthusiastic – a strong character. Pat is a big, powerful Irishman, sensible and quiet – except when he and Martin would start to wind each other up, which was as good as a cabaret for the rest of us.

It did not take us long to realize that we needed still more help, so I added a third extra team: Detective Sergeant Ron Peel and DC Gerald 'Ged' McGlynn. Ron has a similar personality to Pat: quiet with a good sense of humour – the sort that tends to create a situation that would allow the others to be witty. Ged is an individual – a character whose knowledge of the building industry was useful to us during our excavation work.

Everyone blended in very well together, and throughout all those months there was no friction. Every member of that team was as important as the next man. I feel very strongly that they all deserve tremendous credit. Because my face was the one that appeared in the newspapers, the public thought it was my investigation, but in fact the work was shared among us all and the credit should be shared equally, too.

I chose them because they were all proven good detectives and physically fit – the work on the Moors was going to prove long and arduous. We soon became even fitter: any surplus flesh soon disappeared completely, the fresh air tanned our faces, and the three smokers among us – Martin, Ged and Alan – gave up because it made the strenuous physical work far more difficult.

The news came through from the Home Office that Myra Hindley was to be allowed to visit the Moor. It obviously had to be kept confidential, so I told only my close team. My boss, Assistant Chief Constable Lees, was informed, and he notified the chief officers of the force. We all felt excited – this could be the breakthrough that we needed. The visit needed considerable organization, for which I called on the expertise of Detective Chief Inspectors Ivan Montgomery and Chris Baythorpe of CID Operational Support Group. The operation was called Little Chef, after the numerous meals Geoff, Gordon and I had eaten at motorway service areas and roadside restaurants as we had travelled up and down the country.

While we were seeing to all the details I received a phone call from Michael Fisher, to say that his client wanted to see me urgently; he said Hindley needed reassurance. I was alarmed that she might be getting cold feet, so I flew to Gatwick early the following morning and drove immediately to Cookham Wood.

In fact she was not wanting to pull out of the visit, but asking me to speed things up. I couldn't tell her that we were busy setting it up for less than a week ahead, because I couldn't risk her telling anyone and the news being leaked to the press. She said she was finding the crescendo of publicity difficult to cope with. Both she and Brady have always professed to be distressed by publicity, but I have noticed that they both prefer to have it than to be without it. Myra Hindley's reaction to it is schizophrenic: she says she hates it, yet she revels in feeling important.

She told me she was getting herself ready to divulge everything she knew. This was the first time she mentioned, however obliquely, the possibility of a confession. But she stressed that she would need support before, during and after any formal statement. She said she was unable to talk to the Roman Catholic priest at the prison, and that she wanted to be counselled by a Methodist minister who had visited her, the Reverend Peter Timms. Mr Timms had been a prison governor for years before leaving the prison service for the Church, so he seemed an excellent person to counsel her. But Home Office permission was needed for him to visit her freely; prisoners are allowed access to their spiritual advisers, but in her case that was the Catholic priest. I said I would deal with this.

I realized that conditions would have to be ideal before she would confess. Coming to terms with confession would be hard for Hindley: for twenty years

53

she had maintained her innocence, and plenty of people – including her mother, her brother-in-law, her niece, Lord Longford and other friends – were convinced she had been wronged. As well as facing the difficulty of breaking down the barriers she had erected in her own mind, she risked losing all these relationships.

I think she was influenced by the way the media were treating her. They were assuming she had already confessed, or was about to, and although they were not exactly painting a rosy picture of her, their treatment of her was less harsh than it had been. Over the years she had been seen as a hard woman who said nothing and would not help anyone. The press had tended to treat Brady more kindly: he had said more, and had been seen to be suffering. It was also clear that he was not fit for release, so the press campaign was aimed at keeping her inside too.

I was pleased, to say the least, that she was beginning to think about confession, and obviously keen that she should go ahead. I immediately asked the Home Office to let Peter Timms visit her, but here came up against problems. The Home Office did not want to treat her differently from other prisoners. Yet she *is* different: the fact that I had to get permission from the Home Secretary to take her out to the Moors is proof of that – it is routine for the police to take prisoners out of jail to help with inquiries, without needing higher authority. In the meantime, plans for the visit were pressing ahead, but before then I had a call to make: on Ian Brady.

I saw him at Park Lane Hospital, and I think if I had not known who it was I would have found it hard to recognize him. The emaciated, bulging-eyed, ranting skeleton of a man I had met at Gartree Prison had been replaced by a calm, polite, normal-looking person. He was not fat: he has a naturally rangy build. But he had put on some weight, so that he looked healthy; his manner was quiet, he talked sensibly.

But he still did not talk a lot, telling me that he did not feel he was able to help at all. His solicitor, Benedict Birnberg, was present. I found him helpful, but obviously the interests of his client were paramount, and if Brady did not want to talk to me that was his right.

But when I left I still had the feeling that one day we might get somewhere with him. The door was not completely closed. He had agreed that I could come back and see him at a later date, and that alone represented some sort of commitment.

4

Myra Hindley joined the search on Saddleworth Moor for the first time on 16 December 1986. Neither I nor any of the Moors inquiry team went to bed the previous night. We went home, had a meal, showered and changed, and were back at Greater Manchester Police Headquarters by midnight. Then we started briefing all the 135 police officers who had a part to play in the operation.

I would have preferred the visit to have been secret, but I knew this was impossible. Ever since Hindley had said that she was willing to go there, the media had been watching every move we made, as well as keeping a check on the prison gates. They made it clear at our regular press conferences that they wanted not only to photograph her but also to try and talk to her. One newspaper even took Keith Bennett's mother down to Cookham Wood Prison and took photographs of her outside the gates. With this sort of interest there was no chance of keeping the operation secret.

A lot of police officers had to be involved just to ensure safety. To come to any arrangement with the press I would have to offer them a facility to take pictures, and I knew that neither the Home Office nor Myra Hindley would agree to that. So there was always the possibility of the odd irresponsible photographer breaking the rules.

I also knew that if the media could get to her, any crank would be able to do the same. My concern was not just for Hindley, but for all the innocent people around her.

There was no blueprint for me to follow. I suppose the nearest thing for security purposes would be a royal visit – but for that the press and public are allowed a reasonable amount of access. I decided to buy as much time as possible by moving as secretly as possible in the initial stages, but with all the back-up I needed as soon as it became known she was there.

Only a handful of people inside the prison knew what was happening – Myra Hindley herself did not know until she was woken in the early hours of the morning. A small convoy of unmarked cars arrived inside the prison compound, and there were other vehicles ready to intercept any cars that attempted to follow – some journalists had been sleeping in their cars outside the prison gates.

Myra Hindley left at 5.50 a.m. and was driven to the headquarters of Kent police at Maidstone, where the Metropolitan Police helicopter was waiting. Travelling with her were two prison officers with whom she got on well and who had volunteered to accompany her.

The pilot of the helicopter was a senior pilot on loan to the Metropolitan Police from one of the big airlines. I expected him to be skilful and resourceful, and he was. He also had tremendous enthusiasm and great courage without which it would have been impossible to even start the visit.

I was a little worried about taking Hindley on to the Moors. The terrain is rough and hilly, and I was conscious of the fact that she was in her mid-forties and a heavy smoker, obviously not used to much outdoor activity. But the prison medical staff had been consulted and thought she could cope with it.

Also with her, throughout the day, was Detective Inspector Roy Rainford from the firearms branch. I had chosen him as her personal protection officer because he was resourceful, intelligent, and would never allow his personal feelings to interfere with his duty. I had stressed to all police personnel that they must not allow their feelings about her to show – any display of antipathy could jeopardize all the careful work we had done. In fact there was only one such incident in the whole of that day – a policewoman hissed at Hindley as she walked past, but fortunately she did not hear it.

At the same time that she was beginning her journey from Cookham Wood, I started to get my men up on to the Moors. I had ringed the area that we were visiting with observation points, manned by police who would be constantly watching for any intruders.

Snoopy's caravan is up on the Moors all year round, search or no search, selling cups of tea and coffee to passing drivers. The chap who runs it did very well out of the search – for the first day or two he ran out of bacon sandwiches, but he soon had enough supplies to keep everyone going on those cold, wet, miserable days up there. Some of the journalists had moved into his car park, with campers or even just their cars, and were sleeping there – waiting for Hindley. I would have liked to have got them all off the Moor, but in the end I decided that the easiest thing was to contain them on the Moor itself, by putting police officers in the car park with them. They did not cause any problems.

I knew we had to seal off the A635, and a B road that intersects with it, but one of my problems was deciding when to do it. Closing a major road is not something to be done lightly, but I knew I had to give Hindley the opportunity of driving along it, just as she had done all those years ago with Brady, to show us where they had parked and where they had entered the Moor. The closing of the road would in any case be seen as confirmation that the visit was on. If I had done it too early, before Hindley left prison, her convoy would have been besieged at the gate.

Geoff Knupfer, Ivan Montgomery and I managed to get to the control caravan on the Moor without arousing any suspicion. As soon as I had been given permission for the visit I had exchanged our small, basic caravan, which we towed off the Moor every night, for a well-equipped, much larger van which would become a sophisticated permanent base for us. We needed the better communication facilities it offered, both for linking up with officers scattered about the Moor and to keep us informed about the movements of the press. By this time there was at least one hired helicopter in a pub car park not far from the top of the Moor.

The Metropolitan Police helicopter refuelled twice

on the 250-mile journey north, the second time at
Woodford, only about twenty miles away from Saddleworth. I had had to inform every police force throughout the route, and lay on contingency plans in case
anything went wrong. We had identified where all the
hospitals along the route were, and what facilities they
had for dealing with emergencies. Finally, I had
arranged for a road convoy to be following the same
route as the helicopter, just in case it had to put down.

It was bitterly cold. We had tried to plan the visit for
a good day, liaising with the Weather Centre, but as we
had already discovered, it is impossible to predict
conditions on the Moors. The sky was leaden with
cloud, and I was worried that we were going to have to
abort the whole operation, or that I would have to
arrange for Hindley to travel the last twenty miles by
car. The pilot, though, was sure he would be able to
land on the Moor if he could find a break in the cloud.

But apart from that, everything was running like
clockwork. Despite the closure of the road, there had
been no confirmation that the visit was on. The Home
Office had agreed that we would stonewall all inquiries
for as long as possible. But then I heard that David
Mellor, then a junior minister at the Home Office, had
been interviewed on the Radio Four *Today* programme
and had said that Myra Hindley was on her way to the
Moor. It was 7.30 a.m. about an hour before she was
due to arrive. This official confirmation, without prior
consultation, drove a bus through my plans. Although
we were prepared for the news to become public, we
had wanted a good start because there was one area in
which we were vulnerable; the sky over Saddleworth
Moor is not restricted airspace. To have made it so I
would have had to apply for a restriction order, which
would have been published – alerting everyone to the
day of the visit. After David Mellor's interview we
knew it would not be long before hired helicopters
started turning up.

Before Hindley arrived I was joined by Commander
John Metcalfe from the Home Office and by Hindley's
solicitor. It had been easy enough to keep Commander
Metcalfe's visit secret because he was not attracting
any media interest. But Michael Fisher was known to

the press and therefore presented a problem. I had booked him into his hotel under another name, but he ran into difficulties when he tried to pay his bill with a credit card in his own name. When the hotel staff became suspicious he referred them to me – and I had to verify his story!

The helicopter had planned to land at the junction of the A635 and the B road to Meltham, but because of the almost complete cloud cover had to put down two miles away, on the A635. To have landed anywhere on the Moor at this time was a tremendous demonstration of skill on the part of our pilot. I travelled down in a four-wheel drive vehicle to collect the party. Hindley and the two women prison officers were, like the rest of us, wearing black anoraks, black overtrousers, rubber boots and navy blue balaclavas, which were rolled down over our chins so that only a small area of the face was exposed. The weather was so bad that we were glad of them, but the main reason for dressing like this was to foil the photographers – it was difficult to tell who was who unless you were really close.

We drove back to our headquarters compound, where everyone was given hot drinks and sandwiches after their journey. Snow was lying on the ground, and although it was not deep it was blowing in the air. There were a few drifts, and it was in one of these near the compound, just before Hindley's arrival, that police dogs found a photographer who had hidden himself to try to get a photograph. He was lucky to have been found – he was certainly in no condition to have taken pictures, and if he had been there much longer he would have suffered severe hypothermia or worse.

Hindley had told us she was most interested in finding a site on Shiny Brook, near the waterfall, so we set off down a rough stone road made for the Water Authority vehicles. With hindsight, I don't think we should have done this. It was not a route she and Brady had ever followed, so it did not help her get her bearings. But at the time I believed her knowledge of the Moor was greater than it actually proved to be. With her were Michael Fisher, Commander Metcalfe, the two prison officers from Kent, Roy Rainford, Geoff Knupfer and myself, and in a loose ring around us were men from the Moors inquiry team, some of them armed.

At the same time I sent out three decoy parties, each containing at least one policewoman. This had not been part of my original plan, but the knowledge that it would not be long before chartered helicopters were buzzing us made it seem a good idea. (It worked. The following day the *Today* newspaper published a photograph of someone they claimed was Myra Hindley, and the press attacked me for having her dressed in a different coloured hat and mittens from the rest of her group. It was not her at all, of course, it was a policewoman.) All the members of these groups were volunteers, and they knew the risks involved if they were mistaken for Hindley.

The Home Office had insisted that Hindley should be handcuffed to one of the prison officers throughout the visit. But even when walking on the relatively easy surface of the waterworks road, it soon became clear that two people handcuffed together ran the risk of getting injured; the ground was rough, and if one of them had slipped the other would have had a broken wrist at least. The practical and experienced Commander Metcalfe, there to represent the Home Office, took the decision to remove the handcuffs. He could see there was no possibility of Hindley staging an escape, even if she had wanted to.

As we came off the road on to the uneven moorland it became more difficult to walk. The grass grows in tufts, it is springy and boggy, and unless you are on a sheep path you are likely to trip at any moment. Some journalists had written about searching Saddleworth Moor as if it was a village green: they had obviously never been any closer than Watford Gap. I had to walk as closely as I could to Hindley to hear what she was saying, so for most of the day I found myself having to assist her by holding her arm. We were walking parallel to the stream, along the steep bank, so it was even more difficult and progress was slow.

Conversation was not easy, partly because she was struggling to make progress, and partly because we were hampered by the convention of only talking about 'places that seemed to be of interest to Brady'. But soon after we neared the waterfall she asked if she could speak privately to Commander Metcalfe and myself. I immediately became hopeful that she had identified a spot and was going to point us to the site of a grave, especially as she seemed to recognize the area. She, however, only wanted to make it clear that by helping she was not looking for parole or any other concessions. She said she felt she had not got her bearings properly, and she was only able to talk very generally about whole areas. By this time it was very cold, sometimes misty, and there was driving snow. It was all any of us could do to keep walking.

But the day had its lighter moments. There were two dog-handlers from Lancashire Police walking parallel to us, but they were down by the stream bed and ahead of us. Neither of them was young, and I was impressed by their hard work and enthusiasm. Although the stream was not in flood, it was fast-flowing and the banks were treacherously slippery. One of the men fell full-length into the water, to the enormous amusement of his mate. When they went a couple of hundred yards further on, the second one sprawled in. The next day Ged McGlynn turned up with a cartoon of it, captioned 'Lancs County Underwater Dog Section'.

One of the prison officers was by now finding it particularly hard to walk, and Myra Hindley had directed us back towards the A635. Before we got there we had to put the officer on a stretcher, because she had strained her groin quite badly. She was upset – she felt her injury was hampering us, and she could not forgive herself for becoming a burden. Hindley was also distressed: she said she felt it was because of helping her that the officer had been injured. Thankfully it was not a serious injury, and after a few days' rest the officer was fit again.

Inevitably we began to get bothered by helicopters. I believe it was the stretcher that gave us away – I did not have enough stretchers for all the decoy groups to take one. Although they were not my favourite people that day, I have to give the reporters and photographers ten out of ten for effort and ingenuity. As we came off the Moor we had three helicopters over us in the sky, while our own helicopter was up there with them, trying to give us cover. It reflects great credit on the skill of the pilots that there were no accidents. Our attention had to be focused more on protecting Hindley than on getting on with the job – every time a helicopter homed in on our group, we had to stop walking and shield her. Without intending to, the media were severely hampering our work.

When we reached the road she showed us the place where she and Brady used to park. Then we took her back to the compound for lunch. There was a police communications wagon there, a caravan with seating inside, so we were able to warm up and have a hot meal. Hindley's resolution was strong, and she was still enthusiastic about the search, but the weather was getting worse: the snow was settling, altering the shape and dimension of the Moor quite dramatically. It was the worst possible day to be there. But it was not as though I could call the visit off and start again the next day; it was now or never, and I had to make the best of it.

After lunch Myra Hindley wanted to return to an area called Hoe Grain, where they had parked. We drove past it and then returned, approaching from the Manchester direction as she would have done with Brady. Hoe Grain is a deep valley that runs from the road to Shiny Brook, and she told me as we walked that this was the way that she and Brady had come on to the Moor. She pointed out one or two areas that might be significant, but she could not narrow it down. At one place she described a plateau of land: we could not see it, and I was puzzled. But when I walked the same route another day, in better weather and at a different height, I saw exactly what she was describing.

I decided to leave Shiny Brook and go to Hollin Brow Knoll, the stony outcrop near the road where Lesley Ann Downey's body had been found. The fence between the road and the Knoll had been cut, with the farmer's permission, and some planks had been placed across the ditch. We stood at various points and Hindley looked around. I could not discuss with her the site of Lesley Ann Downey's grave, because she and her solicitor were sticking to the convention that she knew nothing about the murders; she also made it clear that she did not want to know the grave site. She mentioned one or two small areas that she thought we should look at closely, and I felt generally optimistic about this section of the Moor because it was so much smaller than the others we had looked over.

While we were there, a hired helicopter dropped a couple of journalists quite close to us; they were challenged and ran off into the Moor. Every sighting of journalists attempting to get on to the Moor was reported to me by radiophone, and each was dealt with on its own merits. There had been some brief tension when Mr Patrick Kilbride, father of John Kilbride, had turned up at a roadblock with a knife on him. But he caused no problem when it was explained that he could not go any further. Mr Kilbride's distress at the loss of his son all those years ago has not abated, and I understand how he feels. On this occasion he was taken up to the roadblock by a couple of reporters, who presumably felt that if they could not get near Myra Hindley they would salvage something from the day for their newspapers. But their actions did them no credit; they were not helping Mr Kilbride.

The temperature was now about freezing, but a strong wind made it seem much colder. There were a lot of glowing cheeks and shiny noses peering out from balaclavas. Our helicopter had had to go back to Woodford. The light had grown very bad, and the combination of that and the very low temperature made it unsafe to attempt to put down on the Moor again, although it was equipped for night flying and would be able to transport Hindley back to Kent from the airfield at Woodford.

So we went back to the caravans, and I made arrangements for a convoy of police cars to escort Myra Hindley to Woodford. She now made a strong plea to Commander Metcalfe and me that she should be allowed to continue the search the following day; she felt she had been getting her bearings, and would like to carry on. But it was not possible: the Home Office order had been for one day only. And frankly I don't believe with the weather and the media attention, that we would have been able to achieve much more. We all felt that Myra Hindley had done her utmost to help.

Although we could not talk directly about the victims, I believe she had tried her best to point us in the right direction. Given the conditions, and the length of time since she had last been up there, she could not have done any better. Yet I must admit I was disappointed: I think my expectations were too high. I realized just how disorientated someone could be after a gap of twenty years and more. I thought that visiting the Moor with murder in mind would have impressed the events and locations firmly into the memory.

After she was safely back in prison I held a brief press conference. I felt the visit had been useful, because it confirmed that Shiny Brook and Hollin Brow Knoll were the two areas where we should concentrate the search. So I was able to be positive with the journalists. We had been working in appalling conditions, and at no time had any of the men or women on the operation complained. I think we were all relieved to go home, have a hot bath and get some sleep.

The weather was deteriorating rapidly, and by the end of the week there was no sense going on with the search. We had equipment up there that needed to be protected. In the end, it was a race against the weather to get the heavy vehicles out of the compound and back down to Manchester; we brought out the last utility vehicle, a toilet block, only a couple of hours before a snowdrift blocked the road.

On our last day I had David Smith brought up to see if he could help identify areas that Ian Brady had seemed particularly interested in. Smith has had a hard life as a result of his involvement with Brady and Hindley. He has been constantly reviled by the people of Manchester, who refused to see him as the man who halted Brady and Hindley's killing spree and was therefore deserving of praise and thanks. I have asked myself on many occasions how many other victims Brady and Hindley would have had if Smith had not taken the action that he did. Rumours about the extent of his involvement persisted: he had found it impossible to get a job, or drink in a pub where he was known, and his home had been vandalized.

His marriage to Myra Hindley's sister Maureen had not survived. In 1969 he was given a three-year jail sentence for knifing a man in a brawl, which he said was triggered by the abuse and attacks he had suffered ever since the trial. By the time he came out of prison his marriage was over and his three children had been taken into care. He remarried, as did Maureen, but in 1977 Maureen died of a brain haemorrhage. At the time of the search Smith had recently moved to Lincolnshire in a bid to get away from the difficulties of constantly being recognized.

From what I had read about Smith in the files of the original investigation, I felt it was unlikely that he had been involved in any of the murders apart from that of Edward Evans, and that after that crime he had gone straight to the police. The date that he met Brady made it impossible for him to have been involved in the Pauline Reade murder, but his name was constantly linked with it because he had lived next-door-but-one to the victim. I also felt that if he had been involved in the others, and had seen how successfully the bodies were disposed of, he would have been unlikely to have gone to the police over the murder of Edward Evans: when a young child disappears there is a massive hue and cry, but teenage boys are always drifting away from home. In that sense, it would have been the easiest murder for them to get away with. So I accepted David Smith at face value: an unfortunate young man who at a very early age became involved in something horrific, and who at least had the courage to go to the police about it.

The day he came up to the Moor the weather was atrocious, with snowdrifts two or three feet deep. He was angry and aggressive when he arrived: he said he had not been told that he was being taken to Saddleworth Moor, only that he was going to Manchester. He threatened to walk all the way back. But he subsided when I explained what I wanted, and he agreed to help us. However, he was obviously deeply affected by the Moor, and it distressed him to remember that time in his life. He said he didn't want to be associated with it.

He confirmed that Hoe Grain was a favourite place to

park the car when he, Brady and Hindley had come up to the Moor. But he was confused, and the snow made it impossible to identify any area with certainty. I had not had very high expectations from this visit, but I had wanted to talk to him anyway and it was useful for that. But whatever he had been able to add to our knowledge, the weather was against us. By the end of that day it was obvious that we could do nothing more on Saddleworth until the winter was over. There were plenty of other inquiries to pursue, but we had all been working very long hours, Christmas was only a few days away, and we all needed a break.

PART TWO

MYRA HINDLEY
CONFESSES

5

Before I saw Myra Hindley again I met the Reverend Peter Timms, the man whose help she had requested. Michael Fisher, Geoff Knupfer and I had lunch at his home a few miles from Cookham Wood on 29 December 1986. He told me he felt it was in Hindley's own interest to confess, for the sake of her mental health and well-being, and he was also very concerned about the families of the victims. While careful not to breach any professional confidence, Michael Fisher, too, indicated he was supporting her.

After lunch we went to the prison, where I told her that I had met Peter Timms and agreed that he should counsel her and that we all felt that several visits would be necessary. She was pleased. I reminded her that the Home Office would have to authorize it – in normal circumstances the prison governor would have the discretion to allow Mr Timms in as a counsellor, but I knew that no decision about Myra Hindley was taken lightly. Her session with Mr Timms would not be open-ended: after a couple of visits I would expect her to be able to tell me whether or not she was going to confess.

As an interviewer, it is always necessary to set up a relationship of some sort with the other person; my experience has taught me that much more can be achieved through a friendly relationship than through an antagonistic one. Ever since my visits to Hindley were made public people have been asking me, 'How could you talk to that woman?' The answer is simple: I had a job to do, and it was in everyone's interests that I did it as successfully as possible.

Myra Hindley and I had a lot of common ground. We both came from Gorton, we had both run errands for our mothers to the same shops, we had both played on the 'red rec', a local recreation ground covered with red shale. My father had a barber's shop on Gorton Lane, and we lived above it. After he died we moved, but we stayed in the area. I went to Sunday School in Taylor Street, just around the corner from Myra Hindley's granny's home where she was brought up. In my late teens I went to night school to learn rock climbing technique at Ryder Brow School, which she attended. I am only two years older than her, so it is quite remarkable that in such a close-knit community we did not meet. As it is, we share a common heritage and there was also plenty to talk about.

She enjoyed being able to reminisce: the Gorton of today is unrecognizable from the place we knew then. It was savagely slum-cleared in the sixties, when Hindley, her grandmother and Ian Brady were moved to Hattersley. All that was good about the community was bulldozed with all that was bad. More thoughtful and caring planners might have chosen to renovate and improve the existing houses, rather than opting for large-scale demolition. Some of the old Gorton, and the hard-working, friendly people who go with it, remains – but not much.

Talking about the places we knew helped to build a comfortable relationship, one where she felt at ease talking to me. Except for the short time that she lived in Hattersley, Gorton was her only recollection of freedom. I think she was surprised to find herself having a friendly conversation with a policeman, and this may have been significant in influencing her decision to confess. So when I was criticized for fraternizing with a woman convicted of murdering children, I could inwardly reassure myself that I was doing it for a good reason. In any case, I was by this stage getting used to letting criticism roll off my back – I had taken enough stick from the media for searching the Moors in the first place.

Although the search was off for the winter months, the Moors inquiry team were very busy. We were evaluating different pieces of equipment that firms had come forward with, all designed to help us find the bodies. We carried out tests with one product on a level field in Lancashire, using a buried animal body. There were numerous 'hits' on flat terrain, and we knew there was only one buried animal. The idea of working with the equipment on Saddleworth Moor – where it is difficult to stand, let alone handle a machine – was unthinkable. Many other devices were considered, but dismissed as unsuitable. I was also aware of the costs of hiring heavy equipment; what sounds like a very modest daily rate soon mounts up to a small fortune when you talk in terms of months. I had been accused of wasting ratepayers' money often enough since the inquiry began.

Great help was provided by the RAF – and it did not cost a penny, despite the outcry in the press. They flew over Saddleworth Moor at my request, taking aerial photographs in exactly the same way as they had been taken during the original inquiry. They fitted the task into their training programme, and so no charge was incurred by Manchester ratepayers. The exercise proved invaluable. Presented with the two sets of photographs and guided by the RAF experts in photographic interpretation, we were able to demolish the claims made by some 'experts' in newspapers that the Moor moves, and that it is not possible to recognize landmarks that were prominent twenty years ago. In fact, not only were we able to pinpoint the same rocks, but vegetation grows so slowly on the moorland that we could even identify the same tufts of grass that were there when Hindley and Brady walked the Moors. It was quite remarkable.

I will never forget the RAF personnel and the way they supported me, particularly at this time when criticism of my actions from some quarters may have caused lesser men to abandon me.

We were advised by several experts, most notably an archaeologist from Manchester University. It was, again, invaluble help. He taught us, among many other things, how to search ground thoroughly, satisfying ourselves that we had not missed anything. I realized that previously we could not only have damaged any grave that we did discover, but completely destroyed it. We were shown how to analyse photographs, looking for signs of disturbed vegetation, and how to devise measuring grids to ensure that all the terrain was covered. It was new ground for the archaeologists, too: they were not used to finding archaeological remains in moorland peat.

There was a great deal of information provided by the public to sift and check. A farmer in Derbyshire, for instance, told us that an area of land near Hathersage had been excavated many years before, probably at the time when Brady and Hindley were free, and that over the years the land had sunk – which can be a tell-tale sign of disturbance. We decided it could be an ideal opportunity to try out our newly acquired digging techniques, so we explored the site under the supervision of the archaeologist. It turned out that there was nothing buried there, although a hole had certainly been dug – but it was a good practice session for us. We had been taught to remove the ground layer by layer, always looking to see if there was any break in the layering. If there was, it was possible to date the disturbance from the layer in which it occurred. The archaeologist became a member of the team, giving up months of his own time to assist and encourage us, and only asking for one thing in return: that his identity was kept from the media. The successful outcome of the inquiry has much to thank this man for.

I next saw Myra Hindley on 27 January, with Geoff Knupfer and Michael Fisher. Although she was not yet ready to confess, she did give me some more information. She told me that none of the murders had taken place in the house in Bannock Street, Gorton, where she had lived with her grandmother before moving to Wardlebrook Avenue in Hattersley. She also confirmed that David Smith had not been involved in the murder of Pauline Reade.

But talking about Smith sparked a reaction that I would see on several occasions, from both her and Brady. Whether underneath it all they blame him for their imprisonment, I don't know; but their old bitterness towards him has not mellowed. Although on this occasion – and subsequently, in her confession – Hindley absolved him of any involvement in the first four murders, she made it clear that she detested Smith.

On this occasion she talked of an incident that David Smith had told the police about – something she had told him about in the first place. When she and Brady had been up on a moorland road – she sitting in the car while Brady was out of sight on the Moor – a police

71

motorcyclist had pulled up and asked what she was doing. She had told him she was waiting for the plugs in the car to dry out. What annoyed her was that David Smith had told the police that when this incident happened Brady had been burying a body. In fact, she told me, he had been practising with the guns and some new ammunition they had just picked up in Bradford. She used this as an example of how, in her view, Smith twisted or misunderstood what was told to him. She disputed the evidence he gave to the police against them. It seemed bizarre, in view of the fact that she was poised to confess her part in the crimes, that she should be so obsessed by the detailed accuracy of Smith's allegations against her and Brady. I did not cross-question her, but just allowed her to tell me what she wanted to. By this time I was sure that she would eventually tell the whole story. So I reckoned it was worth my while to play a waiting game and not to force the issue.

She moved on to talk about the tape recordings made of Lesley Ann Downey. Contrary to popular belief, she said, the tapes had been made while photographs were being taken – not during the torture session. She denied that Lesley Ann had been subjected to any physical torture. Having assessed the evidence at the trial and having heard the tapes, I accepted that they had been made while photographs were being taken; but I told Hindley that to deprive a child of her mother, then strip and bind and gag her, was in my book a form of torture – even if it was not the kind that had grown up in the public imagination. Finally, she confirmed that she believed the general areas in which we should search for the remaining bodies were Shiny Brook and Hoe Grain for Keith Bennett and Hollin Brow Knoll for Pauline Reade.

Our next meeting was some three weeks later, on 19 February. Michael Fisher had called to say she wanted to see me, and from the way he spoke I was sure that the confession was on. I felt we needed some kind of back-up to make any on-the-spot inquiries that seemed necessary, so Geoff Knupfer and I travelled to Cookham Wood with Steve Southward – Gordon Mutch, who had worked so closely with me from the start of the inquiry and would normally have come, was on holiday.

We took with us a police tape recorder, because although I had not spoken to Hindley directly about it Fisher said she had agreed that we could record the confession. Taping was a relatively new departure for Greater Manchester Police – we had the equipment, but had not yet used it. But it was bulky, and when we arrived at the prison I decided to leave it in the car.

It was just as well that we did leave it in the car – if not, we would have had to carry it out again without using it. Both Hindley and Fisher made it clear that, although she was going to make a formal confession, she first wanted to tell me about her involvement in the murders informally – without caution, without any note-taking, and without a tape recorder running. I was disappointed. I felt we had spent a long time talking around the subject, and now I wanted to get on with it. But there was no point in pressing at this juncture. We had made startling progress from my original assessment that I would get nothing out of her, and I did not want to jeopardize anything at this stage.

We assembled in the Deputy Governor's office, a comfortable room with a desk behind which Geoff Knupfer and I sat. It was mid-morning when we met, and early evening when we parted. For all that time Hindley talked, stopping only for a tea or coffee, and chain-smoking her way through the day. She spoke very intensely, very emotionally, and was occasionally very distressed. Peter Timms comforted her often, holding her hand and encouraging her. At times the medical staff brought her doses of medicine, which I assume was a tranquillizer. Sometimes she was unable to carry on until she calmed down, particularly when she was covering details of the killings.

Hindley went through her life story in some detail, dealing eventually with each of the murders. By the time she had finished we were all exhausted – mentally if not physically. Listening may not seem to be a very demanding occupation, but it requires full attention and leaves you feeling exhausted. She agreed that the following day I could return with the tape recorder, and the confession would become formal.

73

Geoff, Steve and I spent that night in a hotel in Rochester. We were elated, for we had learned many things during the course of the day. Some of the theories we had held had been shattered, while others confirmed. But underlying our elation was a feeling of anxiety, a feeling shared by all policemen who had to wait overnight to get a formal statement from a suspect. There is a deep fear that the suspect will have a change of mind. I would have given a lot right then to have had everything we had heard that day on tape. We were up early next morning to return to Cookham Wood by 9 a.m. My fears of the evening before proved to be unfounded. Again, Hindley talking willingly and in great detail – even more than the previous day. I believed that my job as an interviewer had been to get her to this point: from here on I was quite happy to let her tell the story in her own words. The formal interview started at noon, and before she began I cautioned her. The tape recorder was switched on.

It was another difficult day for Hindley, and again she had to have medication to calm her down. Nonetheless she was anxious to press on, and she worked hard. She started by putting on record that she was being interviewed freely, voluntarily and under no duress. We covered a lot of her early life and the first three murders before we finished for the day. We arranged to continue on Monday morning before we set off on the long drive back to Manchester. This time our elation was not tempered by any fear that she would not make a formal confession: we were justified in feeling a tremendous sense of achievement.

On Saturday morning I rang Ralph Lees, the Assistant Chief Constable, to tell him of our success so far, and I am sure he would have passed the information on to the Chief Constable. I spent the weekend quietly; my wife obviously knew what was going on, but we did not discuss it in any detail. There was certainly no celebration as the investigation was far from complete. Although the confession of Myra Hindley was a major landmark, I still felt that my duty – and the purpose of opening the case – was to get as much comfort and relief as possible for the families of the two missing victims.

When we parted on Friday evening, both camps agreed that the confession should remain secret, since any hint of it would have attracted widespread media interest. Everyone stuck to the agreement: I was half-expecting a leak from Cookham Wood, because it is very difficult to keep any secrets in prison, especially where such a high-profile prisoner as Hindley is concerned. But everyone was superb and there was no breach of security.

We left home at 5.30 on Monday morning, and were inside the prison by 11. Hindley had had a very difficult two days; she said she felt exhausted but relieved, and that she had needed medication from the prison hospital all weekend. For her, the implications of the confession were enormous: she knew that when the news came out she ran the risk of attack from other prisoners, and of losing the friendship of those who had believed in her innocence and supported her throughout her sentence.

We worked until 6.30 p.m., and since we still had not finished Geoff, Steve and I stayed overnight again. For part of the day Peter Timms had not been there, but she had carried on nonetheless. Michael Fisher was with her throughout, but at no time tried to interfere or dissuade her from telling us anything.

We returned to the prison early on Tuesday and were able to finish the interview by 2 p.m. On our final journey home we felt we had achieved everything we could have ever have dreamed of down at Cookham Wood. Altogether, on the closely guarded tapes we were taking to Manchester, we had about seventeen hours of Myra Hindley talking about herself, Ian Brady, and the five murders she had been involved in. For the first time, the real story of the Moors Murders had been told.

6

The confession started with Myra Hindley talking about her early life, and how she had met Ian Brady. She was then going out with another boy called Ronnie

Sinclair, whom she had known since she was quite young. Her life up to that point had been blameless, and she emphasized that she was a virgin with very little sexual experience. She was, she said, a normal girl like thousands of other normal girls, and she was a practising Roman Catholic.

She had a job in a typing pool but wasn't very happy, so she decided to leave and work for Burlingtons, a large mail order company. But before she could do so some friends of hers who had gone to work there told her about the job, and she realized it would not suit her. While she was looking around for something else another friend mentioned a vacancy at Millwards, a small chemical company with only about thirty employees not far from her home in Gorton. After taking this job she met a young man called Ian there, whom she found instantly very attractive. He seemed different from the other boys she knew; he was well-dressed, always wearing a three-piece suit and a smart shirt and tie. He obviously made an enormous impression on her.

They were thrown into close contact because his job as a sales clerk meant that he had to dictate letters to her. Hindley was wearing an engagement ring, as she and Ronnie were planning to get married. But her attraction to Ian Brady was developing, and although it was at this stage entirely one-sided Hindley broke off her engagement. When she asked around about Brady, none of the staff seemed to know much about him. He lived in Westmoreland Street, she discovered, and because she had an aunt with a young baby living nearby she spent much of her spare time over there, taking her baby cousin for walks in the hope of bumping into him. She even persuaded a friend to go with her to the local pub, the Westmoreland Arms, in case he was there.

At this time Hindley started to keep a diary, noting down events at work, things Brady had said, and her intimate feelings towards him. Containing entries like 'Please God, let him go out with me', and 'Please, let him marry me', it was the sort of diary many young girls would keep.

She told us how offended she was when she first

heard him swear after losing a bet. That she remembered it so vividly meant that it had clearly shocked
her, and she explained how she detested that sort of
language and behaviour. None the less she was desperately infatuated with him, while he just ignored her –
until the firm's Christmas party in 1961. It was the
usual sort of office party: the staff all went out for a few
drinks at lunchtime, and then came back to the office
for sandwiches and other snacks. Brady had had quite
a lot to drink; in fact everyone was slightly the worse
for wear, including Hindley. Some of the staff were
dancing in the office, but she didn't join in.

Brady asked if he could walk her home that afternoon, and when they reached her street he asked if she
would go out with him that evening. Although she had
a prior arrangement to go out with some girlfriends she
wasn't going to miss this opportunity and she agreed to
meet him at the Three Arrows pub on the corner of
Church Lane and Hyde Road. She was very excited and
bought some new perfume, explaining her feelings to
us by saying, 'It was just like Christmas' – which it was
anyway!

She and Ian Brady went into the centre of Manchester to a pub called the Thatched House. They spent the
evening drinking, moving on to another pub and then
walking home. It was in Ardwick, on Hyde Road, that
he kissed her for the first time. When they reached her
house he wanted to go in with her, but she was worried
because he was quite drunk and she was frightened of
things going too far. They stood on the corner of
Bannock Street until the early hours, kissing a few
times. She expected him to ask her for another date,
but he didn't – he simply said that he would see her
back in the office after the Christmas break. Hindley
had discovered that he was a shy person, and it was to
this that she attributed his apparent lack of interest in
her.

Back at work he acknowledged her, but that was all.
Eventually, however, he asked her to go out with him
the following Saturday evening. They went to the
cinema and then to a pub, and this time when they
returned to her Gran's house he came in with her. It
was then, for the first time in her life, that she had

sexual intercourse, which she said was painful. She explained to us that she had never behaved like this before – she had never allowed a boyfriend to stay the night with her. She had a key to her Gran's house and had the run of the place, but had never abused this facility. On one occasion when she had stayed away from home all night her mother had given her a good hiding. Hindley was at pains to point out that she did not have a bad reputation with the local boys.

After that, said Hindley, she became a 'Saturday night stand'. They invariably went to the cinema, and she particularly remembered being taken to see the film about the Nuremberg Trials. They travelled about on his motorbike, although he did not at that time have a full licence and should not have been carrying a pillion passenger. When the affair expanded from Saturday nights only, he would arrive at her house late in the evening and leave again in the early hours of the morning. Her family were not happy about this, because they realized he was spending the night with her and the neighbours were complaining that they were woken up by the noise of the bike. Hindley's mother asked her why he had not proposed marriage, and even wondered if he already had a wife in Scotland. But by this time Hindley said she had absorbed many of his opinions, and as Brady was opposed to marriage, so was she. Her mother and grandmother did not like him at all, and told her that he was no good. But she felt he was like her father – shy and naturally taciturn.

Despite the fact that no one else liked him, she loved Brady and did not care what they thought. They would drink quite a lot together: he used to make his own wine, and he would also buy bottles of wine. Sometimes they would stay home at her Gran's house all evening, drinking. One night he brought round a Cinzano bottle filled with his own home-made wine. She drank some but it had a gritty sediment in it, which Brady explained was because it had not matured well. She got very drunk, couldn't remember anything and was reduced to semi-consciousness. She said she recalled flashing lights and pain, and the next thing she knew she was waking up the following morning feeling quite ill. She had been really drunk only once before – when she was a child, she and a friend had drunk a half bottle of whisky, and her mother had had to hold her head under the tap to sober her up.

The morning after, she borrowed a bicycle because she felt that a ride in the fresh air would clear her head. In fact, she felt so strange that she fell off after crashing into the back of a bus at traffic lights, but didn't hurt herself. That evening Brady came round and she told him how ill she had been, blaming the wine. When he told her that he had drugged her with her Granny's sleeping pills she was shocked and frightened and demanded an explanation. His old dog was going blind, he said, and he did not want to take it to the vet to be put down – he was going to do it himself. He said he had emptied a couple of capsules to see how much drug would be needed to put the dog to sleep. Humans, he told her, had a stronger resistance than animals, and he claimed he had no intention of killing her. She was very scared, but he assured her that it would never happen again.

After this incident Myra Hindley went to see a close friend, May Hill, whom she had known all her life and with whom she shared her secrets. They used to meet at the Bessemer pub on the corner of Taylor Street and Gorton Lane. May could tell she was upset, but Hindley could not bring herself to tell her friend the whole story. Instead, she said she would write her a letter – if anything happened, May was to take the letter to the police.

After the drugging incident Hindley, worried about what might happen next, decided she wanted to break with Brady and get away from home. She replied to an advertisement for clerical and cafeteria workers for the NAAFI, and after going to London for an interview was offered a two-year contract working somewhere in Germany. The army authorities wanted her to have some dental work done and be ready to fly out in a couple of weeks. When she got off the train at Manchester Brady was waiting for her at the station; he knew about the job interview. They went to her home, and although it was quite late her mother, grandmother and sister were all sitting up waiting for her, anxious to hear how she had got on. When she told them she was going to Germany they were all very upset. This really moved her, and brought home to her how much her family meant to her. She realized that in getting away from Brady she would also be leaving them, and for a long time. So she decided not to go.

Her relationship with Ian Brady continued. It was at about this time that he first took her up to Saddleworth Moor, where she had never been before. She thought it a beautiful and peaceful place, and they would often go up there in the evenings and at weekends, with sandwiches and a flask of tea and bottles of wine.

She was still a practising Roman Catholic, attending confession and mass regularly. As an atheist – Brady pointed out to her discrepancies in the Gospels, and challenged her beliefs by asking how God could allow certain things to happen. After he had demolished her faith, she too became an atheist. But she modified her position to agnostic, deciding that it was presumptuous of her to believe there was no God when in fact she did not know whether or not God existed.

Brady told her that he wanted to better himself. He talked about his Gorbals background and his skirmishes with the law, and said that when he was in Strangeways Prison before being sent to borstal he had associated with men who had been reprieved from the death penalty, with major villains and expert safeblowers. He wanted to get rich and become 'a somebody' – not just do a nine-to-five job working for someone else. The similarities between his own background and that of Adolf Hitler intrigued him, and he told her how Hitler, a postcard painter of low parentage who was only a corporal in the army, rose to be ruler of Germany and almost had the free world on its knees. His interest in Nazism, he explained, was based on an admiration of the way Germany had risen from the ruins of the First World War to become one of the richest countries in the world.

Brady talked often to her about a book called *Compulsion* – later, when I was talking to him, he mentioned the book to me himself. It was the story of two boys from rich families who had wanted to commit the perfect murder, and who had kidnapped and subsequently killed a twelve-year-old boy; they had escaped the death penalty because of their age. He gave Hindley a biography of the Marquis de Sade to read. Brady, she said in answer to a question, agreed with much of de Sade's teachings, and at that time she too accepted them. She believed she had no soul, and that there was no religion. She felt, she told us, that Brady had all the answers.

Hindley recognized that Brady was anti-social, with a chip on his shoulder. But because of this, she said, she felt there was a little child inside him wanting to come out. Brady couldn't express himself properly, she felt.

He first started to talk about committing the perfect murder in July 1963, according to Hindley. I was puzzled by this, because the previous day when we had been talking informally she had told me about a couple of incidents involving her grandmother, which I felt had occurred before this date. She told me about them, but was obviously having difficulty recalling all the details.

She told me first of an incident that exemplified his contempt for other people. When they had been walking along a footpath together he had berated her for stepping into the roadway to let two other people, a middle-aged woman and a girl, go past. He barged ahead, pushing them out of the way. His attitude was that it was up to them to move for him.

When he spoke of the perfect murder she was appalled, especially when he said he wanted her help. But then he produced some pornographic photographs of her – on some of which he appeared with her – which she claimed were taken the night she was drugged. She said that made her realize what the flashing lights were. He threatened to show the pictures to her family and workmates if she didn't help him.

I have seen these photographs – they were in the files on the original investigation – and it is hard to tell whether or not she was drugged. They are certainly pornographic, and would have been regarded as very scandalous in the early sixties. However, that does not mean that I accept this part of her story: I believe that by introducing this element of blackmail she was beginning to make excuses for herself, struggling to make her subsequent behaviour more acceptable. But I said nothing of my suspicions, letting her carry on and tell the whole story.

It was at this time, said Hindley, that Brady threatened the life of her Granny, the person to whom she felt closest in the world. He said he would push her downstairs, and because of the old lady's age people would assume she had fallen. The second incident happened one morning when she was unable to wake her grandmother when she took her her usual cup of tea. Hindley went to fetch her mother and when together they could not wake her Gran they called a doctor. The old lady's health was not good: she had had severe pneumonia once and had led a hard life. But the doctor said she was in a drugged sleep – she must have inadvertently taken her sleeping pills twice.

Brady later told Hindley that it was he who had administered the double dose, adding the tablets to the grandmother's bedtime drink. She realized then that he needed help, but she also inferred that she knew that if she did not comply with his wishes he was quite capable of doing worse to her grandmother.

Although Hindley did not have a driving licence, by July 1963 she had the occasional use of a small van. She used to baby-sit for a man called Benjamin Boyce, who had a Dormobile from which he ran a mobile greengrocery business. Some weekends she would help him, and because of this he let her use an old van he owned.

On 12 July Brady told her he wanted to commit his perfect murder. He drove her home from work on the back of his motorcycle. She had already made arrangements to go with Ben Boyce that evening to recover a broken-down vehicle, but Brady's plans took precedence. He told her to drive the van, and he would follow on his motorbike. When he spotted someone that he wanted her to pick up, he would flash his headlights. He told her to tell whoever she picked up that she had lost a glove while out picnicking, and to offer them some records as a payment for helping her search for it.

They drove down Gorton Lane, and a small girl walked towards them from the direction of Peacock Street. Brady flashed his lights, but although Hindley slowed down she did not stop until they had passed the girl. When Brady drew alongside and asked her why she had not picked up the girl, she told him she recognized the child as Marie Ruck, who lived next door but one to Hindley's mother. Brady accepted that as a good reason to have let her go, and told Hindley to drive on, turning left into Froxmer Street and heading for Ashton Old Road.

Froxmer Street was generally deserted in the evenings, bordered as it was by the outer wall of a huge heavy engineering company, with a lawnmower factory and some wasteland on the other side, and only one small row of terraced houses. Halfway down the road they saw a girl walking away from them, wearing a pale blue coat and white high heels. Hindley told us she did not recognize her. Brady flashed his lights, so she drove past the girl and stopped, turning then and recognizing her as Pauline Reade. She knew the family – Pauline and her mother, father and brother lived a few streets away – but they were not as close or as well known to her as Marie Ruck. She and Pauline would 'let on' to each other if they met in the street, but they had never talked to each other before. Although there was not much of a gap between their ages, it was enough, in their teens, to make a big difference in the groups they socialized with. Hindley had walked to work with Mrs Reade on more than one occasion, and liked her. She described her as very hard-working, like her own mother. The difference between Pauline and Marie Ruck on this occasion, she said, was that she did not live so near to Pauline, and also that Pauline was older. She knew there would be more hue and cry if a seven or eight-year-old child went missing than a teenager, although she said this was not something Brady had discussed with her when planning the perfect murder.

So she offered Pauline a lift, and the girl got into the van. Then Hindley asked if she would do her a favour and come and look for one of an expensive pair of gloves. She offered the records as a reward, and

83

Pauline was keen to have them. She told Hindley she was on her way to a dance, but was in no great hurry and would help search for the glove, which Hindley said she had lost on the Moors while picnicking there earlier in the week.

At this point, Hindley broke with her narrative to tell me very forcibly that suggestions made in a book by journalist Fred Harrison that she had nominated Pauline Reade as a victim, and that the choice of Pauline was premeditated, were totally untrue. Harrison had asserted that Hindley wanted to kill Pauline because the girl was a rival of her sister Maureen for the affections of David Smith. She said Smith and her sister were not involved with each other at this time. But I contradicted her, because I knew from statements made by Maureen and Smith during the original investigation that it was at about this time that they started seeing each other. Hindley was taken aback by this but insisted, none the less, that it was pure chance that they came across Pauline Reade that evening. It could have been anyone, she said, male or female – and that that was the case in all five murders.

They drove up to Saddleworth Moor where she parked in a lay-by, as previously instructed by Brady. We spent some time discussing the site and description of the lay-by – a rocky area on the Manchester side of Hollin Brow Knoll – as it was important in the search for the location of Pauline Reade's body.

Ian Brady arrived shortly afterwards on his motorcycle, and she introduced him to Pauline as her boyfriend who had also come to help look for the glove. She said Pauline accepted this, just saying 'Hello' to Brady. She felt that because he was with her Pauline felt no reason to be suspicious of him.

Brady said he would take Pauline to look for the glove, while Hindley was to drive along the road to the next parking place, a pull-in on the other side of the Knoll and close to it. Nowadays it is difficult to get on to the Moor at this spot because of a deep drainage ditch and a barbed wire fence, but in 1963 neither was there and it was a popular spot with picnickers. Hindley parked and waited in the van. She stressed to us at this point that she knew before she picked up

Pauline Reade that Brady planned to kill her; therefore she considered herself as guilty as he was – perhaps even more so. After what seemed a long time – perhaps half an hour – Brady came over the hill and asked her to go with him. They went up behind some rocks; it was dark and she was frightened. She saw Pauline lying on the ground. She thought there had been a struggle because the girl's shoes had come off, and there was blood on her neck. I asked her if she could see that Pauline's throat had been cut. She said she heard a gurgling noise and saw lots of blood, and that she felt sick and wanted to go away, but Brady would not let her. He said that if she backed out and didn't do what he told her, she would end up in the same grave as Pauline.

Brady told her to stay there while he went to fetch a spade that he had hidden in a trench nearby (at the time she did not know it, but she now knows it was a trench dug for a gas pipeline). She had no idea when he had hidden it, but she guessed that he must have taken it up there on a previous occasion, perhaps hidden under sacks that Ben had left in the back of the van. She noticed that Pauline's coat was undone and her clothes were in disarray, but she didn't want to look at the body. She had guessed, from the time he had taken, that Brady had sexually assaulted her.

When he returned with the spade, Brady told her to go and sit in the van. By this time the gurgling noise had stopped, and she assumed Pauline was dead. When she reached the van she found he had removed the ignition key. She said she had considered driving away and going to the police or her mother when he had first walked off with Pauline. But if she accused him of murder, and he didn't in fact kill her and had a plausible excuse for being there – to search for a glove – then she feared what he would do to her and her family. She said she greatly regretted not going to the police then, because although it might have been too late to save Pauline there would have been no further killings.

When I asked her if she knew beforehand that Brady had a sexual motivation, she did not reply. But she repeated that she had guessed he was sexually assaulting the girl because of the time he took, and because she did not think Pauline's coat had been undone when she went with him. Brady told her later, in the van, that he had at one time nearly called her to help him by holding Pauline's hands down, as she was struggling so much.

While she was telling this story Hindley was very upset. She cried a lot and had to take tranquillizers, and it was obviously difficult for her. I believe this and the murder of Lesley Ann Downey were the hardest of the murders for her to talk about.

I asked her about the spade Brady had used, and she said that they had one spade, bought from a hardware shop in Gorton, that they used for the first three murders, and that they then lost it and bought another one from a store called Volmax in Great Ancoats Street, Manchester. As by this time they were living in Hattersley, in a house with a garden, they had an excuse to buy a spade.

She said she knew Brady would bury the body, because he had already told her that to commit the perfect murder the body must never be found. She said he had wiped the knife he used on the grass, and put it on the dashboard of the car wrapped in newspaper. He put the spade in the back of the van, and together they lifted the motorcycle into the van. The weight in the back made the van difficult to drive. As they neared home they passed Mrs Reade and her son Paul, walking along Gorton Lane from the direction of the hall where Pauline should have been at the dance. She told Brady: 'That's her mother and brother.'

She parked the car on some waste ground at the back of her house, and took the bike out. Brady then insisted that they went round to Ben Boyce's, because he did not want anything to draw suspicion to them. Hindley does not know how she managed to do this: what had happened had been the most devastating thing in her life, but Brady insisted they carried on normally. Ben Boyce was in bed, but she explained that she had had a puncture; he was glad that they had come as he still wanted to collect his broken-down Dormobile. He drove her and Brady over to the Abbey Hey area, and she steered the vehicle while Boyce towed it back. She said she was so upset that she twice hit the back of the van, and drove over the tow-rope on a number of occasions.

After they got home Ian Brady burned his shoes and trousers. She could not remember whether he burned his jacket. She said he cut the clothes up, wrapped them in newspaper and put them on the fire. He washed the spade and burned the handle of the knife, which from her description was a kitchen knife – not as long as a bread knife, but bigger than a knife you would eat with. He tried to snap the blade but it wouldn't break, so he put it on the fire and blackened it. After he had finished burning things he poured water on the fire, then removed the contents of the grate, wrapped them up and put them in the dustbin.

The following morning they cleaned the back and cabin of the van very thoroughly. They took his overcoat to a dry cleaners in Manchester, and then drove out through Stockport towards Macclesfield, where Brady threw the remains of the knife into a stream near the road.

While they were cleaning the van he told her that he had found four half-crowns in Pauline Reade's pocket, and on the journey to dispose of the knife he spent them on twenty cigarettes and a Crunchie bar for her. This terrified her, as the death penalty was still in force for certain murders and a murder involving robbery was a capital offence. So the following day, a Sunday, they drove up to Hollin Brow Knoll again and Brady scattered four half-crowns in the deep, tufted grass in the area where she believed Pauline's body was buried.

Eleven days after the killing of Pauline Reade, Myra Hindley was twenty-one and Ben Boyce gave her the van as a present. It was not taxed, and it had no MoT certificate or insurance. She drove it for a while with the tax disc from another vehicle in the window, which resulted in her being reported by the police and summonsed. Technically the car still belonged to Ben Boyce, and he was charged with permitting the offence, a charge to which he pleaded guilty.

That summer Hindley went on holiday to Scotland with Brady, on the back of his motorcycle. The van, untaxed, was parked on the waste ground at the back of her house. She called at the police station to ask the police to keep an eye on it for her while she was away. She was a familiar figure at the local police station: her puppy was always getting lost, and she popped in regularly to get coins for the gas meter. When she returned from holiday a young policeman called round and asked if she was interested in selling the van. It was a very old van, and she agreed to let him have it for £20.

Afterwards, she told us, she went out with the young policeman a few times. I asked her if she would name him, and she said she did not want to as he was innocent of any involvement in the crimes. Michael Fisher advised her to leave the name out of her confession. She knew that I was aware of the policeman's name, because he had come forward immediately at the time of the original investigation and had been frank about his connection with her. I knew him personally and had worked with him; he is no longer in the police service.

She gave us the impression that Brady did not know about this relationship. She went out several times for a drink with the policeman, and found him a nice young man; he would come back to the house, but he knew she had a regular boyfriend and he agreed that if he heard Brady's motorcycle he would slip out by the back door. She was frightened: Brady never told her when he would come round. They were not living together at this time but he was a frequent, if irregular, visitor, and as a result she had lost contact with all her old friends, and had dropped the roller skating, swimming and dancing that she had previously enjoyed. She said she used to stay at home just in case Brady came round. Her anxiety whilst seeing the policeman was so great that in the end she told him she could not see him again, though they remained friends.

In the weeks after Pauline Reade's disappearance she said she was aware of the local gossip that Pauline had run away with a fairground worker or might have got pregnant. She told me she had read a notice in the personal column of the *Manchester Evening News* from Pauline's parents; it said: 'Please come home, we're heartbroken.' When she saw it she broke down and cried, but Brady became very angry and tried to strangle her. She said she didn't believe he really intended to kill her, but he bruised her neck and she had to wear polo neck sweaters for days. If she displayed any more emotions of this kind, he said, her sister would be the next victim.

By this stage she was very distressed and the interview was falling apart, for she was barely able to talk. I asked her if there was anything else she wanted to tell me about the death of Pauline Reade, and she took the opportunity to deny what the nurse, Doreen Wright, had said about her temper tantrum in Holloway. In fact, Hindley said, she remained very close-mouthed about her crimes all the time she was in Holloway. The only two possible witnesses were not available to corroborate the nurse's story, Helen Kroger being back behind the Iron Curtain and Ethel Gee dead. She asked if I had seen Mrs Wright, and I told her that, although I am sure that Mrs Wright was genuine in her attempt to help, our investigations had led us to believe that what she had said was incorrect.

At one point during the interview she had quoted at length from a document, the text of a talk given to the Medico-Legal Society by William Mars-Jones QC, one of the prosecution lawyers at the trial. She did so to confirm certain things that she had been telling me – about her blameless early life, about her devotion to Catholicism, about the letter she had given to May Hill. Whilst I accepted these points, her reference to this document made me realize that her confession was being carefully controlled. Although she was obviously and genuinely upset, she was still very much in command of what she was telling me. Apart from looking at photographs to try to confirm the site of Pauline Reade's grave, and my asking her more questions about the location of the grave, she had told me all she was going to say about Pauline's death.

7

At the fourth attempt, Myra Hindley passed her driving test on 7 November 1963. Ian Brady was pleased – he had already told her that he 'wanted to do another one'. Despite Pauline Reade's death, Hindley told us that she still loved him very much, and she tried to behave as normally as possible, as though nothing had happened. The killing, she hoped, had been one isolated incident. She believed she was as guilty as him, and she considered herself a candidate for the death penalty. Although she didn't say so explicitly, I understood that she meant she felt she had gone beyond the point of no return, and was committed to helping him.

He wanted her to hire a car, and took her on the back of his motorbike to Warren's Autos on London Road in Manchester. But she was unable to get one because she only had the green slip saying that she had passed her test, not an actual licence. Brady told her to book a car for the following Saturday, the 16th, and he gave her £10 to put down as a deposit. In the event her licence did not arrive in time and it was not until Saturday the 23rd that they picked up the two-door white Anglia they had booked. (As she told me this I was startled by the memory of having hired a white Anglia from Warren's Autos myself in the 1960s, and of taking my young family on holiday in it.)

She picked up the car early that morning and drove to Brady's home in Westmoreland Street to collect him and his dog. They drove to Leek in Staffordshire – among their many photographs are snaps of them taken there that day. Afterwards she dropped him at his home, and he told her he would come round to her house later on. He arrived about 4 p.m., put a spade and a .22 rifle into the car, and they drove to Ashton market. Hindley was wearing a black wig and a headscarf – she told us she had bought the wig at Brady's suggestion after the death of Pauline Reade, because her bright blonde hair was conspicuous. It was later found in the two cases deposited at the left luggage office before the killing of Edward Evans. But she stressed that was the only preparation they made; stories that they had reconnoitred the market before, checking on the habits of the young boys who hung around it, were completely false. They did no research or reconnaissance for any of their murders.

After they had been there five or ten minutes, she said, 'We spotted a small boy, standing by the biscuit stall.' He was buying broken biscuits. Ian Brady strolled over and spoke to him, and they came back to the car together. Brady said to her: 'Do you remember that bottle of sherry we won in the raffle – I've promised it to Jack.'

She said Ian had obviously asked the boy, John Kilbride, his name and he had told him Jack. The boy climbed into the front passenger seat next to Hindley, and Brady went in the back. They drove to the Moors, where Brady had instructed her beforehand to stop in a lay-by on the right-hand side, on the opposite side of the road to where they had buried Pauline Reade. It was about 5.30p.m. when they had picked the boy up, and it was dark.

The boy didn't know where they lived, and apparently believed they were going for the sherry. On the journey up to the Moors Brady had mentioned the lost glove again, and said they would look for it. Hindley had been told beforehand that when she dropped them off she was to drive the car down to Greenfield and wait there for about half an hour, and then to return and flash her headlights three times. Brady would answer with three flashes of his torch. He told her that while she was in Greenfield she should take the gun out of the boot and put it next to her on the passenger seat.

When she stopped the car Brady went to the boot for the torch; he may have taken out the spade as well, although she did not recall seeing it. The little boy stood in the car doorway, and then she watched them walk off together down a slight slope. I asked her if she remembered seeing Brady carrying the spade at this point, but she said she did not think so: she did not think the child would have gone with him if he had been carrying the spade. She said the boy went willingly – in every case, she remarked, the victims had gone willingly to their deaths. She knew what was going to happen, she told us: Brady was going to kill and bury the boy.

She drove down and parked opposite the Clarence pub in Greenfield, stopping before she got there to take the gun out of the boot and put it on the seat. She said she didn't know 'what the heck' Brady wanted her to do with it – he had described it as 'insurance'. She waited near the pub for what she thought was half an hour – she had no watch and no great sense of time. Then she drove back to the Moor and flashed her lights. The torch flashed back at her, from down the hill. She turned the car round. When Brady came up he unlocked the boot and put in the spade and one shoe. He explained he had found the shoe after burying the body – this explains why only one of John Kilbride's shoes was found in the grave.

I asked her if Brady talked about the killing. He told her he had taken out a small knife about six inches long with a serrated blade, and said it was so blunt that he had been unable to use it, so he had strangled the boy with a thin piece of string. The string, which he put with the knife in the back of the car, was white – she said it could have been nylon string, or it could have been the lace from a plimsoll.

Brady told her that he had pulled the boy's trousers and underpants down and given him a slap on the bottom before covering him over in the grave. She asked him what else he had done and he told her: 'It doesn't matter.' She explained that this was a stock phrase that Brady used when he didn't want her to probe, and she knew well enough not to continue questioning. But she said that in her own mind she believed Brady had sexually assaulted the boy. She felt he enjoyed the perverse sense of power that his physical superiority over children gave him, and he also chose them because they were less trouble to kill than adults. But she believed the choice of the victim was of less importance than his enjoyment of killing, burying a body and having secrets that nobody else shared.

When they returned home the spade was washed in the sink and the boy's shoe was burned along with

Brady's shoes and trousers, the string and possibly his jacket – she could not remember whether he had been wearing his overcoat or not. With this killing, for the first time a suitcase had been taken to the left luggage office. She did not know about it until they collected it two or three weeks after the murder. This time Brady had drawn up a disposal plan, meticulously noting down what he was wearing and how many buttons were on his clothes so that he would know if he lost one at the scene of the crime. He burned the handle of the knife after he snapped the blade off, but she could not remember how he disposed of it.

The following morning they cleaned the car, wiping it carefully to remove any of the boy's fingerprints. But they took care not to make it look suspiciously clean. They had lined the boot with sheets of polythene, obtained from work, to prevent the spade leaving muddy marks. Hindley commented wryly that when the foreman of the car hire firm gave evidence at the trial he said that the car had been returned in a very dirty condition, looking as though it had been driven through a football field. She said she had been very tempted to stand up and tell the court they had cleaned it.

After the murder Brady showed her a copy of the *Manchester Evening News*, which he bought regularly for information about horse racing and what was on at the cinema. It contained photographs of volunteers searching in the bracken on the moors just outside Greenfield – Hindley was terrified that, if the search went further up, the body would be discovered.

I questioned her about some photographs Ian Brady had taken of her squatting on the grave, holding her dog. She said she had not known the exact location of the grave – she simply went where he told her to pose for the pictures. At the same time some more pictures were taken on Hollin Brow Knoll, and these had been said at the time of the trial to show where Lesley Ann Downey was buried. But it was clear because of the age of the dog, the clothes Myra Hindley was wearing, and the fact that they still had the motorbike that the pictures were taken before Lesley Ann's death – and this had been a pointer to me that the Knoll was the site of Pauline Reade's grave.

I also asked her about the rifle and the other guns they possessed. She told me that she had applied for the licence for the rifle because Brady had a borstal record, and that she had joined a rifle club at Cheadle, whose President was the foreman at Millwards. She bought two pistols, which she described as 'off the ticket', meaning illegally, from two members of the club. She told me that she, Brady and later David Smith would go pot-shooting with them, shooting at tin cans on the Moors. She believed that Brady intended to use them in the armed robberies he and Smith were constantly planning.

After the death of John Kilbride, she added, there had been reports that a man and woman posing as police officers had gone round to see the boy's mother and come away with some items of clothing. She stressed that it was not them – she said Brady would have been too careful to risk it. Brady had said that whoever had done it must be 'cranks'. But she knew that he did ride his motorbike and park at the top of Smallshaw Lane, where John Kilbride had lived. They did not know which house the boy had lived at, as the newspapers had only given the name of the road. But Brady, she said, had a compulsion to go there and would sometimes sit for ages on his motorbike at the top of the road. John Kilbride was the only victim whom he treated in this way. Later, when they had a car of their own, he showed no interest in driving to the streets where Keith Bennett or Lesley Ann Downey lived.

Early in 1964 they bought an Austin A40 for about £40, and part-exchanged it in April of that year for a Mini pick-up. In June he told her he was ready 'to do another one'.

At this point in the confession she talked about her feelings. She said she did not co-operate willingly with him, but complied with his wishes because it was pointless to object. He had told her that committing murder gave him a feeling of power. If he was in any way slighted or felt that he wanted revenge against the world he would satisfy himself in this way, and as far as she could understand it each murder furthered his feeling of power and satisfaction. She stressed once again that what she did amounted to murder, and that she was as guilty as he was for abducting the children, even though she did not physically murder them. But she wanted to point out that she never encouraged him, or instigated or initiated any of the killings. He asked her if she had a feeling of being 'different', and she said she did, but not in the way he meant – not a feeling of power. She said she felt different because she was virtually a murderess, abducting children to their deaths. 'How many women do that?' she asked herself.

On the night of the murder of Keith Bennett, Hindley said she could not remember whether Brady was already at her house, or whether she drove round to pick him up at his home in Westmoreland Street. She remembers driving into a side street and, when no one was about, putting on the black wig. On this occasion he had again taken the suitcase on his own to the left luggage office, and gave her no details of any plan he might have, except that she knew they would be going up to the Moors again.

Brady sat in the back of the Mini pick-up, and told her that he would tap on the window at the back of the cabin when he saw someone he wanted her to pick up. She drove down a road leading off Stockport Road – it might have been Morton Street or Grey Street – where they saw a little boy walking on his own. Brady tapped, but she knew he would before he did. She wasn't sure of the time, but thinks it was about 7p.m.

She stopped the car and asked the boy if he would help her carry boxes from an off-licence – a story Brady had rehearsed with her. She said she herself would never have been able to think of anything to say. She told the boy she would then drive him home. He climbed willingly in to the front seat and they drove a little way until Brady tapped on the glass and asked her to put the boy in the back with him. She told the boy her boyfriend was helping with the boxes, too.

The awful thing about all these children, she said, was that none of them ever queried anything, or objected to anything they were asked to do. 'It was probably because of me being a woman – they never had any fear.'

She drove up to the lay-by on Saddleworth Moor at the top of Hoe Grain, where Brady had told her to go. He and the boy got out of the back of the vehicle; Brady had already told her that he would once again use the story about looking for the glove. The two of them walked on to the Moor together, Brady with a camera round his neck. Hindley described the boy as going 'like a little lamb to the slaughter'.

She locked up the vehicle and followed them, quite a way behind, carrying a pair of binoculars. They walked down the stream until they were a long way from the road, crossing the water from side to side but mostly travelling along the right-hand bank. They reached a point where Brady signalled to her to stop and scan the horizon with the binoculars, because shepherds and hikers might be in the area. Brady had no spade with him – she believes he must have hidden it on his own at the spot he had chosen on a previous occasion. She again made the point that no child would have gone with him had he been carrying a spade.

She stayed there, sitting down and keeping a watch for anyone approaching. Brady and the boy went into a dip about twenty-five or thirty yards away. At one time she thought someone was coming, but it was only a sheep. She said she did not know what she would have done if anyone had come up. 'I don't know how long I was there,' she told us. 'It seemed like ages. It could have been thirty or forty minutes.'

When Brady came back he had the spade with him. When she asked him how he had killed the boy, he said he had strangled him with a piece of string. He never volunteered any information, she said, never bragged about what he had done. Brady told her he had taken a photograph and that he had sexually assaulted the boy, but added: 'Why, does it matter?'

I asked her about the photograph. She said there was blood on the boy's body, and because of that she had not looked at it closely. But she had seen that the boy was lying on his back with his trousers down; she could not tell whether he was alive or dead. Brady was emotionless when he showed it to her two or three days after the killing. He had developed the film at his own home, because there was no bathroom where she

Before their arrest – Myra Hindley
and Ian Brady seemed ordinary,
carefree young lovers

By the time of her committal for
murder, twenty-three-year-old Myra
Hindley looked middle-aged before
her time

Ian Brady was obsessed by stone and bleak country in his youth — a number of pictures were taken of him relaxing in the countryside before his arrest

Ian Sloan, later to become Ian Brady, must have found the moors the greatest possible contrast to No.56 Camden Street, Gorbals, Glasgow. (The Sloans' tenement is on the right of the picture)

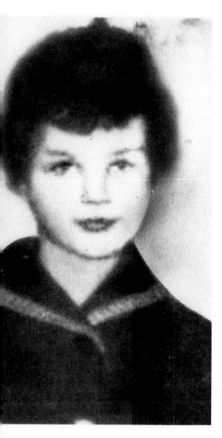

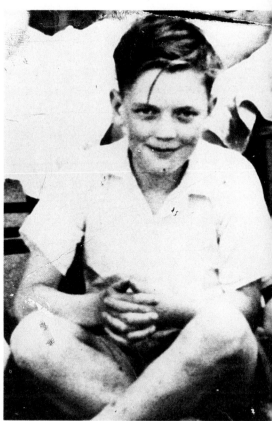

Lesley Ann Downey (*above, left*), whose recorded last words so horrified all those who heard them, was murdered in December 1964

John Kilbride (*above, right*), whose body was found in October 1965, two years after his murder

Edward Evans (*right*) the final victim, whose murder is described in more chilling detail in Hindley's recent confession

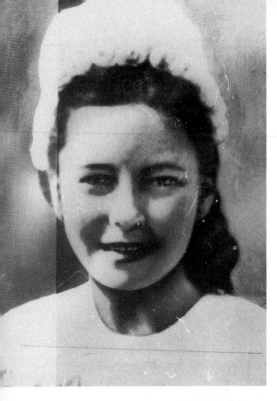

Pauline Reade, whose body we found in the summer of 1987, twenty-four years after her murder

The poster which was widely circulated in 1964. Neither Hindley nor Brady were able to locate his grave in our searches of the moors

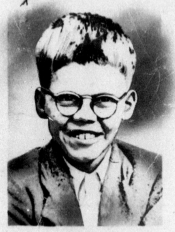

HAVE YOU SEEN THIS BOY?

MISSING FROM HIS HOME IN CHORLTON-ON-MEDLOCK, MANCHESTER, SINCE 8.0.pm. 16th JUNE, 1964

KEITH BENNETT (MAY USE NAME **JOHNSON**), 12 YEARS, 4ft. 8ins., PROPORTIONATE BUILD

BLUE EYES, FAIR HAIR, VERY SHORT SIGHTED (IS NOT WEARING SPECTACLES); WEARING WHITE LEATHER

JACKET, ZIP FASTENER WITH POCKETS EACH SIDE, BLUE JEANS, STRIPED LILAC 'T' SHIRT, BLACK PLASTIC

SHOES.

ANY INFORMATION TELEPHONE CHIEF CONSTABLE, MANCHESTER CITY POLICE, CENtral 1212

Mrs Ann Downey, watching the search for Lesley Ann's body on
Saddleworth Moor. The body was found in October 1965 – following a
massive search operation (*below*)

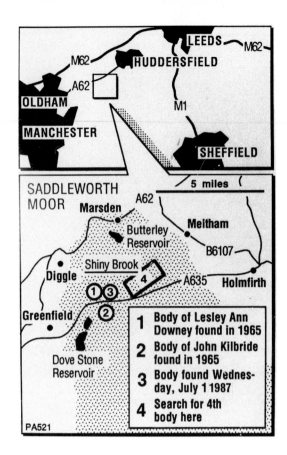

Where it all happened

1 Body of Lesley Ann Downey found in 1965

2 Body of John Kilbride found in 1965

3 Body found Wednesday, July 1 1987

4 Search for 4th body here

Looking very much a product of the early Sixties, David Smith and Hindley's sister Maureen, pose with their dog and cat

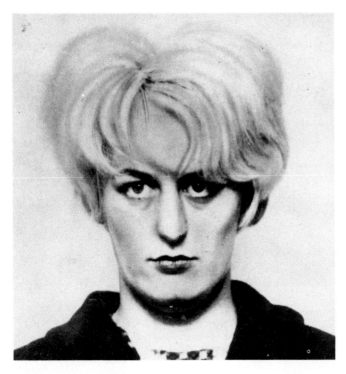

Myra Hindley – the notorious and still instantly recognised photograph taken at the time of her trial

Ian Brady, another instantly recognisable image, on his way to the committal proceedings

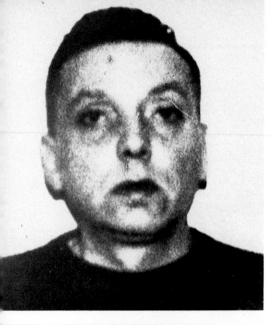

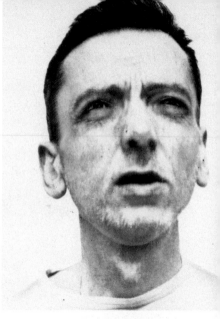

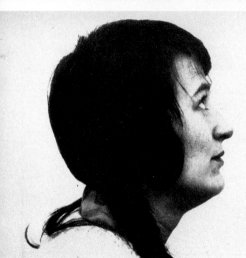

Images of prison: recent photographs of the now emaciated Brady, and Hindley in 1973 – a contrast to a more recent photograph of her in Cookham Wood Prison (*below, left*)

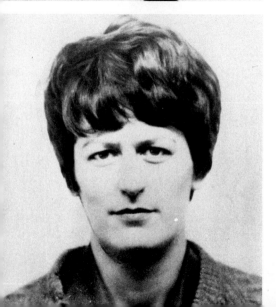

Right: Following the discovery of Pauline Reade's body, on 2 July 1987, I answer questions from the press

and her Gran lived. He told her he was going to destroy it because it was blurred.

Hindley and Brady walked back together along the stream bed, Brady carrying the spade. He told her he was going to leave it, and buried it in a bank of shale or peat. I spent a considerable amount of time going over with Hindley the details of the location of the grave; this was very important, as Keith Bennett's body has never been found. She drew a rough sketch for me to try to pinpoint the locations of both the body and the spade.

When they returned home, she told us they both had to burn their shoes. I asked if she had seen the boy after he had been killed. She denied it, and said she had last seen him alive, with Brady. She said her shoes had to be burned because she had been on the shale, and had been close to where Brady and the boy were. I put it to her that burning the shoes suggested she had been to the actual spot of the killing, but she said this was not so.

Again Brady counted the buttons on all his clothes to satisfy himself that he hadn't lost one up on the Moor. He tore and cut up the trousers while Hindley burned them. Then he ticked off the items on his disposal plan; she told us she did not know where he had kept the plan, because she had not seen it before that evening. He also threw on the fire a piece of string, which she assumed was what he had used to strangle the boy. He had told her the killing had been the same as the murder of John Kilbride, but without the knife. When he was satisfied that everything had been accounted for, he burned the plan.

They tidied the vehicle that night, but did not clean it properly – they both had to go to work the next day. The following evening Brady cleaned it out thoroughly. Two or three weeks later he recovered the suitcase; Hindley did not go with him, but he told her he had done it. She said that by this time he was confiding in her slightly more, telling her about collecting the case. She did not know the exact contents of the case, but believed it held the pornographic pictures of the two of them, a pornographic book and 'anything incriminating'.

She said she later discovered that the 'incriminating' evidence in the case was the notebook in which he had written John Kilbride's name, and an address book full of names and addresses of people he had met at borstal and in Strangeways. She said she hadn't known of the existence of the notebook until the trial, and had no idea why Brady had written down the name of one of the victims.

The suitcase intrigued her and she had been tempted to look inside it. On one occasion she had pulled it out from under the bed, but then realized that a hair had been placed across the lock – if she had opened it the hair would have fallen off, and he would have known she had looked inside. So she never saw the contents. She said she looked for the hair because she had read James Bond books in which this sort of thing was described.

As an example of how meticulous Brady was, she told us how on one occasion they had driven to a small village near Halifax, where a borstal friend of his called Gilbert Dears lived. This young man was later thought by many, including senior policemen and journalists, to have been another victim of Brady's. But as a result of our inquiries we discovered that he was not; he was drowned in a Sheffield reservoir in 1977. Journalists have always referred to him as Phil Dear, but in fact he was known as Gil.

Gil's father did not approve of his friendship with Brady, so when Brady wanted to make contact he sent Hindley to the house to claim that she was an old girlfriend trying to get in touch. The father told her that his son was not there, and when she reported this to Brady he told her to go to the house again and leave her name and address, asking if Gil could get in touch with her on his return.

A couple of weeks later a letter arrived, addressed to her. She knew what it was from the postmark and therefore steamed it open, knowing that, although it had her name on the envelope, Brady would regard it as his. The letter was not from Gil but from his family: it simply said that he had not reappeared – apparently it was not unusual for him to be away for weeks at a time. Later, when they were in a cinema in Oldham, she gave Brady the letter. He went to the Gents to open it, and when he came back he challenged her about steaming it open. After that he did not speak to her for a week.

This marked the end of our first day of formally recording her confession. I felt an enormous sense of relief that we had got it all on tape, especially as she had dealt with the two outstanding murders. Even if she changed her mind over the weekend we had the important part, and I had achieved one of my original objectives of solving those two cases.

When we resumed again on the Monday morning I reminded her that we had been talking about Keith Bennett's death, and I asked her some more questions about it. I wanted to know if she had heard anything, any shouts from the boy. She said no.

I asked if she thought he might have been gagged: the Moor is a quiet place, and I was puzzled that she had heard nothing. She said she had been aware of the noise of the wind and the grass, although it had not been very windy that evening. She could not remember whether she could hear the stream from where she was sitting, but she was adamant that she had heard nothing from the boy – no screams or shouts or conversation.

I asked her if Ian Brady had marked the grave. She said she found out later where the spot was, when one day they went up there with the dog. They had taken sandwiches and a bottle of wine, and Brady put the wine in the stream to cool. The dog disappeared into a dip and was found sniffing around a dead lamb. 'Brady kicked the dog away and picked up the lamb and threw it as far as he could away from the spot,' she said. Then she knew that this was the place where he had buried Keith Bennett.

The next murder to deal with was that of Lesley Ann Downey, the first one where a victim had been taken back to Hindley and Brady's house. Hindley revealed that she would find it the most difficult to talk about; compared with this one, her involvement in the other killings had been minimal. Even as she explained this she began to get upset, and she showed a lot of emotion all the time that she was talking about the death of the little girl. She had managed to stay quite calm while talking about John Kilbride and Keith Bennett; Pauline Reade had upset her a lot, and now Lesley Ann Downey would prove to be the worst of all for her.

She stressed straightaway that she did not know that Brady's tape recorder had been running until afterwards. There had been so many interpretations of what was on the tape, so many conclusions drawn and imaginative conjectures made. She knew it was the tape that had made the Moors Murders into 'the most horrific case of the twentieth century'. She wanted to put on record that the torture the child had suffered was only mental torture – there had been no physical torture. She had no defence for her behaviour, except that she was frightened that the child was making a noise and she was terrified the neighbours would hear. She realized how awful this excuse sounded in the light of what happened to the little girl.

Just before Christmas 1964 she and Brady went one lunchtime to a branch of Tesco's in either the Miles Platting or Newton Heath area of Manchester, because the store had been advertising cut-price wine and spirits and they wanted to get some. On the way they saw posters advertising a funfair.

On Boxing Day her Gran wanted to visit one of Hindley's uncles, Gran's only surviving son from her first marriage. It was his birthday, so traditionally Gran spent the day with him. When she was younger, both Hindley and her mother used to go, too. But she did not get on well with this uncle: he was only a half-brother to her mother, and although theirs was a close family she did not feel as close to this branch of it. She drove her grandmother to the uncle's house in Dukinfield shortly after lunch, and told her she would return to pick her up about 9p.m.

Brady had already told her that he wanted to 'do another one'. She said that after the occasion when he had threatened to strangle her – after the murder of Pauline Reade – she 'tried to acquiesce rather than demur'. Brady said they would use the fairground that had been advertised, and they debated its location; she did not know that area of Manchester very well. 'He said he would bring back whoever it was we picked up to the house, and we'd take photographs, which he called blue photographs, which he said we could sell.'

They drove to the fair and parked nearby. Hindley was wearing the black wig and headscarf – she had to wear the scarf to keep the wig in place, because it did not fit very well. Both of them were carrying boxes, as though they had been shopping. They looked around for a likely victim, and again she insisted that Brady had not stipulated which sex: it could be anyone, as long as he or she was alone and approachable.

It was between 5 and 6p.m., and she remembered that as they looked around them the music that was blaring out from the loudspeakers was a Rolling Stones record, 'Little Red Rooster'. Then they spotted a little girl on her own by the dodgems. They watched her for five or ten minutes, to see if she was waiting for someone to get off the dodgems. When it was clear that she was on her own they walked towards her. The fair was busy, but not packed. Hindley explained that Brady had always told her that the most obvious approach was the least likely to be suspicious. So they walked up to her, and when they were near they dropped some of the shopping. They asked the little girl if she would help them carry the boxes back to the car and then to their house, and Hindley said she would give her some money for doing it.

They put the little girl in the passenger seat and piled the boxes around her, so that anyone looking in would not see much of the girl. They drove home to the new house in Wardlebrook Avenue, Hattersley, where Hindley knew Brady had already set up his camera, tripod and lighting equipment. She told the little girl to take the boxes up to the bedroom, where Brady had already gone. Hindley told us she now realized that he had switched the tape recorder on when he first went up there. She said she was going to follow the girl up, but the dogs had run into the hall and she did not want them to go upstairs. It took her a couple of minutes to lock them in the kitchen, and by then she could hear loud screaming from the girl. Ian Brady was either trying to take her coat off or had told her to take it off.

101

When she went into the room she could not see the tape recorder: it was beneath the divan bed, which had a sheet reaching down to the ground concealing it. At this point in the confession she challenged the court transcript of the tape, because it was said in court that the first voice on it was a woman's. She said it could not have been, because she was not in the room at that moment.

This led her on to a long digression. She talked about the time of her arrest, and how she had first heard the tape when she was in custody. She had not seen her solicitor since her remand the week before, so she did not know that Lesley Ann Downey's body had been found. The sight of hundreds of people queuing at the police station shocked her: when she had been remanded there had been virtually nobody there. When her solicitor asked her if she knew anything about the discovery of the body of a little girl on the Moors, she had said 'No' – because she thought he was asking if she knew about the discovery, not the murder. But she added that she did not tell her solicitor the truth. She talked about the television cameras that had been set up outside the police station, and about how she and her mother were pushed to one side by a police officer to avoid being filmed.

She did not see Brady from the time of his arrest until they were in the dock together. I felt that she was talking about her arrest now because it troubled her too deeply to go on talking about the actual murder. Then she told us how she felt when the Brady pictures of Lesley Ann Downey were shown to her at the police station, and how when the tape was played she burst into tears and said she was ashamed, but could not say more because she was frightened. She was terrified of the police who interrogated her at the time: she understood their attitude towards her, but said their methods 'left a lot to be desired'. She said they 'frightened me to death'.

I brought her back to the subject of the night that Lesley Ann Downey was killed. Hindley told us that after hearing the screams she ran into the bedroom and saw the little girl crying as Brady tried to take her coat off. 'I know I should have tried to protect the child and comfort her but I didn't. I was cruel, I was brusque and I told her to shut up because I was frightened people would hear. I just panicked.'

She said she had not expected anything like it. She described how Brady tried to put a handkerchief in the girl's mouth, and how the child was pleading with him. 'Oh God, this is a nightmare to have lived with so long,' she said. The girl was pleading for her mother. When Brady held the back of her neck and tried to push the handkerchief into her mouth the girl said it hurt, Brady got a bigger handkerchief and tied her up, but the girl was still crying and making noises.

Myra Hindley said the window was open, and she described the geography of the housing estate, pointing out how near the other houses were. She said it was because she was so frightened that she kept telling the child to shut up. She put the handkerchief in her mouth and told her to bite on it hard or she would pack it in more tightly. It was nothing else, just a handkerchief, she insisted. She said she would swear 'on her mother's life' that was all it was.

Then she went downstairs – she didn't really know why. It was only when she heard the tape later that she heard the child ask, 'What are you going to do?' and Brady reply that he was going to take some photos. The little girl told him that if she was not home by eight o'clock she would get killed, and Brady told her it would not take that long. The girl grew calmer, she said, and she put the radio on to try to relieve the tension.

As she was telling us this story, Hindley could hardly talk for sobbing. It was impossible to go on for a while. When we did resume, she told us that she tuned the radio to Radio Luxembourg, where a recording of 'The Little Drummer Boy' was playing. The girl was now sitting on the bed.

To change the subject slightly, she then discussed suggestions made at the trial that the music on the tape had been superimposed afterwards. She denied this. She told us there were several things said about the tape that she and Brady would like to have challenged, but it was such an emotive tape that it was felt the less it was played in court the better. Michael Fisher asked at this point about suggestions that there had been more than two adult voices on the tape, and she replied that this was just speculation: only she and Brady had been present.

At this stage the girl had not been physically harmed or hurt, she assured us; she accepted that when Brady held the back of her neck it hurt, but it was not physical assault or torture. She acknowledged that the child was 'mentally terrified out of her life, hysterical and frightened to death', and again said that she had no defence. She would regard as justified any derogatory adjective used to describe her behaviour. Although she was unfeeling, the only thing she could say for herself was that she was frightened.

I asked her what happened next, and she said that when the girl became calmer Brady plugged in a very bright light. The tripod was in the bedroom, and the three loud cracks heard on the tape were the opening of the tripod's legs – again, these noises, she said, had been misinterpreted as blows being struck on the child. I inquired whether the child was clothed or unclothed: at this stage she had her clothes on. Then Hindley corrected the sequence she had just described: she now said the tripod legs were pulled out *before* the light was switched on. There was only one plug in the bedroom, so when the light went on the tape recorder went off.

Brady told the girl to get undressed, which she did, and then tied a scarf round the bottom half of her face in an attempt to conceal her identity. Pictures were taken, in what Hindley described as 'various unpleasant poses, not only for a child but for anybody else'. She believed Emlyn Williams, the actor and author, had described them as failing miserably as pornographic pictures – an abuse of the child's dignity. I asked her if any pictures were taken of her or him, and she said that none were; the police had recovered all the pictures taken.

Then Brady told her to go and run a bath for the child, to get rid of any dog hairs or fibres on her body. He told Hindley to wait in the bathroom. She heard no noise, but after she had waited twenty minutes or half an hour the water had gone cold, so she let it out and

104

ran some more. Eventually Brady came into the bathroom, and she went into the bedroom.

Lesley Ann Downey was lying half on and half off the end of the bed, facing down on to the bed. There was blood on her legs, from which Hindley realized that the girl had been sexually assaulted: when she first had sexual intercourse, she explained, there had been blood. The scarf was still tied round the child's face. Brady picked her up and lowered her into the bath to wash the blood off her legs. Hindley noticed there was blood on the sheet. Brady told her to wash out the bath, then he carried the small body into the bedroom and took the scarf off. There was a deep red mark around her neck where he had strangled her, and the piece of string that he had used to do it. He wrapped the child in a sheet, putting her clothes in with her. After Hindley had cleaned out the bath he told her to bring the car nearer to the house.

As she brought the car round she saw it was snowing; it hadn't been earlier, at the fairground. She thought that by now it was about 8p.m. There was nobody about: it was Boxing day evening, and very quiet. Brady carried the bundle that was Lesley Ann Downey's body and clothing and put it in the back of the vehicle – a Mini Countryman which they had traded in for the Mini pick-up.

Then they set off for Saddleworth Moor. It was very cold and the roads were very slippery, so driving was difficult. On a hill where other cars were struggling they got halfway up, quite close to where her uncle lived in Dukinfield, and then realized they could not get any further and would have to take the body back. Brady told Hindley to phone the AA to ask about road conditions, particularly on Saddleworth Moor. She was advised not to travel unless it was essential, so they decided to wait until the next day.

Hindley said she would have to go and fetch her grandmother, but Brady pointed out that that was impossible. So they drove to an area of level ground nearby, and she left Brady in the vehicle while she walked to her uncle's. She told him that she had tried to drive there but it was impossible since the gritting lorries had not been out.

105

Her uncle was 'a bit cross' at the implications of this. Hindley explained that he had had a son who had died at the age of twenty-one after a blow to his skull, which was exceptionally thin. His parents had turned his bedroom into a shrine, and would not let Gran sleep there. It was suggested that she should sleep on the settee. Hindley's uncle came outside and looked at the road conditions: there was not much snow to be seen, and he said he didn't know why Hindley couldn't take her. During her trial he gave evidence that in his opinion they could have taken Gran back with them.

They returned to Wardlebrook Avenue and took the body of Lesley Ann Downey up to Hindley's bedroom. She said she never slept in that bedroom again; after that night she hated going into it, even to clean it. Brady developed the photographs straightaway and showed them to her, and she heard the tape recording. She pleaded with him to destroy them and he said he would. She believed he had until she saw them again, following her arrest.

The next morning the gritting lorries had been out, and conditions, according to the AA, were better – although still not good. In the late afternoon, while it was still light, they loaded the body into the back of the vehicle and put in a new spade that Brady had bought as well. She drove them up to Saddleworth Moor and parked in more or less the same spot she had been in when Pauline Reade was taken up there. There were few vehicles on the road, but from where she was parked she could clearly see any traffic approaching from either direction.

Brady got out and ran up Hollin Brow Knoll with the bundle, coming back in a minute or two for the spade. She said he had practised carrying bodies with her on the Moor, telling her to make herself as limp as possible and then putting her over his shoulder and walking with her. The other three victims had all walked to their deaths on the Moor.

Hindley stayed in the vehicle, keeping watch. She had little idea of the time, but said it was getting dark and it was too cold to get out. She told us that now, after so long in prison, she had no concept of time – except in years. The snow on the ground was several inches thick. Brady returned, with the sheet, and said the girl's clothes were in the grave with her. She said she did not know what he did with the bloodstained sheet. He could not burn it because they now lived in a smokeless zone.

Although this was not the first murder, she said it was the one that had the most powerful effect on her. She was very distressed, and as a consequence she was confused about what happened afterwards – she could not describe the disposal plan in detail, as she had with the other murders. But she knew that they went back home before she collected her grandmother, and that Brady washed the spade and said he would start making the dinner. He was going to visit his mother, a late Christmas visit, and he did not come home that night. She assumed he disposed of everything while he was away.

Once again, she said, the suitcase had gone to the railway station left luggage office before the murder. Michael Fisher then asked her if she knew where Brady kept the left luggage ticket, and she said she assumed it was in his wallet. She said she was not aware that he kept it in the back of her prayer book until after the last murder. The book, she said, had sentimental value for her, as her aunt had given it to her to commemorate her first communion, and even though at this stage she was agnostic she was still attached to it. Brady knew how important it was to her, even though he knew she no longer went to church.

After a break for lunch, Hindley began to talk about Pat Hodges. Pat was one of seven children from a not very well-off family whom she met when they moved to the new house at Hattersley. Hindley became friendly with their mother, and the children came round to borrow flour or sugar. She took two of the younger ones out for rides in the car, went shopping with them and let them and the two Waterhouse children, Carol and David, who were also neighbours, wash the car for sixpence or a shilling.

'Patty', she said, seemed to be a lonely girl and she was fond of her. The child used to watch television with her and her grandmother when they first moved to Hattersley in September 1964 – Brady did not move in full-time with her until the following February. Until then he would go home on his motorbike to his mother's house after work, and Hindley would pick him up later in the van. Patty, who she thought was about twelve or thirteen (in fact she was eleven), often asked if she could go with her. Hindley said the three of them had an affectionate relationship, but there was nothing sexual about it.

Brady had two nephews – his foster-sister's boys – of whom he was very fond: he would hide money in their bedrooms for them to find as a surprise. Hindley said, not for the first time, that he was shy, but he felt affection for both his nephews and Pat Hodges. She explained that when they travelled with the girl in the van Patty sat on his lap, and he never interfered with her. If he had, Hindley pointed out, the girl would surely have stopped coming with them.

Patty did, in fact, suddenly stop visiting them. But when Hindley asked the girl why, Patty was very embarrassed and said it was because she had made friends with twin sisters who had moved into the area, and was too busy. It was not until she was in court that Hindley heard that Brady had told Patty off for using their garden as a short cut. She said she asked him if he had interfered with the girl, and he replied that he would not be so stupid. Hindley referred again to the document produced by the Legal Medico Society, in which it was asserted that Brady had sexually assaulted Pat Hodges in her presence: she denied this categorically, and said she did not know where the story had come from: it was completely untrue.

She told us that Carol and David Waterhouse had only been taken on to the Moors on a couple of occasions. Again, they were neighbours' children, and she became friendly with them after Carol asked to help clean the car. She had taken them for rides in it, and for a picnic. She said the photographs Brady took of them on the Moors were not significant: he took pictures all the time.

Then I asked her about the theory that Brady would take children up to the Moors shortly before a murder was due to take place (they took Pat Hodges up on Christmas Eve, less than forty-eight hours before the murder of Lesley Ann Downey). But Hindley could not remember the dates the Waterhouse children were taken on to the Moors, and she did not believe there was any pattern to their visits: Brady had certainly never mentioned it to her.

She told us that Brady taped Patty Hodges reading an item out of a local newspaper about the disappearance of Lesley Ann Downey. It was on New Year's day or the day after, a week after the girl's death. Gran was at a neighbour's, and Patty came round. Brady had said that when Patty was there he would put the tape on as a joke, and play it back to her afterwards. She said she was sitting in the living room by the fire, peeling potatoes, while Brady was beating eggs in the kitchen: they were going to have an omelette. The girl pulled out a pile of newspapers and magazines, and then told Hindley that her friend knew the missing girl. Hindley said she didn't look over to see exactly what Patty was reading, but assumed the missing girl she was talking about was Lesley Ann Downey. She stressed that Patty talking about the case was pure coincidence, and not, as the prosecution had alleged at the trial, deliberately engineered so that they could obtain pleasure from hearing another child talking about the murder victim.

That was all she wanted to say about the Lesley Ann Downey episode, Hindley said. But I asked her about a reference made by her sister in court: Maureen said that when she talked to Hindley about the £100 reward that had been offered for information about Lesley Ann's whereabouts, Hindley had laughed. Hindley herself said she was certain this was not true, and when she was reconciled with Maureen years later they had talked about it. Maureen had said Brady was with them at the time, and he had laughed, and she assumed Hindley must have laughed simply because he did.

The only other thing she told us about the Lesley Ann Downey case concerned an allegation made in a book by an ex-prisoner, who claimed that he had heard another inmate read out from Brady's prison records a reference to a tape recording of a child screaming while

109

her fingers were being cut off with garden shears. Hindley wanted to stress again that this kind of physical torture just did not happen – had it been so, it would have been revealed at the post mortem. This, she said, was another fabrication that had grown up around the case, part of the public's obsession with a kind of torture that had not been practised. With that, she said she had finished talking about Lesley Ann Downey and would move on to the final murder.

8

When she was telling us about the Lesley Ann Downey murder, Myra Hindley ruled out any possibility that David Smith had been involved – despite all the rumours and innuendoes that had circulated around Manchester in the years since the trial. Now she started to explain how Smith and her sister Maureen became so closely involved with her and Ian Brady.

She said the four of them used to go out together socially. She had approached the council for a flat for her sister and brother-in-law, and after they moved to live nearby in Hattersley the four would spend days out together, in Blackpool or the Lake District. She said they would also sometimes go to Whaley Bridge – and the mention of this little Derbyshire town prompted me to ask her some specific questions about that area. David Smith had told us that when they were in Whaley Bridge Brady would go off on his own, and I had wondered whether there was another grave there.

But Myra Hindley said she did not believe there was – the only times Brady went off on his own were to answer a call of nature. She stressed the stark contrast between the scenery of Saddleworth Moor and that of Whaley Bridge. Brady had frequently visited the Moors with her, and had been up there many times on his own, on his motorcycle. He found it peaceful, quiet and yet wild, and she felt he went there for a renewal of his power, which he believed came from the know-
110   ledge of what they had both done there. Once again she

stressed *both* – she said she was as guilty as he was for having made the abductions possible.

Whaley Bridge, on the other hand, had a completely different atmosphere – it was a place for congenial picnics. I asked her about a churchyard at the nearby village of Taxal; I had understood from Smith that when Brady went off on his own it was in this direction, and the carvings on the old church tower might have been of interest to anyone involved in Devil worship. The churchyard has lots of old raised stone box graves with heavy slabs on them, and I had noticed that many of the names on the graves were, by coincidence, Bennett. I felt it was impossible to know what was in the mind of an evil man like Brady – it might have pleased him to offend against the sanctity of a churchyard by burying a victim there. Trying to look into the mind of such a complex man who has kept his secrets for so many years is difficult, and there was little I did not believe him capable of. A trained dog had already examined the churchyard and found nothing, but I thought it was worthwhile double-checking. Hindley said she did not know the village or the church, and was sure in her own mind that it had no significance. She did not believe Brady was interested in Devil worship, but she did give us an example of his contempt for religion.

One Christmas Eve she had wanted to go to midnight mass – they were on Gorton Lane and could hear the church bells. She tried to persuade Brady to go with her, just as an observer; but he said he would not go into a Roman Catholic church because if any religion had any claim on him at all it was the Protestant one. So they went to St James's Anglican church further along the road. When they came out of the service they wandered through the cemetery; then Brady went behind some trees and urinated over the gravestones, telling her: 'That's what I think of established Churches.'

She said it was alleged that the only books they ever read were pornographic, sexually intimidating or sado-masochistic. She referred to the remarks of the Attorney General, Sir Frederick Elwyn Jones, who led the prosecution at the trial and said he was not going to

111

advertise the books by naming them in court, but handed copies to the jury. She pointed out that these books
belonged to Brady or Smith – there had been no suggestion that any of them were hers.

I asked her about the Saddleworth Moor map reference of 0666, and again she said she did not believe
this had any significance. Although Brady had nothing
but contempt for religion, he had never mentioned
black magic or Devil worship to her. I believed what
she was saying – I have discussed religion with Brady
myself, and although he claims to be a non-believer he
has never suggested any interest in diabolism.

Then she told us about the friendship between Brady
and Smith. She could not at first remember when they
first met, but after some deliberation she said it was
before Smith's marriage to her sister. Maureen had a
job at Millwards while she was courting Smith and,
because of this Brady met Smith several times when he
arrived to meet Maureen after work. Hindley remembered that Smith would get angry on occasions, because he thought that some of the men at work were
making advances to Maureen. The four of them went
out together in the evenings, either going to the house
in Wiles Street, Gorton, where Maureen and David
lived with David's father – next door but one to Pauline
Reade's parents – or to Wardlebrook Avenue. They
would watch television, play cards and drink wine.
Maureen and Hindley would often go to bed at around
11p.m., leaving Brady and Smith downstairs together.
The next morning they would find them still there.
Smith said in court that it was during these evenings
that Brady began his indoctrination, giving him books
to read, expounding his own theories and philosophies, and planning bank robberies.

Hindley remembered one evening when she and
Brady were watching television: the BBC were running
a series of Shakespeare plays covering the Wars of the
Roses, and this particular one was *Richard III*. It was
late in the evening when David, Maureen and her
mother came round to break the news that Maureen's
first baby had died. Brady was angry that they had
interrupted his television viewing, so she took the sad
little party to an uncle's in Stockport. Hindley was

upset about her niece's death, while Brady was not at all sympathetic.

By this time, she said, David and Maureen were living close to them, at a block of flats called Underwood Court. David never held a job for long, and the couple were poor.

She talked about their chaotic domestic situation – they were always embroiled in problems and arguments. On one occasion Brady and Smith argued, and Brady told her he was fed up with being annoyed by Smith's constant domestic difficulties. He said he was going to get rid of Smith – to kill him. She said she had no idea what his motive was, but she persuaded Brady not to kill him because of the love her sister Maureen had for him, despite their differences.

Smith often came round to their home uninvited and was made welcome, usually going with Brady up to Hindley's bedroom, which was used as a bed-sitting room. (This contradicts the statement that Smith made to the police, when he said that access to the house depended on the mood that Brady was in. 'He's a very temperamental sort of fellow,' Smith said.) On one evening in October 1965, Hindley said, the two of them had been up there when Brady came down with the blue suitcase in his hand, because he was taking it to the left luggage office. He told her that he and Smith were going to commit a robbery at an Electricity Board showroom, and they wanted all incriminating articles out of the house. The suitcase was taken to the usual place at Central Station.

The following week – she remembered it clearly because it was the day that Edward Evans died – David and Maureen Smith received notice of eviction. Smith came round with the notice, which was for non-payment of rent, but the letter from the council also alleged there had been complaints from neighbours about 'teddy boys' frequenting the Smiths' flat. Maureen was pregnant with her second child at the time.

When I pointed out to her that two suitcases were in fact taken to the station the day before Edward Evans' death, not the week before, she was surprised and said she must have had a lapse of memory. But she recovered quickly by saying that she was confusing the

113

murder with the robbery, which was not due to take place for another week after the suitcase was taken to the station.

She said when Smith came round with the eviction letter, he and Brady had a discussion about it. They realized they could not carry out the robbery on that particular night because they had planned it for the day before the takings at the showroom were deposited in the bank. She had no money – she had just paid the car insurance. Brady had no money either. There was none in the house.

Brady said, 'We'll have to roll a queer.' She commented that in those days, before the Wolfenden Act, it was an offence for homosexuals to practise, even in private, so if they robbed one he would not go to the police because he would have to admit to his homosexuality.

I asked her who was present when this conversation took place; herself, Brady and Smith, she said, and they were in the living room of the house at Wardlebrook Avenue. Brady told Smith that he and Hindley would go into Manchester to try to pick someone up.

They left the house at 7.30p.m. She said that as she got into the car Brady was still talking to Smith, but she could not hear what they were saying because the engine was running. She went into great detail about an incident that happened on the journey to Manchester: a dog jumped out into the road and the car in front of theirs hit it. Both cars stopped. The dog ran off, and Brady and she went after it. The couple who owned the dog caught it and said it was OK. Hindley offered to take it to the vet, but they said there was no need.

In Manchester Brady said they would look at Central Station, and he would buy a couple of bottles of wine or beer to take back with them. She parked on a double yellow line, and Brady said he would not be long. She added that to park legally cost 3s 6d (17½p) in those days, which for her was quite a lot of money. When a policeman came up she told him her boyfriend had just gone to the station buffet; if she was still there when he came round the block again he would book her, he said.

Luckily Brady returned soon afterwards. She told

him about her encounter with the policeman, but he said it didn't matter. He introduced her as his sister to a youth he called Eddie, who he said was coming back to the house for a drink. They drove back to Hattersley, and she pulled the car up where she normally parked. As she was locking the car Brady told her to go and get Smith. She walked around to Underwood Court, and when she spoke into the entryphone she said it was Smith who answered her.

Although in her confession Myra Hindley exonerates Smith from having taken part in the first four murders, I was aware when dealing with both Hindley and Brady that they still harbour deep grudges against Smith, and I accept that she has possibly coloured his role in this murder more vividly than it warrants.

She insisted it was Smith who spoke to her and released the door, allowing her to go up – although at the trial Smith said it was Maureen who did this. She also said that when she got upstairs Maureen was in her nightie, but David was dressed except for his shoes and jacket. He had told the police and the court that he was in bed when she called, but Hindley made the point that he could hardly have got dressed in the couple of seconds it took her to get up to the flat. She said he had been waiting for her.

She told him that Brady was waiting for him. When Maureen walked in she had to make some excuse about why she was there so late, and she told her sister that Brady wanted to talk to David. Then she gave Maureen a message to give to their mother, to say that she would be round on Friday to do her hair, and she also talked about borrowing a pair of her mother's shoes. She explained to us that Maureen at this stage worked with their mother, and so would be seeing her the next day.

She told us that Brady had told her to stay round at the flat at Underwood Court for a while, which was what she intended to do. But then she remembered that all the street lights on the estate went off at 11p.m., and that unless she went with Smith she would have to walk back on her own in the dark. She was making the point, I believe, that she really should not even have been in the house when the murder was committed, and if it had not been for her fear of the unlit streets she would not have been.

She said that Smith picked up a stick about one and three-quarter inches thick and between two and three feet in length and with a piece of string looped around the end. He used it when taking the dog for walks. They walked back to the house together, and she knocked at the door. Contrary to Smith's evidence that he had to wait across the road until she flicked the landing light on and off, a signal for him to go in, she claims they both went in together. Brady had told her to knock rather than use her key, and he answered the door.

Hindley then said she went through to the kitchen to feed the dogs, closing the door behind her to keep them in. Smith went into the living room with Brady. The house had a serving hatch, connecting the kitchen to the living room, and it was in a cupboard underneath this hatch that the dog food was kept. She was opening a can when she heard a chair crashing across the living room and scraping on the floor: as she looked through the hatch she saw Brady and Edward Evans struggling, each holding the other's lapels.

She ran into the hallway and saw Smith standing in the doorway. She shouted to him to help Brady, and then as he ran into the living room she dashed back into the kitchen and shut the door behind her to keep the dogs in. What happened next she described as 'all hell let loose'. She could hear very loud screaming, which she assumed was coming from Evans. She said she could not see what was happening, and when I asked her where Brady and Smith were all she could tell me was that they were in the room with Evans.

She had no idea how long it lasted, but when the house was quiet again she went into the living room. Everywhere 'was one complete pool of blood', she said. Evans was sinking face down to the floor. As she went in her little black and white dog which she called Poppet, and which figured on so many of the photographs of moorland scenery with her, dashed past her into the room. The other dog followed it.

She could not go into the room. She said she could not stand the sight of blood: anyone who knew her well would vouch that she had never been able to stand it.

116

She ran back into the kitchen and was 'horribly sick'. Brady came through and went to a drawer where tools were kept, and pulled out a piece of electric wire, the flex from an old iron.

'He told me to pull myself together because he said I had to clean the place up,' she said. She told us she thought he went back with the flex to finish Evans off. I asked her what he had been hitting Edward Evans with; afterwards she found out it had been an axe that they used for chopping firewood. They had had it in the household for some time – it had not been bought specifically.

She re-emphasized that he said the place had to be cleaned. Her Granny had shouted downstairs to ask what all the noise was about, and she was frightened that if her grandmother came downstairs and saw the mess she would die of a heart attack. She called up that she had dropped the tape recorder on her foot and that the dogs had started barking.

Brady once again said the place had to be cleaned up, but she couldn't face it. She managed to refill the bowls and buckets with clean water and throw out the dirty water, which was full of blood. She believed that Smith had claimed in his statement that she said something like 'Eddie's a dead weight' or 'Eddie's a brainy bastard' as they cleaned up the mess around his head. But she denied saying it. (In fact, Smith alleged only that Brady made the remark about Eddie being a dead weight, although he also claimed that Hindley joined Brady in laughing at the remark.) According to Hindley, it was Smith himself who made these remarks. After they had finished cleaning up Brady told her to get some polythene sheeting. They had some which had come off bags of chemicals at Millwards, and which she used to protect the interior of her car.

She said she hadn't been able to see anything through the restricted vision of the serving hatch. Brady had said that he hit Evans with the axe, and the boy just kept on shouting so he kept on hitting – the more they tried to quieten him, the more noise he made.

I asked her if she knew why he had hit him in the first place. It puzzled me: she had claimed they had

117

planned a robbery – they were going to 'roll a queer'. But you don't bring someone back to your house if you are going to rob them; you do it on the street.

She replied, 'I think they wanted to kill him.'

'Was the intention all along to kill him, and not to rob him?' I asked.

She said it was to do both. She thought Brady and Smith had been discussing killings, although she said they had not talked about it with her. The whole explanation of this killing does not ring true to me, and I do not believe a lot of thought had been given to it. No criminal, however stupid, would take someone they intended to rob back to their home. If Smith and Brady had been planning to do a robbery together they would have gone out together.

At this point Michael Fisher interjected that a passage about murder in Smith's writing had been found in a notebook that was in the suitcase left at the station. He had also written about the killing of infants in their cradles. Hindley recapped on Smith's criminal history and personality saying that he had a police record for minor violence and a reputation as a violent person. Both Hindley and Fisher were making the point that it was quite possible that Brady and Smith had planned a murder, not just a robbery.

I brought the conversation back to Edward Evans. Hindley said she went to get sheets and polythene to wrap the body up. Brady told her that Evans had resisted when he had asked him for money and a fight had started. Brady had weak ankles and was limping quite badly, and he said he could not dispose of the body that night. They put cold compresses round his injured ankle.

Then Smith and Brady carried Evans' body upstairs, and Hindley held her grandmother's door closed in case she came out of her bedroom to go to the bathroom. They put the body under the window in Hindley's bedroom, and went downstairs to complete the cleaning up. She went into the kitchen to make a cup of tea, and then they all sat down in the living room. She was at pains to point out that, although Smith said she was sitting with her feet on the mantelpiece, this was not true. She believes it is these minute details that have built up the public perception of her as a monster.

She said Brady was sitting on two chairs at the end of the room, with some notepaper on the coffee table. He was writing a disposal plan. I asked if this was the plan to bury the body. Then she remembered something that she had forgotten to tell us earlier: Brady had opened Evans' jacket and removed his wallet. Although Brady knew his victim's first name, and later said in court that he knew Evans visited homosexual bars in Manchester, it was from the wallet that they discovered his name was Edward Evans and that he was an apprentice of some sort. She said she did not know whether there was any money in the wallet. Brady, she thought, might have known Evans previously.

I asked her about the electric flex and she said she saw Brady use this on Evans. The youth was lying face down with a cushion cover over his head. Brady leaned over, put the flex round his neck and pulled it from behind. She said the string from Smith's stick was used to tie up the body, but she only became aware of this at the trial.

She said there was almost as much blood on Smith's clothes and stick as there was on Brady's clothes, whereas there were only a few spots on her shoes, which came when she went into the room to try to get the dogs out. At the trial, she said, it had been alleged by the prosecution that she must have been in the room because one spot on her skirt was arterial blood, which must have come shooting out when one of Evans' arteries was severed. She stressed again that she was not in the room, and said that in cross-examination Smith had conceded it was possible she was not there, that he could only see the rest of the room out of the corner of his eye, and that he might have thought the birdcage on its stand was a figure.

Then she went back to the point we had reached a few minutes earlier: the body was upstairs and Brady was writing out the disposal plan. She said his first idea was that they should hide the body in some bushes on a very dark road nearby that she knew – they could make it look like a hit-and-run road accident. She claims that David Smith said the best thing to do was to bury the body. She thought he didn't know anything about it, so commented sarcastically: 'Where, in the garden?' Smith said 'No, Penistone.' She said she thought that 'PB' on the disposal plan that was produced in court stood for Penistone Burn: she did not know about the prayer book until the court case.

I asked her if she knew what 'WH' stood for on the plan. She thought it meant Woodhead, which is on the way to Penistone. I asked her if, in the light of developments, she now thought it stood for Wessendon Head on Saddleworth Moor. She did not think so, since she and Brady did not know the names of specific areas up there: they just knew the whole area as the Moor.

Brady's ankle, she said, was very painful, so they had to leave the disposal for the following day. She said Smith showed no fear or apprehension – nothing to indicate he was appalled, frightened or sickened. She felt she would have noticed it if he had.

By the time they had finished making the disposal plan, according to Hindley it was three o'clock in the morning. Brady told her she would have to go to work the next day, as it would look suspicious if they both stayed off – he could not go because he could not walk. It was decided that she would pick Smith up in the car on Hyde Road at 5.30p.m. the next day, and they would drive round to his grandfather's house where his dead baby's pram was kept. They would use this to move the body, which was much bigger and heavier than Lesley Ann Downey's.

Smith then said he would go, and would see them both the next day. Brady insisted that Hindley went outside to lock the car up properly and put the anti-theft device on. But she did not want to go out, so he agreed to do it himself. The following day, when the police took the car away, they found Brady's wallet on the dashboard; in it was the disposal plan. Looking back, she believes the wallet fell out of his pocket when he was padlocking the wheel, and that he put it on the dashboard and then forgot it.

She did not sleep that night, but spent what was left of it in an armchair downstairs. The next morning she started to get ready for work and took a cup of tea up to her grandmother, as she always did. Brady was writing a letter to his boss, explaining that he could not manage

120

to get into work because of the injury to his ankle. Then there was a knock at the back door.

9

Myra Hindley would, she told us, normally have been suspicious of a knock at the back door so early in the morning; but she was still in a state of shock from the events of the night before. When she answered it, a man in a baker's overall asked if her husband was in. She said she didn't have a husband. He asked her if there was a man in the house. She said all she could think was that they didn't get Sunblest bread – they had Mother's Pride. Then the bread man told her he was a policeman, and that he wanted to see her boyfriend. She took him into the living room, where Brady was sitting up in bed (they had a sofa bed downstairs), and told him the police had arrived.

Superintendent Bob Talbot told them he had information about an act of violence involving guns that had taken place there the previous evening. Hindley believed David Smith had told the police they had guns. She told Talbot there had been no such violence. He asked to look round the house, but before that happened she was searched by a policewoman in the bathroom. She took the police upstairs, but asked them not to go into her grandmother's room. When they insisted, she opened the door to show them that the old woman was in bed; she told her grandmother not to worry, and said she would bring her another cup of tea. The police tried the door of the room where the body was, and found it locked. They asked Brady for the key, but he didn't answer. Hindley told them that the key was at work, and they offered to drive her there to get it, at which point Brady told her that she had better give it to them.

When they came downstairs the police told Brady they had found a trussed up body, and that they were arresting him on suspicion of murder. After they cautioned him they told Hindley they wanted her to go to Hyde Police Station with them. A neighbour was called in – Hindley made some excuse by saying there was a problem over a hit-and-run accident – and it was arranged for her grandmother to be taken to a friend's. The police said they wanted the house empty, so the older dog, Lassie, went with her grandmother while Hindley was allowed to take the little one, Poppet, with her to the police station.

When she was questioned about what had happened the night before, she said it was an accident and that she didn't want to talk. She asked for food for her dog, and some was brought, and she learned from her questioner, Detective Chief Superintendent Arthur Benfield, that David Smith had told the police the whole story. Her mother arrived at the police station, and said: 'Myra, they say you are in a lot of trouble because you won't talk to them. They are talking about bodies being buried on the Moors.'

This, she said, upset her. The police carried out the usual tests to which anyone suspected of taking part in a murder is subjected: saliva tests, blood samples and so on. Later Hindley was told that Brady had been charged with murder. She said Brady had made a statement admitting he had had a fight with Edward Evans, and that David Smith and he had killed the youth between them. Hindley, he said, had only done what she had been told. But she was still not prepared to talk to the police.

At one point it was suggested by the police that she was a prostitute and that Evans was a client who had refused to pay up – so her boyfriend had killed him. This she denied. She said if there had been any sexual activity in the house that night, she had not taken part in it. There was evidence, she said, that three people had been smoking at the house that evening, but at this stage of her life she did not smoke: forensic tests, she told us, had shown she had the same saliva group as the victim, Edward Evans.

Now, at Cookham Wood, her solicitor asked her about the medical examination she was given, and she told him that the examination showed that she had not had sexual intercourse. She said she had not had sexual relations with Brady for at least two weeks. Peter Timms had to leave at this stage because he had another appointment; Hindley accepted this with equanimity and said she was willing to carry on with her confession without him present.

Later on the day after the murder, she continued, her mother and prospective stepfather came to Hyde Police Station again; her mother brought clothes for Hindley to change into, because the police wanted the ones she was wearing for forensic examination. Then she was allowed to go, but was told to return the following day for further questioning.

Over the next few days she was at the police station every day. She asked if she could have her car back, but was told that it was still needed for forensic examination. She took some food and books to the police station for Brady, and asked for her driving licence to be returned so that she could hire a car. She explained that she was having problems getting about between her mother's and her uncle's where she was staying and the police station; but the police told her they were unable to find her licence.

Brady, she said, had glimpsed her walking into the police station at one point with a policewoman on either side of her: he assumed she had been charged, and asked for the same solicitor as Hindley. In fact at that stage she had not been charged, but when she was they did indeed share a solicitor – which, she said, enabled them to communicate with one another. She was initially charged with being an accessory to the murder of Edward Evans, and was held on remand at Risley.

I asked her about the period between the murder of Edward Evans and the time she was remanded – she was at liberty for four full days before being charged on Monday, 11 October. Had she, in that time, disposed of any evidence? She said she knew Brady had some papers which he had told her he had forgotten to put into the suitcase. They were nothing to do with the murders, but she believed they were plans for robberies, listing times that money was delivered to various banks and the registration numbers of the delivery vehicles. Her part in the planned robberies was that of getaway driver.

On the Saturday morning she went to Millwards to

collect her wages and Brady's, and asked to be sacked so she could go on the dole. Then she went to a cupboard near the fireplace where some very old records were stacked, found Brady's papers and burnt them in an ashtray. She said they were in an envelope which she did not open. Brady had not told her to burn these papers – she did it of her own accord. I asked her if Gilbert Dears, the youth who lived near Halifax and had been in borstal with Brady, had been part of the robbery plans; she thought he had, although he had never actually come on the scene.

I told her that our investigations had shown that the missing Dears had drowned, and she was relieved to hear that his death could not be connected to Brady or herself, which over the years various commentators had suggested. At the time of the original investigation, she said, the police had questioned her about Dears, but all she had been able to tell them was that he was a friend of Brady's.

We talked about Brady and any other possible victims. Had they ever had any failures – had they ever approached any children who had run away from them? She said they had not, and that this was why she wanted to write a book – so that she could give a warning to children that anyone who approaches them, man or woman, however plausible they might sound, should be ignored. Children should not go with such people.

I inquired if Brady had ever discussed any other killings with her. She said no, very firmly. Then I asked if she had been involved in any other killings. She replied emphatically: 'No, I swear I haven't.'

Michael Fisher asked her if she knew about Brady being haunted by 'the green mask of death'. This was an allegation made by the journalist Fred Harrison, who, after interviewing Brady, claimed that his subject told him that 'the green mask of death' demanded sacrifices from him. Hindley said Brady had never mentioned anything like that to her.

I asked her if she suspected that Brady was involved in homosexual activities. She said she used to wonder what he did downstairs all night with Smith, but nevertheless felt that when he wasn't with her – when he went into Manchester on his own or when he did not come round to her house – he was probably with other women.

I explained that I was putting these questions because, after the murder of Evans, Brady had said: 'That was the messiest one so far,' which suggested that there might have been others apart from the children. She reiterated that she had not been involved in any others, but she wondered whether Brady had; he had allegedly confessed to others to Fred Harrison, but she said she did not know whether this confession was true.

Prompted by Fisher, who asked her how affectionate Brady was towards her, I asked if her relationship with him was normal. She explained that, when she first met him, she didn't know what a normal relationship between a man and a woman was. He didn't show a lot of interest in her sexually, but for the first few times they had normal sexual intercourse. There were times when he had just wanted her to relieve him, and on a couple of occasions he had forced her to have anal sex with him, which she described as 'dreadfully painful'. On other occasions he liked her to insert a candle into his anus while he relieved himself.

He never showed overt affection towards her, she said. The most they would ever do was sit in the car or stand kissing. Kissing was as much as she had ever done with other boyfriends. Brady, she said, didn't even know how to kiss properly – it seemed to her that he had never had any experience of it. She told us that if she was ever out with Brady and she linked her arm through his he would take his hands out of his pockets and say, 'Don't do that. Walk normally.' But there were times, she said, when he was loving and affectionate. He would call her 'kiddo' as a term of endearment. Despite everything he had done, she told us she could not think of him as wholly evil at all times. Sometimes he was kind, and he would surprise her by bringing home unexpected presents.

She pointed out that Smith had made a statement that, although they were both very fond of dogs, he had never known Brady show any sentiment over people.

On the whole he despised human beings; he respected very few – people like Hitler and the Marquis

125

de Sade. Brady himself told me on another occasion that he hated Winston Churchill. Hindley revealed to us how on the day Churchill died, he went out and bought a bottle of Drambuie to celebrate. However, he was very fond of the foster-family who had brought him up in Glasgow.

She felt there was a little child inside Brady, she told us, and she had tried to bring out love from him by showering him with her affection, to reach inside him and bring out what was there. Nevertheless, she said he was 'always cloaked in an aura of mystery and secrecy' that she could never penetrate. This was in many ways what fascinated her and made him so attractive to her.

I brought the conversation back to the possibility of other victims. According to Smith, Brady had told him there were two types of murders: in one type the victims were approached in the street and disposed of quickly, while the others were the ones in which Hindley was involved. When Brady discussed the killing of Evans with Smith he had said 'This one doesn't count', and that he 'wasn't due one yet'. This would suggest that the killing of Evans was out of sequence.

I also knew that they had hired cars on three occasions, one of which was when John Kilbride was abducted and murdered. Hindley told us that Brady had paid for the hire of the vehicles, and that he had tried to cover every contingency, stressing that they should hire vehicles even on occasions when nobody disappeared. She said she could not explain what he meant when he said he was 'not due one yet'.

When asked about their holidays in Scotland she said they had been five or six times, maybe seven or eight, travelling sometimes on the motorcycle and sometimes by car. She did not think he had ever killed anybody in Scotland, and to illustrate this point she explained how on one trip, when they had driven beyond Loch Lomond and were camping, she had asked him why they didn't take a couple more days off work. He said he did not want their colleagues at work to know they were living together, and grew angry with her for suggesting it. When she saw a child walking past and asked him, 'Don't you want to do another one?' he retorted that he could not kill one of his own –

meaning anyone Scottish.

I asked about Smith's connection with murders other than that of Edward Evans. To the best of her knowledge, Hindley said, he had not been involved in any others. She said she had done him irreparable harm in court by accusing him of bringing Lesley Ann Downey to the house and taking the child away again, unharmed, after Brady had taken photographs of her. This explanation had grown out of a statement by Brady that there was another man involved: it was he, she said, who had started the lies about Smith, and she had carried on with them. She said she would one day like to write to Smith and ask for forgiveness for the damage she had done to him. But the statements he had made to the police and in court about the Evans murder, she pointed out, had accused her of a deeper involvement than she in fact had in that killing, and she believed he made things as bad as possible for her.

Years later, when her sister was in the process of divorcing Smith, Maureen had told her that he had said that he wasn't going to go down with Brady and Hindley. This had eased Hindley's conscience about what she had tried to do to him. She confirmed again to us that David Smith had not been connected in any way with the murders of Pauline Reade, John Kilbride, Keith Bennett or Lesley Ann Downey.

Brady and Smith had first met, she went on, when she got her sister Maureen a job at Millwards. Smith, who never really worked, used to call for Maureen and she would often drive all of them home together. But she felt that the friendship between Brady and Smith did not become really firm until after he married Maureen. She did not know if they met at other times, without her or Maureen knowing. The marriage was not approved of by the Hindley family, so she did not attend the ceremony. But she and Brady took the newly-weds to the Lake District for a day out. The pregnant Maureen sat in the front beside Hindley, with David and Brady in the back. They travelled for hundreds of miles in this way, and became regular visitors to each other's houses.

We talked about the grave sites on the Moors, and she told us that as far as she knew Brady did not use markers to locate the graves. She felt she would have been able to help us more on her visit to the Moor if the weather had been better and if we had not been hampered by the attentions of the media. She said she was 99.9 per cent certain that if she was given a clear day on Saddleworth Moor she would be able to locate the graves and save months of digging. We discussed the half crowns that he had left in the area of Pauline Reade's grave, which she said he had 'strewn' around, throwing them as far as he could. She wasn't there when he did it, but walking on the rocks.

At this stage Michael Fisher read out a long extract from David Smith's writing, found in the suitcase that Brady had left at the station. Hindley felt the writing – a précis of de Sade's philosophies, backed up her assertion that Smith was close to Brady and shared his philosophies.

There was another document in court during the trial, she reminded us – a diary that Smith had composed. She remembered a section in which he had written something like 'Infants should be murdered in their cots.' Although she had pointed this out to her solicitor in court, she said, Smith was not questioned about it. She felt it illustrated the extent to which he was prepared to think certain things, and that he had a similar bent mind to Brady's.

Throughout the investigation, dealing with both Brady and Hindley, I found that whenever David Smith's name was mentioned they would verbally throw things at him – as though even now, after all these years, they still feel that if it hadn't been for him they wouldn't be where they are. Even Myra Hindley – who was openly confessing to her part in all the murders, and was clearing Smith of involvement in any except the last one, and talking about the great injustice she had done him and how she would write to him for forgiveness – still had to blacken him as much as she could.

I asked her if she knew whether Smith had been given books to read by Brady. She said it was possible; alternatively Smith could have bought his own. They did, she told us, spend a lot of time together in the bed sitting-room which had been her bedroom, but she was not with them so could not say whether Brady encouraged Smith to read any particular sort of book.

At this point she wanted to put on tape that I had not offered her any form of immunity from prosecution, and that she had asked for none. She was upset by newspaper reports that she had been promised a deal. She said she wished Mrs Winnie Johnson had written to her fifteen years earlier, when she first broke contact with Brady, and that the police had visited her then. The police had seen her since she had been in prison, but that was in 1967 and she had not been prepared to tell them anything then. Because of that, the parents of Pauline Reade and Keith Bennett had endured twenty-two years of agony, she said.

She restated that she would not be applying for parole in 1990. Both she and Michael Fisher pointed out how difficult it had been for her to confess after such a long time, and that there might be details that she had forgotten that she would want to bring up at a later date. It had taken long sessions with her solicitor and with Peter Timms to prepare her to face the ordeal of making a confession. Hindley herself described confessing as 'like watching a malignant tumour being removed without an anaesthetic, feeling the pain as you are watching it being done'. She said she knew this was only the beginning of her pain – the worst was yet to come. But she felt she had been lightened of an intolerable burden. She appealed to God that the bodies of the two missing youngsters should be found, to ease the minds of Mrs Reade and Mrs Johnson. She knew she was twenty-two years too late, but, at least, she said, she was trying to redeem herself and make her peace with God.

It was late in the evening by now, and I would have liked the whole interview to end. The information she had given had prompted a great many new avenues of inquiry, I had a lot of investigation to initiate and I wanted to get on with it. I would like to have parted at that point, having made arrangements to come back and talk to her again if we found there were any details that needed elaborating. But she said she had more to tell. She had blocked things off in her mind for so long, and now it was all coming back. She wanted to see me the next day to add more, and to explain her position in greater detail. Hindley was agitated, and her voice dropped to a mumble. It was clear that she did have more that she wanted to say, so I agreed to return.

10

When Geoff Knupfer and I went back the following morning we were expecting to get away fairly quickly. Hindley told us she wanted to add a few comments on the evidence she had already given, and that she would like to make a statement about herself and her confession. She said if she seemed at all hesitant while speaking it was because she was reading from her notes. Then she started, and we soon realized it was going to be a long statement.

She told us that when she went to prison she still maintained the same feelings for Ian Brady, despite what he had done. She had prayed that she would get life imprisonment herself, as she could not envisage life without him. She did not mean she would miss her involvement in his murders, but simply that she had no other friends, no boyfriends. Her only contacts were a few neighbours and colleagues.

When she was first remanded, and charged only with being an accessory to the murder of Edward Evans, their solicitor told her that she might be acquitted or given a short sentence. Brady told her that if she were, he had no intention of serving the life sentence he knew he would get for killing Evans. He had already spent three months in Strangeways Prison and some months in borstal: he told her he would kill himself by using the glass from a jar of jam his mother had brought him in a food parcel rather than endure a lengthy prison sentence. When she was given life, she begged him in one of her letters not to commit suicide. Brady said he would not. 'He said he would not leave me to endure the fate that he himself would not endure.'

About nine months before she broke off contact with him, (they wrote to each other regularly until early 1971), he sensed that she was beginning to drift away. He wrote and asked her if she remembered a question he had asked her in a country pub in Whitefield, when, after a week of not speaking to each other, he had passed her a note at work asking her to meet him that night. They went to the pub on his motorbike, and he asked her if she wanted to finish with him. Her reply then was no. Now he was asking her the question again.

She explained, that although they had drifted so far apart, she felt he had nobody else in the world apart from Lord Longford and another prison visitor. He would not allow his mother to visit him because he was protesting to the Home Office about inter-prison visits (i.e. the lack of freedom for one prisoner to visit another in prison) – he protested about everything connected with the Home Office. She said she felt sorry for him; he would be left with virtually nobody if she finished with him, so she replied that she didn't want to finish with him.

She said her feelings towards him had changed: whereas she had once loved him passionately her emotions had become quieter, and she quoted a passage from a poem by Wordsworth about the first wild ecstasies of love which mature into a more sober passion. 'He wrote back to me and told me he had waited for my letter to arrive so he would know where his fate lay, because if my answer had been yes, that I wanted to finish with him, he would do what he had originally planned.'

She realized this was emotional blackmail. He had said from the very beginning that it was her and himself against the world, and in a real sense it was. Although she had had some very difficult times in prison, she had not been on Rule 43 – segregation from other prisoners – after the first month. She had made some very good friends, she had met Lord Longford, and through other friends she had met people who

131

were regular visitors and correspondents. She felt she was quietly supported while she was in prison, but that Ian had nobody. She said that even though she knew he was blackmailing her, she could not desert him.

At the start of her sentence she said she passionately wanted inter-prison visits with him, and so did he. But she had never resorted to hunger strikes or stopping her mother visiting, as he did as part of his protest over not being allowed to see her. After a while she felt she did not want to see him anyway, but for his sake she kept up the formal request for inter-prison visits.

When, in January 1967, Manchester Police asked if they could visit Holloway to interview her, she refused to see them. The governor of the prison told her she was under no obligation to do so. Hindley said she just wanted to get on with her sentence (she had at that stage only served ten months of it) as she knew it was going to be a long one. She wrote to tell Brady of the police approach, and he replied that he had had the same request. He told her she must see the police, in the presence of their solicitor; otherwise, he argued, it would look as though she had something to hide.

So she agreed to see the two senior detectives. They questioned her about Pauline Reade and Keith Bennett, but she told them she had already been questioned extensively during the original investigation and had nothing further to add. She told them they should go and see David Smith – this, she told us now, was another injustice she had done him as she always knew he had nothing to do with Pauline Reade's death. The police asked for proof that Smith had killed Pauline Reade, but she said she had none.

She pointed out that at the trial Brady had tried to exonerate her – within the limits of what he was prepared to admit. He told her counsel during cross-examination that she was his typist in the office 'and this tended to wrap over' – meaning that his views would prevail in their private lives as well as at work.

She said that when she told him she had gone back to her religion he had responded that it was her business, but that he hoped she would not be disillusioned. She wrote him a coded message saying she had been to confession but had not revealed anything. As time went by he started to accuse her of preaching to him and trying to convert him. He wrote what she described as nasty letters to her, asking what colour hair-shirt she was wearing that day, what was her penance for the day, and what was her answer to the fifty million people in China – where did God fit them in, in heaven, if they didn't believe in God? They were very abusive letters, she said, and in the end she realized there was no need to continue to correspond. She wrote to him saying she would always care for him, always wish him well, but that there was no need for him to write to her again as she would not be writing to him. She also told him she didn't believe he would kill himself – he wouldn't consider it would be worth killing himself. If he did write, she told him, she had given the prison governor instructions to return his letters unopened.

It was while she was still corresponding with Brady that her sister Maureen, who at the trial had given evidence for the prosecution, wrote to her. Hindley said she had always been close to Maureen and had never hated her for what she did: 'She was almost as dominated by Smith as I was by Brady,' she said. 'I was just very hurt by some of the things she had said.'

Maureen had told her in a letter that she knew she had done wrong, and Hindley inferred from this that Maureen was regretting giving prejudicial evidence against her. When she told Brady about this he told her to send the letter to their solicitor, saying that Maureen was implying that she was involved with Smith in other things. Hindley said she knew this was not what the letter meant, so she did not send it to the solicitor. And despite the fact that Brady regularly mentioned in his letters that he hoped she would not write to Maureen again, the two sisters kept in touch.

She made a reference to Brady's alleged confessions to a journalist, in which Brady had apparently said there was as much blood on David Smith and his wife as there was on himself and Hindley. She said he had also accused Smith of taking Polaroid pornographic pictures of Maureen, and she did not believe this was true. But she said it didn't matter any more, as her

133

sister was dead. Brady, she said, hated Maureen for giving detrimental evidence about them.

In either 1968 or 1969 their solicitor approached them both to say he had been offered a considerable sum of money from a national newspaper to buy 'the tartan album', a photograph album with a tartan cover which had contained many pictures of her and him together, and which had been returned to them after the trial as part of their personal property. She wrote to the solicitor and said 'absolutely no way'. Brady wrote to say the money would be useful for her on her release. 'But I said I didn't want the album selling. I didn't want my pictures in the papers again.'

They had another approach, from a subsidiary of Paramount Pictures in America, who wanted to make a film of the Emlyn Williams book about the case, *Beyond Belief*, to be directed by William Friedkin. They sent her a contract to sign, which would allow her name, likeness and those of her family to be used and portrayed by actors and actresses. 'They left a pound sign blank, indicating that I could name my own price. But I sent it back and said I could not believe anybody could contemplate making a film out of a book of that nature.' She wrote to Justice, the organization that campaigns on behalf of prisoners and ex-prisoners, as well as to her solicitor.

Brady was again quite cross, because he said they were going to make the movie anyway so she might as well have the money. She wrote back and said she did not want 'blood money', and she was relieved when MPs representing the families of the victims stepped in and had the film project dropped. Brady wrote and accused her of becoming too intractable, she told us. He did not like the fact that she was by now able to say no. She said she realized that he needed her as much as she needed him.

She stressed she was not trying to put the blame for what happened solely on him, because she accepted her responsibility. She said that she did not have his excuse – that there was something mentally or psychologically wrong. 'I didn't have any traumas in my childhood as he may have done. I didn't have a grudge against the world or society. I had no excuse for my actions. It was out of fear in the beginning, and after that just to remain safe, and hoping that between murders he would display affection and never fancied anybody else.'

She did not believe anybody to be wholly bad, and she was not trying to blame everything on to him. But she said she knew without one shred of doubt that if she had never met him she would not have become involved in any of the things for which she was eventually sentenced. Although she could never be sure, she doubted if she would ever have gone to prison for anything. She would possibly be married and have a family by this stage, and that was why she mainly blamed Brady for what had happened, but she blamed herself for her part in it. She had done it, she said, and there was no disputing that.

Her attitude before her arrest and for the seven months that she was on remand was one of non-cooperation with the police, she said – partly because she was frightened and partly because the legal advice from her solicitor was to say nothing. She claimed the police were not meticulous about allowing her solicitor to be present when they questioned her, but she confirmed that this criticism had already been aired in court at the time of her trial.

She said she knew the police were justified in thinking of her as hard, tough, callous and unbreakable; yet it was a case of fear, combined with adhering to legal advice. I am not sure that this is true – I think she would get that legal advice only if she was telling her solicitor she was innocent. If she had told the truth – the fact that she had been involved in the murders, and the nature of her role – she would have been advised to help the police. I have never known a reputable solicitor who would have advised her to say nothing in those circumstances – and I believe her solicitor was a reputable member of his profession.

She said she maintained her attitude in court, particularly in the dock, where she felt she was under the microscope because there was so much publicity surrounding the case. In those days the defence could not ask for closed committal proceedings. (The law later was changed, largely as a result of this case. Hearing

135

the committal in public meant that most of the prosecution case had been reported in the press long before the trial, although the case for the defence had not
been presented.) From December to the trial in May
there was non-stop publicity based on prosecution evidence, and she believed the Lord Chancellor at the
time had described it as 'undoubtedly trial by newspaper'. The press were issued with tickets for the trial,
she said, the courtroom was fitted with carpets to help
the acoustics, microphones had been set up, and she
was frightened to death because they had put up a
bullet-proof screen round the dock, with a ring of
policemen standing outside it. She said there was no
bullet-proof glass around the witness box, which de-
feated the whole purpose of the exercise – both she and
Brady gave evidence from the witness box.

When she saw the queues of people as she was going
in and out of the court – both at Hyde, where the
committal was heard, and at Chester – she felt like a
fish in a bowl, her every movement and expression
being watched. So she tried to remain expressionless,
she told us, not wanting to add fuel to the fire she
believed was already being stoked – and therefore she
was condemned as hard-faced. Every time she left prison for court she was given medication to stop her from
being sick, and a nursing sister would travel with her.
Every day when she had to go into the witness box she
felt sick from nerves and fear. She used to try and hold
on until it was over. But nobody knew about these
things, she said: they just imagined she was completely
callous and indifferent.

At this meeting she remembered something that she
had forgotten to tell us about the five murders. She and
Brady did not have arguments, but there were times
when he would just stop speaking to her. And then he
would buy her a present, which they would call an
anniversary present, and she would apologise to him,
even though she had not been in the wrong. On the day
of each murder or the day before he would buy her a
record, and again they would refer to the day as an
anniversary.

The record he bought for her on the day of Pauline
Reade's death was the theme music from *The Hill*, a

film about an army prison in which soldiers had to keep climbing a hill as a punishment. She remembered seeing the film as part of a double bill, with *The Day of the Triffids*, at a cinema in Oldham. On the day of John Kilbride's death he bought her Gene Pitney singing 'Twenty-four Hours from Tulsa', for Keith Bennett it was Roy Orbison's 'It's Over' and for Lesley Ann Downey it was Sandie Shaw's 'Girl Don't Come'. The day Edward Evans died he gave her Joan Baez singing 'It's All Over Now, Baby Blue'.

He did not tell her when he gave her the records that they had any significance, but she knew afterwards that he was going to kill someone. Sometimes, she said in answer to questions, she knew before he gave her the record that he intended to kill someone, because he had told her that he was 'going to do one'. She did not believe the records contained any hidden clues to his motives. She said that he never asked her what record she wanted, even when he was buying one for her birthday.

We talked again about the timing of the murders, and about the ten months' lapse – 'the most peaceful time in my life' – between the killing of Lesley Ann Downey and that of Edward Evans. The fact that Brady had told Smith he was 'not due one yet' made her wonder whether he had, in fact, committed a murder during that time without her knowing. (Ten months was the longest gap between any of the murders, which occurred at irregular intervals.)

Then she said she wanted to talk more about Patricia Hodge, the girl who had lived next door but one and who had taken the police to the area of the Moors where the bodies were buried. She said the little girl used to come with them when they went on to the Moor with sacks to dig for peat. Many of the householders on the new estate did it, she said: the gardens were full of clay and bricks, so it was necessary to improve the soil for anything to grow. They would park in the lay-by near to where John Kilbride was buried, and then cross over to dig for peat on the other side, the Hollin Brow Knoll side, where Pauline Reade and subsequently Lesley Ann Downey were buried.

It sounded in court, she said, as though they had

137

plied the child with wine, and she wanted it put on record now that Patty was only given the occasional glass. Hindley said there was an off-licence midway between Hyde and the estate which sold its own wine 'out of the wood'; they would buy one particular kind, apricot wine, which was very sweet. She liked it herself and so did Patty, so she would let the girl have a glass. Although it was quite potent the child had never got drunk. I was surprised that someone who was admitting to being involved in the killings of children should be so concerned to make it clear that she would not be irresponsible in this way.

On Christmas Eve 1964, two days before Lesley Ann Downey was abducted and killed, she took presents to the Hodges' house for the children. Brady suggested a trip up to the Moors. Hindley had already described how he liked to sit at the top of Smallshaw Lane, near John Kilbride's home, and she said he also liked to sit in a lay-by near the spot where John was buried. They would often sit there, listen to the radio or just talk, and then drive home. On this occasion, they took Patty with them. They had a bottle of wine and gave Patty a drink, but Hindley was at pains to point out that she would never have got the child – or any child – drunk. Then they took the girl home, got some blankets because it was very cold, and went back to the Moor. They spent the night sitting in the car, which was uncomfortable and freezing – they did not keep the engine running to heat the car. She said there was no sinister significance in taking the child up there.

Hindley then told us she wanted to talk about the impression that the press and public had received, that she had never shown any remorse for her involvement in the killings. In the early seventies, she said, there had been a lot of publicity in which Mrs Ann West, the mother of Lesley Ann Downey, had figured prominently. Hindley made an application to the governor of Holloway for permission to write to Mrs West, so that she could tell her that what the woman believed had happened to her child, from the evidence of the tape recordings, was in fact wrong – many rumours had been circulating that the tape was made during a torture session, and not while Brady was merely taking photographs. 'I wanted to tell her that I knew that she would never forgive me,' Hindley said, 'but that nothing I could say could express my remorse, genuinely and deeply felt.'

But in those days prisoners were only allowed to write to people they had known outside – close friends and family. To make an exception to this rule, Home Office permission was required. Hindley said she had come into prison with no close friends, because she had been so close to Brady that she had lost her former friends. The governor felt it would not be a good idea for her to write to Mrs West as the letters could be given to the press and quoted out of context. None the less, she passed on the request to the Home Office: they, too, turned it down. They also turned down out of hand a request from Hindley that Mrs West be allowed to visit her.

We talked at length about visits she had made to Saddleworth Moor with Brady, David Smith and Maureen, trying to pinpoint locations that would help now in the search for the remaining two bodies. Hindley's solicitor quoted from statements that Smith had made which had been printed in the *Medico-Legal Journal*. I was particularly interested in one of his claims – that Brady had told him he had been on the site of one of the graves: questioning Hindley established that Smith could have been on the site of Pauline Reade or Lesley Ann Downey's grave, as they had all picnicked on Hollin Brow Knoll, although she felt it was not as far on to the Moor as Pauline Reade's grave. And one night he and Brady had walked in the direction of John Kilbride's grave to relieve themselves, while she and Maureen stayed in the car.

I also asked about the possibility of Pauline Reade's body being buried in the trench which at the time was being dug across the Moor to house pipes for a new gas supply. Hindley thought it was unlikely that he had buried her there. (So did I, but as, over the next few months, my search of Hollin Brow Knoll grew unproductive I began to think more seriously about the possibility of the body being in the pipe trench.)

Then she said she wanted to talk about the plea for parole she had written in 1978 and 1979 for the Home

Office Joint Committee of Parole Boards. The thirty thousand-word document submitted to the then Home Secretary, Merlyn Rees, protested her innocence. Now she told us that on the whole the document was a pack of lies.

But she referred to it to explain her relationship and feelings for Ian Brady. She believed they were fundamental to this case, and she had never been able adequately to express them; she still couldn't. She knew that very many people found it difficult to understand how she could feel for a man who had done such things, involved her in them, and subjected her to the kind of lifestyle they led.

Before she went out with him, she said, there had been an altercation in the office in which she was inadvertently involved, and he had ceased speaking to her. She said he went out of his way to insult her and make detrimental remarks – she felt at first belittled and humiliated, and then angry and indignant. Experiencing feelings that were completely new to her, she began to use shorthand pads as diaries into which she poured out her feelings – they ranged from loving him desperately to almost hating him; the utter despair and hopelessness of unrequited love to 'wild and passionate hopes and prayers that he would somehow begin to share and return my feelings'.

For nearly a year, she said, she lived with 'this agonizing obsession', and finally reached the point where she thought she could no longer endure any existence as it was, and decided to leave the job, forget about him and make another kind of life. She went on to admit that she felt that what she had said so far about her feelings for Brady sounded a bit theatrical, ridiculous, exaggerated – but she was trying to give some idea of how, to an emotionally immature eighteen-year-old, one man could become the sole centre of existence, her *raison d'être*. She quoted directly from her parole plea:

I feel it is crucially important that the whose essence of such feelings and emotions is understood and appreciated fully for what it was, for it is this that is at the heart of the whole tragic case in which everything that transpired had its roots, and those roots

began their growth in virginal, vulnerable soil
nourished, as it were, by unassuaged grief and despair and a painful hopeless yearning of a young and
inexperienced heart which was almost overwhelmed
by the strength and fierceness of hitherto unknown
emotions.

She said she could not stress strongly enough how
totally obsessed and besotted she was with Brady. After he finally invited her out and she became, in her
own words, 'a Saturday night stand', she would spend
the week in a fever of anxiety waiting for Saturday
night to come round again. She said she could not
explain the infatuation, but it stemmed partly from the
fact that Brady was so different from anybody else she
had met.

> Within months he had convinced me that there was
> no God at all: he could have told me that the earth
> was flat, the moon was made of green cheese and the
> sun rose in the west, I would have believed him,
> such was his power of persuasion, his softly con-
> vincing means of speech which fascinated me, be-
> cause I could never fully comprehend, only browse
> at the odd sentence here and there, believing it to be
> gospel truth.

He convinced her, she said, that her faith and all religion was superstition instilled in people's conventional minds; religion, he said, was a crutch people used to
hobble through life, the opium of the people. 'I believed him because I thought I loved him. His argument was so convincing it demolished my tiny precept
with a single word, so he became my god, my idol, my
object of worship. I worshipped him more blindly than
the congenitally blind.' She said that when she wrote
the parole plea, at the age of thirty-six, she looked back
with incredulity at the teenager she once was – a teenager who allowed her whole world to revolve solely
around one man who became the sole focus of her
existence.

She then started reading from the parole plea about
the photographs and tape recordings of Lesley Ann

141

Downey, saying that the general consensus was that they were the ultimate in torture and obscenity. Whilst she was not denying that they were both degrading and grossly insulting to the child, and that her actions were indefensible, she wanted to put the incident into some kind of perspective. She said that she, too, was terrified, and instead of helping the child she made it worse by frightening her. She quoted from the document, saying that she had drifted away from all her friends and totally built her life around Brady, and 'in his absence I felt utterly desolate'.

She was filled with shame and disgust and despair over the tape. When confronted with the photographs and tapes at Hyde Police Station she had cried from sheer fright and remorse, and when the barrage of questions began she explained that she 'took refuge behind the mists that swirled in my mind'. She remembered very little of what transpired in that room, except that 'my instinctive reaction to escape the unbearable reality was construed as arrogance and hard defiance'. She did not blame anyone for thinking that of her, but the hardness was only a veneer – a veneer that she had to maintain throughout the trial when she was being observed by the press and public and the celebrity writers who were there preparing books about the case – one of them was even watching her through a pair of opera glasses. 'I needed that veneer more than ever,' she told us. 'I could not express my ravaged self,' she said. It had taken many years to dismantle the shield she had built around herself, but, she said, 'I can now hold up my head in the face of God, in spite of the hostility and antagonism that remain.'

Hindley went on to deal, at some length, with the evidence given against her in the Edward Evans case by David Smith, which she described as 'contradictory'. She referred to the fact that Smith's version of events changed from the initial statement he made to the police – which implicated her heavily in the murder – to the evidence he gave in court, when he said he was not sure whether or not she was in the room when Evans was killed. His original assertion that she had been so close to the axe-wielding Brady that she had sustained a graze to her head from the axe was not corroborated by the police surgeon who examined her the next day and made no mention of a graze.

But just as bad, she said, were Smith's accusations that she and Brady treated the whole matter as a joke.

She had wondered whether her own life was in jeopardy, because she believed there were things going on between Brady and Smith that were totally separate to what went on between herself and Brady. She now considered it quite possible that she could have finished up as a victim: she felt she could have become a liability, involved in too many things, and ultimately dispensable.

She had previously felt that Brady did his best to exonerate her at the trial, but she now felt that he only did this within the limitations of what he was prepared to admit: 'Beyond that he was prepared to sacrifice me to my fate – and what a fate it's been.'

The evidence that Evans' murder was premeditated rested mainly on the disposal plan, which she claimed she knew nothing about, and had only seen for the first time in court.

She also referred to the fact that Smith had a vested interest in her and Brady's convictions. As revealed at the trial, he had signed a contract with a newspaper for a large fee and syndication rights for publication of his story if Hindley and Brady were convicted; he had already, by the time of the trial, enjoyed perks such as a foreign holiday and accommodation for the duration of the trial in a five-star hotel – all at the expense of the newspaper in question.

She discussed an interview that Smith had given on London Weekend Television some years after the trial, in which he had talked about how he and Brady had discussed killing a youth he knew. She said that all the evidence against her in the Evans case rested on the testimony of this man, Smith.

She was still quoting from the parole appeal written in 1978 and 1979, long before she had confessed her full role in the murders. But she believed that the sections she was quoting had kept their relevance.

Even if people were confronted with the truth, she said, their emotions and prejudices about the case would remain unchanged. She said she knew from her

143

own experience that she had placed Brady on a pedestal where he was out of reach, and had loved him blindly long after she had been sent to prison.

Flaubert said we should never touch our idols, for the gilt always rubbed off on our fingers. One day I gained the courage to reach up and touch, and the gilt did rub off. He crashed from his pedestal, and the dust and ashes of a dead love flaked around my feet and I stepped from it shaking the last remaining specks from myself. It was unbearably painful, it always is when one prepares to face reality squarely.

Hindley then told us that while in prison she had had various psychiatric and psychological evaluations, but that these had unearthed no symptoms of schizophrenia or psycho-sadism 'or any of the other syndromes that come to mind when my name is mentioned'. Unlike Brady, she said, she had no excuse for her actions. Brady was naturally secretive and introverted, and she had long ago learned not to trespass on those private areas of his life that he was not prepared to share with her. Time in prison, she said, had given her the opportunity for self-analysis and deep critical introspection – a luxury often denied to people outside, who are too busy leading their lives.

Although I could never say I have ever had peace of mind, but I believe I have been forgiven by God. I want to say it is the most profound relief, in spite of the unbearable pain of making these confessions, that I have been able to get them off my chest to you, and I thank God that you did come up and ask me, and that they could progress as they did. And I just hope to God that the case can be concluded and finally laid to rest, and I just hope that some day, in some way I can be forgiven for making those families wait twenty-two years.

I asked if there was anything more she would like to say, and she replied there was something she would like to read out. One day soon, because of the renewed interest in the case, she would like to write a book – not just about the case but about how easy it was to become involved in the activities which led to it. She said she wanted it to be a warning to people. She talked about the millions of words that have been written about her already, in books and newspapers, in evidence. The theories expounded and value judgements passed were all the product of somebody else's imagination: at no time did any authors or journalists approach her, she said, to ask for her contribution to their books and articles. She had been told she was public property, about whom many things had been said, but without any right of reply. But now the rules had been changed and prisoners were allowed to write for publication, provided they fulfilled the criteria laid down by the Home Office. She said her book would fulfil these criteria, and read out a passage from the foreword. It described how her book was intended not to 'titillate with nightmarish horrors' but rather to end speculation and 'lay the whole thing to rest'.

Continuing to quote from her foreword, she said she had received a letter from Mrs Winnie Johnson and then a visit from me which was totally unexpected. I had explained to her that the case had been reopened and that in the next few days we proposed to start digging in an effort to find the bodies of Pauline Reade and Keith Bennett. She said that when she was asked to help she agreed.

Many people have written asking her to write this book, she said, but, until our visit and the letter from Mrs Johnson it would not have been a truthful account. She had never told the truth of this 'whole sordid story' before because she had not been able to face up to it publicly. 'This does not mean I'd hide the truth from myself. On the contrary, it was something I had to live with for over twenty-four years, or for twenty-seven years if I go back to when I first met Ian Brady.' She described her crimes as 'heinous and despicable', and said how much she regretted deceiving her family, her friends and her loved ones.

At this point the tape ran out – I think if we had had endless tape and endless time she would have gone on talking longer. But this drew the whole confession to a

145

satisfactory conclusion.

I had now heard everything Myra Hindley had to say about the crimes. I believed she was telling the material truth about the circumstances of the murders and the whereabouts of the bodies. I was sure that, in all the information she had given me about trying to locate the graves, she was doing her best to be helpful. But I had some grave reservations about some of the other things she had told us.

11

My feelings about the confession were mixed. I could not deny that it had taken a lot of courage to go ahead with it after spending twenty years convincing her family, her supporters – notably Lord Longford – and her fellow prisoners that she was innocent of anything more than being Brady's lover. She knew that she was possibly throwing away a lot of the friendship and support that had kept her going in prison all those years (though in fact, with the exception of her brother-in-law and young niece, I believe all her friends have stood by her). But I was left wondering whether she had told the truth, the whole truth and nothing but the truth.

Had she been truthful about her own role in the killings? Or had she only told me as much as was necessary to convince me that she was telling the truth? I never had any doubts that she was giving me as much information as she could about the causes of death, the times of death and the places of burial. I also believed her version of how the young victims were abducted – even after Ian Brady later gave me a different version. But I could not help feeling that she had overlaid all this information with an interpretation of her own role that was calculated to put her in the best light possible, to make her own behaviour understandable.

I was struck by the fact that she was never there when the killings took place. She was in the car, over the brow of the hill, in the bathroom and even, in the case of the Evans murder, in the kitchen. She always removed herself from the scene of the crime. I found this hard to believe – and Brady himself contradicted it.

Her behaviour during the confession was of a type I have never seen before in many years' experience of hearing people confess to serious crimes. She showed tremendous emotion at times, very deep emotion – but it was coupled with complete control. Usually such strong emotions lead to loss of control, but she never lost hers. Even at the most moving moments she considered very carefully everything she said, and was always ready to quote from documents that she believed corroborated her own version of her role. I shall always remember the words she used when she finished talking about the Pauline Reade murder, one which seemed to upset her a great deal: 'Well, that, as far as I remember, concludes the first murder, which was Pauline Reade.' It was as though she were giving a company report to a group of shareholders – not, as she herself described the experience, 'having a malignant tumour removed without anaesthetic'. In the final analysis, I was left feeling I had witnessed a great performance rather than a genuine confession.

It could be that she has told the whole truth, but has overdone the mitigation. While she openly admitted that she was as guilty as Brady, and came back to that point regularly, she always tried to give an excuse for her actions, so that, even if they are not forgivable, they are understandable.

With the first murder, the killing of Pauline Reade, she put forward threats to her own life and that of her grandmother as the reason she participated. It is impossible to check whether these threats were real. But even if they were, and even if she had real reason to harbour such fears, she had ample opportunity to go to the police. Brady also gives a very different version of her frame of mind at the time of this murder.

She also claimed that Brady had taken pornographic photographs of her while she was drugged. It is impossible to tell from these photographs whether or not she was drugged. I think she claimed that because, as with everything else she is involved in, it is at odds with the person she now believes she is. She was making another excuse. Although she put the threats to herself and her grandmother as her main reasons for getting involved in the first murder, she also said he threatened to reveal these photographs. But she was intelligent enough to assess whether he really could have done this: after all, he himself is on some of the photographs. And even for the others, questions would be asked about how he obtained them. Revealing them at work would have condemned him as much as it condemned her. Revealing them to her family would have been shocking, but surely that was not enough to persuade anyone to commit murder – the subsequent shock to her family of learning about that was much greater.

All the way through her confession, she tries to counter the effects of those aspects that have made the case so infamous. She was well aware that the main evidence that set the case apart was that dreadful tape recording of Lesley Ann Downey: it has had a tremendous impact on the way the public feels about the Moors Murders. She was at pains to point out on several occasions that it had been misunderstood, that the girl was only being photographed at the time of the recording, and that she was not physically tortured.

Geoff Knupfer, Gordon Mutch and myself listened to that tape very carefully. We had the sound quality improved – many advances in sound engineering have been made since the sixties, and modern techniques of eliminating background noise could be applied. Everyone who has heard that tape has been deeply moved by it, and we were no exceptions. It is an experience nobody would want to have, and one that I would have preferred not to have had. Lesley Ann spoke like any child would – pleading for her mother, pleading to go home. She said 'I'll get killed' – that's an expression many children from Manchester would say if they were late home.

I have also carefully studied the photographs of Lesley Ann, in which she is bound and gagged. I have looked at the expression on her face. As a father myself, I believe that the full horrors of what happened to that child have not been misunderstood. Although, as

Hindley points out, no fingers were cut off, and what was being forced into the child's mouth was a gag – not, as some people have construed, Brady's penis – torture certainly took place. When you think of the effects of what they did to that defenceless child then you can only conclude that she was dreadfully tortured. My heart goes out to Mrs Ann West, who will never and perhaps should never forgive them for their actions.

If ordering a child to strip, binding and gagging her, photographing her and then subjecting her to sexual abuse is not torture, what is? I viewed Myra Hindley's attempts to put herself in a favourable light with great suspicion throughout: in the case of Lesley Ann Downey I do not believe that anything she could say would ameliorate her position. Her voice, clearly to be heard on the tape, is harsh and brutal: she blames her own fear for that. She never stopped to consider the fear on the face and in the voice of the young child she had in her power.

Myra Hindley has said that the children all went to their deaths like 'lambs to the slaughter'. Lesley Ann certainly did not. She protested all the time, until she was gagged. Why should we believe Hindley about the others? We do not know how they went to their deaths. But we know this little girl resisted as much as she could.

According to her the other killings were all easy. She was so close to Keith Bennett at the time of his death, yet she says she heard nothing. That could be so, but the Moor is a quiet place: apart from the wind and the noise of water, there is nothing else. Sounds carry well. Even if the boy did not cry out, she should have been able to hear any normal conversation he had with Brady. I particularly questioned her about it, but she denied hearing anything. I have no way of saying that she is not telling the truth, but I am surprised.

Throughout the confession she always had a good excuse. The one murder she had a big problem explaining was Lesley Ann's, because there is a tape recording and photographs – evidence. Talking about that killing caused her the most distress – but was it because of her feelings for what happened to the child, or because it

149

was so much harder to explain away?

She seemed genuinely shocked when I suggested that what she burnt at Millwards, in the days during which she was free after Brady's arrest, were photographs that could have helped locate Keith Bennett's grave. She said she did not open the envelope and look at its contents, believing it to be plans for bank robberies. But it was strange not to have opened it anyway: paper burns more easily if it is separated. It also seemed odd to be worrying so much about plans for robberies that had never been carried out, when there were murder charges hanging over their heads.

All the way through her confession she admitted she was as guilty as Brady, but in a subtle way she was trying to make out that she was not. She did not try to shirk her guilt in law, but all the time was trying to put herself on the higher moral ground.

I never had an open confrontation with her about her claims: it would not have helped the inquiry, or the search for the bodies of Pauline Reade and Keith Bennett. It was in my interests to gain all I could from her, so I purposely avoided challenge. I had managed to persuade her to confess, which took time and patience and, I believe, luck. I was pleased to have the confession – most of all for the families of the victims – and I do not wish to undermine its value. But I believe that, however cleverly she tried to do it, her strategies show up in the confession, and leave her motives and her truthfulness in question.

I made it clear to her at the beginning that public interest in the case would never abate until the mystery was cleared up and the bodies of the two remaining children found. I believe she has given me enough information to unravel the mystery. But at the same time I believe she hopes that, once the case is closed, people will be left with an understanding view of how a young woman could be completely taken in, threatened and misused by Brady. In my view, one of her over-riding motives in making the confession was to seek a sympathetic ear, to put herself in a different light, and in the long term to win her freedom. She said she did not want parole, and did not want to be considered for it even in 1990. Yet I gained the impression that she hopes she will one day be free to mix with her new-found friends in society – friends she would never have met had she stayed in Gorton or Hattersley.

She says herself that she confessed for the peace of her inner soul, and to help the victims' families. If that was the case, why did she have to keep quoting from documents that suggest she was an innocent young girl, misled by Brady? Why did she not just come out with a straight confession, give us the facts and do anything she could to help us find the bodies? Why not leave it at that?

However, I must not take away from her the fact that her general account of the murders is correct, as far as our detailed inquiries have been able to corroborate. Her description of the death of Pauline Reade, and the cause of death, were confirmed beyond doubt when Pauline's body was found. She did not try to mislead me, and I would like to balance my misgivings about what she told me with the good she did for the inquiry. I believe we would have found the body of Pauline Reade with or without her help, but she certainly did everything she could to assist us and we probably found her sooner than we would otherwise have done. Hindley never asked for anything in return for her confession – no favours, no privileges, no immunity from prosecution.

She bases her involvement in the killings on her initial infatuation with Ian Brady. I think this is easy to understand: she was young and impressionable, and there is no doubt that they formed a very deep relationship, sharing their thoughts and feelings as couples do who are close to each other. I believe her when she says that she was initially very much under his influence.

But knowing her as I now do, and looking at the way she has handled twenty years in prison, I am in no doubt that she is a very strong character. If she really had been the little girl lost she is trying to suggest, then she would have broken down under the questioning that followed her arrest – if not before – and the whole story would have come out. After Brady was arrested he was unable to give her any support, but she for her part remained steely and silent.

151

I have seen some very hard people in prison over my years in the police force. The isolation affects people deeply, and yet Hindley managed to maintain her hard front for over twenty years. Prison has not damaged her in the way I would have expected – it has certainly damaged Brady. She is a very strong-minded individual, and I find it hard to believe that she just did what she was told during the murders.

She is an intelligent woman who has used her time in prison to gain an Open University degree, and has strong views on most subjects. It is hard to accept that she could not have got out of the situation she was in with Brady, if she genuinely thought it was so abhorrent. A woman of her intelligence and resources could have escaped from the 'trap' in which she claims he had her.

I know that when she met him he offered her an excitement she had not previously known: Brady seemed sophisticated, he always had money for wine, he had a motorcycle and he encouraged her to get a car at a time when there were not many car owners about in areas like Gorton. But I do not believe the impression he made on her was enough to justify what she did. However deep and committed the relationship, most people would simply say no if their partner suggested anything that involved endangering the lives of others, let alone murdering them. We have all from time to time met people who have influenced us, but we have also been able to resist the influences when necessary. She crossed a line that very few others would cross, and she cannot say she did that simply because of her feelings for Brady.

She claims, and she believes, that she would never have become involved in murder had she never met Brady. That is probably true. But if she had not given a favourable reception to his ideas, would he ever have developed them as far as murder? Even if he had wanted to kill, could he have done it without her? He needed an accomplice, and he really needed a female accomplice to make the abduction of the children possible. It might be just as true to say that if Ian Brady had never met her, he would never have become a murderer. He was in need of help, and even though she

152

was young she should have been able to recognize this, and not to feed his madness.

Several times she told me how much she regretted never getting married and having children of her own, and how she felt that if she had not met Brady she would have settled down to a normal life. I cannot say whether this is likely or not: all I know is that she had a capacity for participating in the sort of things the rest of us would run a mile from. David Smith, a man from a very tough background who had already been involved in violence, went to pieces when he discovered just what Brady and Hindley were involved in. There's a line that cannot be crossed, except by a very few people. Whatever she says, she is one of them.

The tape recording of her confession runs over seventeen hours. Occasionally she repeated herself and went back over things. But all in all it was a very controlled, very well worked out performance in which, I believe, she told me just as much as she wanted me to know, and no more.

PART THREE

CAT AND MOUSE WITH IAN BRADY

12

With the confession in my hands, I felt it more important than ever that Hindley should visit the Moors again. On her first visit we had been severely hampered: the weather had been against us; the media had distracted us; and we had been working under the phoney constraint of only talking about 'places of special interest to Ian Brady'.

Now, with her admission of her involvement in the killings, we could talk openly about actual burial sites. We could talk in specifics: where she stood, what she saw, what she did. Her previous visit had been useful in familiarizing her with Saddleworth Moor again: now I wanted to take her back up there and see if she could locate the graves. Any doubts I might have had about the strength of her intent to find the bodies had been dispelled: I knew she was completely committed to the search.

With the agreement of Michael Fisher and Peter Timms, the news of her confession had been kept secret. I did not want a fresh round of publicity to jeopardize the chances of another, more successful, trip to Saddleworth Moor. I applied again to the Home Office for permission to take her there, telling them about her confession.

While I was making plans for Hindley's second visit I was also making arrangements to see Ian Brady again: it was obvious that I needed to talk to him. Although Hindley had insisted she was shouldering her share of the blame, she had inevitably strongly implicated him in the crimes, and her allegations needed to be put to him.

On 11 March I went to Park Lane Hospital. I knew that over Christmas Brady's mental state had deteriorated. On one occasion when I wanted to speak to him I was told by the medical staff that it was pointless, as he would not be able to understand what I was saying and would be incapable of answering. So I arranged a meeting with the acting Medical Director, Dr Hunter, Dr Strickland, who was Brady's own doctor, Robert

Fitzpatrick, his social worker, and his solicitor, Benedict Birnberg. I could have made a formal approach, insisted on seeing him, and cautioned him – I was dealing with two murders that he had never previously been charged with. But I instinctively felt – and my dealings with Hindley had confirmed this – that to see him when he was willing to see me, and when the medical staff felt he was in a reasonable condition to do so, would get us further.

I also wanted the staff who had to deal with him every day to be aware of the effect that news of the confession might have on him. The recent deterioration of his health had probably been due to the renewed interest in the case, the publicity about Myra Hindley's visit to the Moors and the renewal of the search for bodies. News of the confession could have an even worse result.

Dr Hunter and Dr Strickland both felt that he was well enough to see me, as did Mr Fitzpatrick. Birnberg agreed that he would see his client and put my request to him. He spent an hour with him, and returned to say that, although Brady was a little confused, he was willing to see me that afternoon. He stipulated that the interview should be informal, and that there should be no other police officer present.

Over the next few months I spent many hours with Ian Brady – far longer than I spent with Myra Hindley – and I was to learn a lot about the way his mind works. I am not a psychiatrist, so I cannot say medically what is wrong with him. But I became used to dealing with his devious thinking and his paramount need to feel that he is in control of everything he does.

That afternoon I told him of all the developments since I had seen him in November – the most important being the confession, which implicated him; I explained that he could help find the bodies of the two missing children. He said that he could not remember seeing me in November, which surprised me – he then told me he had been ill and was suffering from amnesia.

He said he did not accept or believe that Hindley had confessed, feeling that anything she had done or said would be in furtherance of her claim for parole. I

157

realized at this point that Brady's solicitor was taking detailed notes of the interview; because of the conditions they had imposed on me, however, I had no back-up to take notes on my behalf. Mr Birnberg said there was nothing sinister in it, and although I did feel uneasy that a one-sided record was being made I agreed to continue when they accepted that, if necessary, I could call on them for a copy of the notes. By refusing to have another police officer present, I realized in retrospect, Brady was trying to establish his dominance.

I told him again that I thought he could help us accurately pinpoint the two graves, thus relieving the great anguish of the children's families, and that this would clear up, once and for all, the mysteries of the case. He was still very sceptical about the confession until I outlined the story of Pauline Reade's abduction. As he heard the details he was visibly shocked and his mannerisms became agitated. He has a facial twitch, which he blames on the medication he is given, and this became more noticeable. But he didn't throw up his arms and ask me to leave; he was calm enough to talk, and he continued to be polite.

He told me that he was prepared to confess provided it could be on his own terms. He said he would make a written confession on condition that afterwards he was immediately given the means to kill himself. He believed this would be the ideal solution to the whole problem.

I explained, and so did his solicitor, that this was not possible. I told him that he was an intelligent man and must therefore have known that this was an unrealistic condition when he imposed it. We talked for hours, going round and round the possibility of a confession but always ending with the same ultimatum: 'I'll tell you as long as you help me to end it all afterwards.' In his eyes he was putting the ball into my court: he was in control. He had not refused to co-operate – it was me who was refusing to meet his condition. He had known all along that his condition was preposterous, but it allowed him to feel that he was making a reasonable offer and that I was the one who was being unreasonable.

Benedict Birnberg told him that his doctors felt it would improve his health if he confessed, as he was clearly tormented by the memory of his crimes. I then pointed out that a confession would eliminate media speculation about the murders. Brady was indifferent to this: he felt the media would never leave him alone, even when the truth was out. I explained that journalists would no longer have a mystery to probe, so gradually their interest would die away. But he could not accept this, and continued to comment on the treatment he received from some quarters of the press.

He told me that he, Myra Hindley and David Smith had talked about killing in a very matter-of-fact way – Brady was critical of the police officers who had taken part in the original investigation: he said they had failed to find blood on the carpet at Wardlebrook Avenue, which he reckoned they should have been able to do easily.

He asked if Hindley had told me about the evidence he asked her to destroy while he was in custody; I told him about the envelope at Millwards which she had burned. He said she had failed to get into the house at Wardlebrook Avenue because the police were there, and had therefore not been able to get the ticket for the suitcase at the left luggage office. Hindley and he had agreed to kill David Smith, he said, because he knew too much; he had also wanted to get rid of Maureen, but Hindley had been against murdering her sister. Later, when they were both in custody, she had agreed to Maureen being killed: he said this was contained in code in letters between them.

I presented my arguments in favour of confession to him in many different forms, urging him to see the benefits to the families, to the public and to himself. I stressed the torment he would suffer when the search of the Moors was renewed and if armed with the fresh details from Myra Hindley, we found the bodies.

He returned constantly to his disbelief that she had actually confessed, although he found it hard to continue not to believe when confronted with the information she had given me. I was careful not to give him too many details, and although he did not ask me for more he would have been very happy to listen had I been prepared to run through the whole confession for him. He frequently interrupted with: 'That's not right. I now know she's not telling the truth.' But he would never say why she was wrong, or what the truth was. I said I would give him the details of one crime in full as she had told it to me, and then he could give his version – but he refused. He never ruled out confession, though – in fact he came back time and time again to his 'perfect solution', the confession followed by suicide.

We talked for nearly five hours, and parted with an agreement that if he wanted to speak to either his solicitor or me the hospital staff would contact us. He was lucid throughout the time I was with him, but I was not sure what the effect of learning about Myra Hindley's confession would be over the next few days – I felt he might withdraw completely into himself. I did not leave Park Lane feeling that Brady's confession was imminent, although I still felt it could not be ruled out entirely.

It took a number of visits to London and a lot of very positive arguments on my side to convince the Home Office that Myra Hindley should visit Saddleworth Moor again. I could understand their hesitation: the previous visit had not been an unqualified success, and it made them an easy target for public criticism. But I was convinced, and eventually swayed them. We agreed that this time there would be no media involvement: if questioned about it, the official line would be that it was not policy to disclose the movements of prisoners. But they made it clear that if pushed very hard they would have to confirm the visit; I accepted that. At least I was reassured we would not have a repeat of the events surrounding the previous visit, with a government minister announcing it to the nation early in the morning.

We needed a two-day operation, so I had to find somewhere secure for Myra Hindley to stay the night. I knew there was no question of her attempting to escape, but I none the less needed to find somewhere that demonstrably precluded escape, and where the movement in and out of police vehicles would not be conspicuous or out of the ordinary. Greater Manchester Police Training School at Sedgley Park, Prestwich, provided the answer: the Commandant in charge had a flat on the premises that was only occasionally used and was therefore ideal.

Arrangements were made for Hindley to leave Cookham Wood in the late evening, and to travel by road to meet me in the early hours of the morning – I decided a helicopter would draw too much attention. I had assigned Roy Rainford as her personal bodyguard again. An unmarked convoy of cars went into the prison to pick her up; as they came out, they were spotted by a journalist who went up to one of the cars and asked if Myra Hindley was leaving the prison. He was told no, but undeterred, he climbed into his own car and followed the convoy. When I heard about this I was worried. It was the worst possible news – all our hopes of carrying out the operation in secrecy seemed to have been dashed at the outset. When I reported the incident to the Home Office they asked me if I wanted to call the whole visit off. They left the decision to me, and I opted not to cancel as so much time and energy had been invested setting it up.

The small convoy of cars, followed by the journalist, drove to the nearest police station, where they pulled into the yard as though they were local policemen. It was a very clever ruse: the journalist was completely thrown by it and gave up, and after a brief wait the convoy was able to carry on with no one following them. We were not sure that he had not phoned his newspaper to alert others, but we gambled on the fact that he was working on a tip-off from a not necessarily well-informed or reliable source, and that the convoy's little manoeuvre had convinced him. I had the necessary manpower available, should the whole operation become public, to take care of press, television and radio journalists the way we had on the previous occasion, but I was fervently hoping it would not come to that. For the rest of the night, the presence of that pressman at the prison gates was a nagging worry.

The control room for the operation was on the ninth

floor of police headquarters, where my office was. I left work at 5p.m. and went home for a shower and a meal, meeting Geoff Knupfer back at the control room at nine to brief staff. We tried to get a couple of hours' sleep in sleeping bags on the floor. The rest of the team had been sent home for some sleep and reported for duty at 4a.m. when we started liaising with the officers who were with Hindley for the rendezvous on the Moor. We listened intently to the news bulletins on the radio, but there was, to my relief, no mention of the visit.

Hindley had been taken in the early hours to Sedgley Park, where it was planned that she would have some sleep – but in fact she did not get any. Reviewing our arrangements hour by hour, I felt it would be better if we started on the Moor at first light, earlier than planned, just in case our friend the journalist had tipped somebody off. We knew the Moor was clear, so it was vital not to lose valuable searching time.

It was 5.40a.m. when we met up. We were dropped off near Hoe Grain, a deep-sided valley that cuts from the road down to Shiny Brook. A small party of us stayed close to Hindley, with the rest of the inquiry team placed strategically around. There was a very heavy mist, and we could not see more than a few yards in front of us at the best of times. We walked about the Moor to give her the opportunity to look around, but it was very difficult, even for those of us who had become so familiar with the area, to recognize landmarks in the mist. It was cold, but not bitingly cold as it had been for her first visit. We walked around until 9.30 when we had a break for tea and sandwiches.

Within a few hours there were quite a few journalists on the Moor. They did not know for certain that she was there, but they had been tipped off that she might be. It was the turn of the mist to help us now: if some of those journalists ever realized how close they came to her without seeing her, they would regret it for the rest of their careers. Fortunately, we were all wearing civilian clothes.

I was in a vehicle with Hindley at my side when a journalist approached and asked Roy Rainford, who was in the front passenger seat, if we had seen anything of the police or knew anything about a visit by Myra

Hindley. Roy put on a convincing performance and the journalist, who was only two feet away from Hindley, accepted his reply and walked away.

Hindley was very keen to concentrate on Hoe Grain, despite my asking her if she would like to look at other areas. She felt sure this was the most important place to search for the body of Keith Bennett. But despite searching until 12.30 she could not be positive about any particular spot. She was trying to put herself into the position she had been in as look-out, but although she found spots she thought were promising she could not be sure.

After lunch we went to Hollin Brow Knoll. It was still very misty – although the Knoll is close to the road we were not spotted. We stayed there for some time, but again she could not come up with anything certain. She was very enthusiastic, very keen to help, and therefore very frustrated that she could not give us an exact location. She went to great pains never to commit herself totally, in case she was wrong and the information she gave was misleading. She did not seem elated to be out of prison and in the fresh air: her only concern seemed to be to get on with the job in hand.

Although, if we believe her confession in detail, she was quite close to the burial of Keith Bennett, she was not close enough when Pauline Reade was buried to have anything more than a vague idea of the area. Early in the afternoon I called off the search and she was taken back to Sedgley Park. She had had very little, if any, sleep, followed by a physically tiring day on the Moor – and that went for the staff who were with her, too. We had successfully kept the whole operation away from the media: it was not until the next day that they were able to confirm that Hindley had been there. Later, when it was revealed that she had stayed on police premises, there was an outcry promoted by one MP: it was totally unnecessary – there were people with her all the time, and both the building and the grounds were secure.

Before she left Sedgley Park the next day she asked to see me; I was reluctant, because I did not want to draw attention to her, and at this time the press were interested in every move that I made. She wanted to go

163

over what she had told me on the Moor, reaffirming that we had got the right two general areas – Hoe Grain and Hollin Brow Knoll. Hindley travelled back to Cookham Wood on the morning of the 25 March, again in a small unmarked convoy. It was an uneventful journey: she was not spotted at any stage, even as she re-entered the prison.

Once again the visit had been blighted by poor weather, and at the end we had nothing concrete to work on: she had not been able to point a finger directly at a grave site. But my over-riding impression of that visit was of her willingness to help. I knew for certain that, however cynical I might feel about some parts of her confession, she was committed to helping us find the bodies. She wanted the case resolved, whatever her motivation. She had done her best that day, there was no doubt about that.

The weather was getting better every day. It was time to start searching the Moors again. After discussion with the team, I decided to start searching the areas on Hoe Grain that Myra Hindley had thought were possible sites. We all agreed that we were more likely to find Pauline Reade than Keith Bennett, but we were still optimistic about Keith, as was the archaeologist we had consulted. So I chose to start looking for him, believing that, as we would be working deeper into the Moor than Hollin Brow Knoll, where Pauline was buried, we would be shielded from the photographers and cameramen.

Not for the first time, I had underestimated the determination of the media and their enormous interest in this story. They followed us, with all their equipment, right on to the Moor. And as we started work excavating one side of the Hoe Grain valley, they lined up on the other bank for a grandstand view. It was a strange feeling for all of us, knowing that telephoto lenses were focused on us the whole day. It was private land, and I could have had them removed, but I felt that would have been an overbearing attitude to take and would have achieved no benefit in the long run.

We were using the new digging techniques that we had been taught by the experts, removing the topsoil and then using a trowel and a hoe to identify the different layers of soil and looking for signs that the natural layering had been disturbed. There were problems – the valleys and depressions we were working on had suffered slippage which had caused disturbance of the layers – but it was still a very effective method. Working conditions were, as usual, terrible. The heavy rain that summer made conditions worse than they had been the previous winter. We wore boiler suits, with anoraks and waterproof over-trousers: the choice was not to wear the waterproofs and to be soaked by the rain, or to wear them and be soaked in perspiration. We were not only looking for the two missing bodies: we also spent many hours searching for a spade that, according to Hindley, Brady had buried up there. We made quite a few finds of clothing, but nothing significant: over the years lots of people have left sweaters and anoraks up there.

We were criticized by some conservationists for what we did to the Moor, yet every bucketful of earth was carefully restored before we moved on, and if you go up there today you will find most of the areas we excavated have grown over with grass again. Where the ground was left open, it was with the consent of the landowner. We put the earth on large plastic sheets, moving it in a human chain of buckets uphill of where we were digging. We moved the ground more quickly than I had expected: naturally, competition developed between the lads as to who could do the most. It was filthy work, and by the end of the day we were caked in mud. But at least when we were working in the Hoe Grain and Shiny Brook areas we could stand in the stream and wash ourselves down before we started the long trek back to the road. The walk back was not popular: after a day's hard work we were often faced with trekking a mile or so over difficult, springy, treacherous terrain, carrying our spades and other equipment.

There were also health risks. Before we started we were all given anti-tetanus vaccinations, and I insisted that everyone had a clean set of clothes each day. As

165

we were digging we released natural methane gas from the earth, and we would get home in the evenings unable to taste anything but methane. We had a number of small injuries: cuts that needed stitches; bruises, trapped fingernails and so on. But thankfully there was nothing serious, and in all the time we were on the Moor not one of the team had a day off for illness or injury.

There was light relief, plenty of jokes and banter. Ged McGlynn, being a bit of a perfectionist, wasn't happy with the spade issued to him by Greater Manchester Police and brought his own from home. The other lads teased him about it unmercifully. One day they daubed his precious spade with the yellow marker paint with which we coloured areas of interest: poor Ged spent all that evening restoring his spade to its former glory.

There was one personally sad moment for me, when I realized I had lost my wedding ring while we were digging. There was no point looking for it, as we had covered quite a large area of Moor that day. Barbara and I got married when we were both twenty-one, and the previous year we had celebrated our silver wedding. I thought she might be upset, but she wasn't – she realized it could not be helped. The following weekend we went out together and bought a new one.

The lads took turns driving the van up to Saddleworth, and we became regular visitors to an excellent pie shop on the way. Our wives were also kept busy providing enough food – our appetites were enormous with the hard physical work we were doing. Hot drinks were made from water heated on a gas stove; chicken soup was the favourite in cold weather. There was competition as to who had the best lunch box, but we all surrendered to Gordon when we discovered that his wife actually peeled his oranges for him. When the weather became hot we would stop at a newsagents in Greenfield, the first village we came to on our way home, and raid his fridge for ice-cold cans of drink. We showered back at police headquarters, and occasionally we would go for a pint together after work; but most days we were too exhausted, and it was straight home for a hot bath, a hot meal and an early night.

My relationship with the press was difficult. I did not expect immediate results; they did. I made it clear to them that I was anticipating a long, arduous search, but they did not appreciate this – or chose not to. As before, they wanted instant results, and when we could not produce them they turned on me again. Nevertheless there were quite a few reporters and photographers with whom we developed a good rapport. They shared the same problems that we did, up on the Moor in all weather. They respected us for what we were doing, and we were able to respect them. We asked the photographers to leave us alone during our breaks and after their first round of pictures for the day, and they did. But the newspapers felt obliged to keep the story going, and reporting on another day of routine digging was not enough, so the attacks started. I was more used to it this time round, and able to cope with it. But I still felt angry on behalf of the team. And, as before, we were even getting whispered criticism from our own colleagues: the joke going round the force was that my next task would be to find Glenn Miller.

In April Michael Fisher released the news that Hindley had confessed. There had been plenty of speculation, and finally he confirmed it. Through him she put out a long statement, giving a brief account of her life since her arrest – her breaking away from Brady's influence, the strengthening of her religious faith, and her meeting with Peter Timms. She talked about the letter from Mrs Winnie Johnson, and then the approach from me – she described my attitude to her as 'professional, but kind and sympathetic'. She said she had informed the Home Office that she did not wish to be considered for parole in 1990 when her case was next due for review.

The news of the confession briefly deflected criticism from the search, but we were still an on-going attraction for the media. I was on the Moors with the team every day apart from visits to Brady, with whom I was now developing a much closer relationship. Although the day-to-day running of CID had been handed over to my deputy, I was involved in other inquiries and had other decisions to take. Usually, after a day on the Moor, I would have to spend a couple of hours back at my desk sorting out the rest of the day's problems.

After six weeks in the Hoe Grain and Shiny Brook areas we moved the search to Hollin Brow Knoll – not because we had exhausted every possibility but because, quite simply, we were washed out. The weather, which had been on our side for a couple of weeks – we were all beginning to look as though we were just back from a fortnight's holiday, rather than doing the hardest work of our lives – turned suddenly and dramatically against us. We arrived on the Moor after a wet weekend to find all the places we had been digging were awash with floodwater. So we moved to the Knoll, a high piece of ground from which the water drained away more easily.

We were optimistic when we started work. I planned literally to take the whole of the surface off the Knoll, working around the area of Lesley Ann Downey's grave. Hindley had said she was not there when Pauline Reade was buried, but the natural limitations of the area would, I felt, make everything much easier.

By this time we had modified our digging technique. A Danish scientist, an expert in buried body detection who had worked for some years for a police force in America, came to see us. At his suggestion we were now making more use of an implement called a Shillington hoe, a tool with a pickaxe handle and a broad blade at right-angles with the handle. It enabled us to move even more quickly across the ground, shifting hundreds of tons of earth.

It was the peaty areas of the Knoll we were searching. Lesley Ann Downey had been buried in peat, and digging peat is so easy compared to digging the grass-covered earth up there that it would seem crazy for anybody to have buried a body anywhere other than in the peat beds. But Hindley had told us that when she last saw Pauline Reade the girl was lying on grass. This little gem of information was nagging away at me: I asked myself repeatedly if she was trying to tell me something but could not bring herself to be specific. I also felt from her description that we were definitely interested in the top area of the Knoll, and I felt sure that it would be out of sight of the road –

Lesley Ann Downey had been buried just out of sight of the road.

Despite the height of the Knoll, conditions were still bad; even though the rainwater was draining away from us, it was hampering our progress. There was no stream to wash away the worst mud, so we were driving home caked in it. But I felt we were moving away from what I thought was the 'hot spot', the most likely area, and the team agreed with me.

By this time the only journalists left with us were the stalwarts, the ones who had come up every day. Of course the *Manchester Evening News* was represented, but by this stage it was mounting a fierce campaign against me. As if that wasn't enough, the Police Federation magazine, *Police*, read by policemen all over the country, ran an article by an expert from Leicester University criticizing me for the way we were working and for not giving sufficient consideration to the scientific equipment and techniques now available. The *Evening News* were glad to seize on this criticism. Geoffrey Dickens, one of the MPs whose constituencies cover Saddleworth Moor, was also willing to weigh in with criticisms of the search whenever asked. I felt gratified when our own expert archaeologist, who had given us so much of his valuable time, wrote back to *Police* magazine, of his own volition and answered in detail all the criticisms made of us. The magazine published his long letter in full – unfortunately, readers of the *Manchester Evening News* did not get the same opportunity to read it. It was these readers who were the friends and neighbours of all the team and their families, yet not once did any of the team waver in their support of me or the belief that we were doing the right thing.

Our archaeologist's letter to *Police* said that he had been advising us for nine months. 'The Greater Manchester Police have consulted widely and well,' he wrote. 'I really admire the attitude and calm of the CID members, who are working under very trying conditions.' He talked about two common fallacies held about the search. One he described as the Silver Bullet Theory, the belief that there was some way of targeting the bodies, some machine or magic formula that could

169

find the exact spot. The second he called the Treasure Island Map – the theory that there was a marked map in the heads of the people involved. He pointed out that after such a long lapse of time it is possible to be totally disorientated in a landscape like the Moors.

He detailed the techniques that we had learned from our advisers: stratography, excavation, use of trowel, cleanliness of excavation, high-angle photographic interpretation. Nine machines had been tested, he said, but none had been found to be useful. His conclusion was: 'I have been impressed with the readiness of the CID to accept advice, though not blindly, to evaluate many differing skills and techniques and choose between them, to treat the search as a police matter and never let the boffins take over.'

Relations with the *Manchester Evening News* disintegrated even further when they published an editorial describing our work as 'a farce'. The following day, when a reporter from the paper turned up at my press conference, I told him to leave, first giving him a message for his editor: 'If it is a farce, why is he wasting his own resources covering the search?' I believe then, and I would still believe it today even if we had not found a body, that it would have been improper of me not to carry out the search after the information I had been given by Myra Hindley. To have ignored it would be to have neglected my duty, and would have been unfair to the families of Pauline Reade and Keith Bennett. The editor of the *Evening News,* Michael Unger, asked for a meeting with me to try to sort the matter out. But before we could arrange it, the search had changed from a farce into a highly acclaimed success – with the discovery of a body. Unger apologised, which I appreciated.

But I had more to worry about at this time than a squabble with a newspaper. I had been over the whole story many times with Myra Hindley, but I still felt that she might be holding some clue in her subconscious that would help us. I knew that she was consciously doing her best, but we were drawing a blank.

As I knew that it would be impossible for her to make another visit to the Moor – the Home Office would not have considered it – I had a video made on a clear, sunny day. It showed all the areas and possible sites that she was interested in, with me standing in for her at locations she had visited. Superimposed on the film were some of the numerous snapshots that Brady had taken. Detective Sergeant Ron Pulford had made a brilliant job of editing the film. I had not had time to show the video to Hindley, but the media were speculating that she had seen it.

On 17 June she rang me while I was working on the Moor. But reception was bad, so I rang her back from the nearest police station. She wanted to talk about newspaper reports that she had seen the video, and about a letter she had written, sent via the BBC, appealing to Ian Brady to help. I explained that reporters had seen the video being made and were assuming, wrongly, that she had been shown it. She also wanted to tell me that she had written a letter to Mrs Winnie Johnson, Keith Bennett's mother.

While she was on the phone I went over with her again everything she could remember about the night when Pauline Reade was buried. She again confirmed that the grave was further into the Moor than Lesley Ann Downey's, that she could not remember whether or not she could see the road from the location where she had last seen the body, and that it had been dark when Brady buried the body. She said she did not think he had buried the body in the gas pipeline trench, but that she could not completely rule it out.

I asked if there was anything else she could remember, and we discussed again the place where she was sitting on the grass at the side of the body. Then she said for the first time that she could clearly see the rocks of Hollin Brow Knoll silhouetted against the night sky. Just a few words. Not something she had deliberately withheld. But those few words were to prove of great significance in the search for Pauline Reade.

13

I was not on Saddleworth Moor when Pauline Reade's body was found, on the afternoon on 1 July 1987. I was at Park Lane Hospital, talking to Ian Brady.

After Myra Hindley's clue about the silhouette of the rocks on the skyline we had moved the digging further into the Moor, concentrating on the grassy parts and making sure that we kept the outline of the rocks in view. Brady was being very difficult at this stage, informing me that he knew exactly where Pauline Reade was buried but would only tell me in return for impossible conditions. He was hinting that the body was buried in the gas pipeline trench.

While I was with him I was called away to take a phone call from Geoff. He was excited, and I knew from his voice that it was good news. At about 2.45p.m. a slight change in the vegetation had been noticed – the telltale sign that we had been taught to look out for. After a few minutes' careful work with a spade they had seen part of a white high-heeled shoe. They did what I had instructed them to do if such circumstances occurred: act normally, do not excavate any further, and come off the Moor at 4.30 or 5p.m., as though it was the end of a normal working day.

This was very important: I did not want to alert newspaper and television journalists before I had had the chance to talk to the victims' parents. It would be terrible for them if the first they knew of a discovery was when it was flashed on their television screens. So two of the team hid themselves on the Moor, near to the site, as a precaution against any journalist checking on the progress of the search.

Before I left Brady and returned to Manchester I used the opportunity to put even more pressure on him to help. I did not tell him anything specific, but made a point of going back to see him to say there had been a 'significant development'. He could interpret that however he liked.

There was a lot to do. Back in Manchester I met Geoff and the rest of the team, and then started on the round of official notifications that I was required to make: Mr Brian North, the coroner; Dr Geoffrey Garrett, the Home Office pathologist for the area; Dr Mike Green, the pathologist who had been so helpful at the start of the inquiry; forensic experts, the police photographic and video teams; and, of course, my senior officers.

In the early evening we went back to the site, about 150 yards in from the road, where the discovery had been made – much further into the Moor than I had originally expected. We started slowly excavating the body, digging round it very gently and uncovering it. It was a fine, light summer's evening, so we could see clearly what we were doing. Dr Garrett was there, and during the course of the evening Dr Green and his assistant arrived and so did the Deputy Coroner.

We came across some clothing, and then a foot and a shoe. Already, even at this stage, we could see that the body was remarkably well preserved. She was lying on her left side, facing the road, with her left arm across her front and her right arm along her side, her knees bent. Only one foot had a shoe on, and we found that the foot without the shoe was much better preserved than the one with the shoe. The shoes, I was aware, had been bought on the day she died, and they still looked so new that we could clearly see the manufacturer's gold writing inside, as though they had just come out of their box.

I knew it was Pauline Reade. It would not have been proper to rely on a visual identification, and later a scientific examination revealed the colour of the clothing, and the age of the body was calculated. But even before we had this sort of confirmation I was sure that I was looking at the body of the young girl who had died on her way to a dance, a girl who would have been a forty-year-old woman had she been allowed to live. It was a moving moment for all of us. Whilst we were elated to have discovered the body, our feeling of achievement was tempered by sadness and even anger that a young life could have been ended so arbitrarily.

We could see that she had died from a throat wound, which was how Myra Hindley had described the murder. From the position of the body, and the way the clothing had been pulled up and pushed down, I felt

173

there had been sexual abuse, although at this stage that was only my opinion. By late evening we had removed the body from the ground and it was taken to the mortuary at Oldham District and General Hospital. By this time there were a small number of pressmen on the Moor, watching our progress from afar. It was the early hours of the next day before we went home; obviously some men had to be left on the Moor to guard the site, so a tent had been erected to give them some protection from the cold moorland night.

All the Moors team were there that evening. It was a tremendous feeling for all of us. Thoughts of the Reade family were in our minds. Mrs Joan Reade was in a psychiatric hospital: none of us knew that evening just how important the discovery of her daughter's body was going to be on her road to recovery.

But even without that knowledge, we felt proud. Months of hard work in appalling conditions were justified. We had been subjected to a barrage of harsh criticism and mockery: the search had been called a sham, a show, a farce, a nonsense, a waste of public money and police time. I always felt I could have justified the search even if we had found nothing. But the discovery of the body vindicated the views of Dr Mike Green, who from the outset had been confident that there could be recognizable remains, sufficient for a dog to find, and also the archaeologist and Danish scientist whose professional assessments had tallied with his. Their opinions had been constantly sniped at, and I felt pleased for them.

Looking round the site area, I realized how close we had been to discovering the body in the November and December search, when the dogs had investigated a place very near to the body. If only we had found it then, so much would have been saved for so many people. What effect such an early discovery would have had on Myra Hindley and her subsequent confession, though, I could only speculate. I felt sympathy for the dog teams: they had put in so much effort, and had come so close to a remarkable success.

After we had taken the body to the mortuary I went to see Amos Reade at his home. I told him there had been a development: I did not want to say more because there had been no positive identification, but I wanted to prepare him for the fact that we had found Pauline. Mr Reade, who was alone, took it quietly. He expressed gratitude and relief, but he was restrained. There was already one pressman outside his house, so I made arrangements with the local police station to protect Mr Reade from the press that night and in the days that followed.

I then had the difficult task of telephoning Mrs Winnie Johnson and explaining to her that we had found a body, but that it was not her son. She broke down and cried – but she was also very relieved on behalf of the Reade family. I reassured her that we would continue the search for her son.

The following day we went back on to the Moor and fully explored the grave site to make sure we had missed nothing. Samples of the soil were taken away. The media were there in great numbers by now – so great that they were causing traffic problems along the A635. It was refreshing to find they were now on my side. I asked them not to identify the actual grave site in their pictures, as this would only attract ghouls. The photographers and their editors respected my request. When I was satisfied that the grave had been thoroughly excavated and measurements and police photographs taken, the earth was replaced and the Moor put back to its original state.

The pathologists told me that finding a body in such good condition after so many years was remarkable, and it created a lot of professional interest. But there was also an unusual problem: the body, although so well preserved, had gone very stiff and hard. It had to be softened by immersion in a solution of polyethylene glycol before a post-mortem could be carried out: Unfortunately this chemical was used by pathologists only rarely and they did not have any in stock – certainly not in the large quantities we required. I contacted the Shell Chemical Company, through an ex-colleague of mine who was now working as their chief security officer, and they very kindly agreed to supply enough in the correct strength. It was normally stored in solid form and had to be liquefied specially for us – they did it immediately and delivered it the same day. Without their prompt help serious damage would have occurred to the body; they went to considerable trouble and made no charge, for all of which I was extremely grateful.

A few days after the discovery of the body, the Chief Constable, Jim Anderton, came up to the Moor. He had always supported my review of the case and the search, but this was the first time he had visited us and it was a great morale-booster for the men. With his suit trousers tucked into wellington boots he walked deep into the Moor, looking at the work we had done and at what lay ahead of us in the search for Keith Bennett. He spent a few hours up there, and afterwards talked to the press.

Even my arch-critic, Geoffrey Dickens MP, asked to see me after the body was discovered. He had been making public statements claiming that he had evidence of the involvement of a third person in Pauline's murder – I knew that one source of the information was Pauline Reade's brother, Paul. When questioned by the press I said that if Geoffrey Dickens had any evidence it would have been proper for him to pass it to me, not talk on radio and television about it – and I assume that is why he asked to see me.

I arranged to see him at his house in Greenfield after coming off the Moor on 17 June. Geoff Knupfer was with me. We were still in our boiler suits and we saw him at the back of the house because we were too dirty to go inside. He held out his hand and greeted me like a long-lost friend, addressing me as Peter, although I had never met him before. He said he was sorry to have criticized me so much, but that he had been acting on the wishes of his constituents. It was a brief meeting – he gave me some letters he had received from the public with alleged details about the third person. They contained no surprises or new evidence: we investigated them and they came to nothing. Given the information Myra Hindley had provided – and also by this time what Ian Brady had confirmed – I was not excited by any of the third man theories. I was not prepared to discuss the case with Mr Dickens, especially as at this stage there was still the possibility of a new trial for Brady and Hindley.

Shortly after the discovery of the body Myra Hindley's champion, Lord Longford, made an astonishing statement to the press. He talked about the possibility of her release on parole. 'It isn't right to keep her in prison just to satisfy mob emotion. To say she is an evil fiend is completely wrong. With a possible inquest and trial coming up, I am not suggesting that she should be released immediately. But with a saner approach to her character it should be possible in the future.'

It was a totally inappropriate remark to make at the time, and it certainly did not help Myra Hindley's cause, if that was what he was hoping. I was amazed that someone of Lord Longford's standing and intelligence could be so insensitive towards the victims. Before my first approach to Myra Hindley I had thought about asking Lord Longford to mediate with her, to appeal for her help for the sake of the families of the victims. But people who knew him, and knew his relationship with her, advised me against getting involved with him, and now I realized how sound their advice had been.

The discovery of the body was bound to have a profound effect on Ian Brady. My relationship with him had been improving, particularly in the month prior to finding Pauline, and by the time we found the body I was hoping that he would confess and take me straight to the graves.

After press reports early in June saying that he had refused to help me with the search for bodies, he had written to me denying them and saying that he was willing. I replied straightaway, dropping the ball back into his court: if he was willing, I would arrange for him to visit the Moor. On 9 June, the day the letter arrived at Park Lane Hospital, one of the staff rang and left a message that Brady wanted to speak to me. I phoned him that evening.

He told me he had read my letter, and wanted to know what form of transport would be used to get him up to the Moor. I explained that we would have to work that out carefully. With a helicopter, he said, the journey would be over in thirty minutes, but I pointed

177

out that this would attract attention to the visit. I refused to discuss the arrangements over the telephone, and asked if I could come and see him.

He did not answer directly, but asked a strange question. Did I, he wanted to know, have jurisdiction in places other than Greater Manchester? I told him that as far as this inquiry was concerned, I was in sole charge. He particularly wanted to know if I had jurisdiction over the border in Scotland, and I replied that if he wanted to talk to me about things that happened there I felt sure the Scottish authorities would leave the interviewing to me. He said that something had happened, and he was puzzled why he had never heard more about it. There were other special circumstances, he said, but he did not wish to go into any details over the telephone.

He complained that he was having difficulties with the hospital over visits: he said he was being treated like a category A prisoner (those who have been convicted of serious crime and are imprisoned under very strict conditions), and that his visitors were having to go through stringent procedures to which he objected. He asked me if the Chief Constable was directly involved in the Moors case, and if he had called me off the search of Saddleworth Moor. I told him that, although the Chief Constable was ultimately in charge, the day-to-day running of the inquiry was entirely my responsibility, and that the search had not been called off.

This was, in many ways, a typical conversation with Brady – he would hop about from one subject to another all the time; I became quite used to it over the following months. I asked if he would see me the following day, to which he was agreeable as long as his solicitor was present. I explained that there was a problem: Benedict Birnberg was having trouble getting legal aid fees and expenses for his visits to Brady, and until that was sorted out he might not be able to be there. (On a previous occasion I had spoken directly to the Law Society to explain how important it was to the inquiry that Brady co-operated, and that he be legally represented). Besides, Birnberg was a busy lawyer who could not necessarily drop everything to travel from

London to Liverpool at Brady's beck and call. (Michael Fisher, Myra Hindley's solicitor, was prepared to work for her unpaid.)

Brady told me that he knew nothing of all this. His solicitor, he said, was holding stocks and shares of his which could be used to pay for the visit (I gathered from this and things he told me at other times that Brady had saved money from his small prison allowance, and had invested some of it on the stock exchange.) But he said that he would see me anyway, on a one-to-one basis, if he could talk with Birnberg on the telephone beforehand.

In fact both of us spoke to the solicitor – I promised that I would only be discussing with Brady details of a visit to Saddleworth Moor, and not trying to persuade him to give details about his crimes. Benedict Birnberg was doing his job, which was to protect his client's interests.

Once again, Brady asked for a deal: all the facts about the killings in return for the means to end his own life. Once again I told him this was not an option. He said he was willing to go to Saddleworth Moor and point out two areas – he took great care not to use the word 'graves'. Again, the conversation rambled from subject to subject. He asked once more about my jurisdiction in Scotland, but this time he wanted to know if it made any difference if the victim was English. I explained that any crime committed in Scotland was the province of the Scottish police, but that any interviewing of him could probably be conducted by me. In any case, as he was in custody he could to some extent control who he would see and who he would speak to.

We talked about transportation to the Moor and I sensed that he was looking for some way out of the corner he had backed himself into: his unequivocal stand that he would only confess if he was allowed to kill himself. He was seeking a compromise. He asked me if it would be possible for him occasionally to have a meal of his own choice, accompanied by an alcoholic drink. He explained that there were precedents: there were patients in the hospital who were allowed Guinness, Mackeson and even one who – he thought for medical reasons – was allowed a glass of whisky. I

179

asked if this was a condition he was putting on his visit to the Moor. At some stages in the conversation he said it was, at others he said it wasn't. After a lot of discussion I told him that I would approach the Home Office for permission to take him to the Moor. I made no promises about putting his request for food and drink to the authorities.

It had been, like most of my conversations with Brady, long, confused and muddling. Sometimes he had said he would go to the Moor unconditionally, and seemed eager to help. At other times he was defensive, and put problems into the way of any visit. I became aware at this interview of his paranoia about secrecy: he would always insist that our conversations were totally confidential, telling me that if I breached that trust he would refuse to see me again. He was very sensitive about what appeared in the press: occasionally journalists would speculate on matters that came quite near to what we had been talking about. He was very suspicious and would question me at length about any possible leak. I never did breach his confidence: in the end it was he who released 'confidential' details to the media.

Brady would not allow me to take notes during our talks, which was part of his need to feel in control of the situation. Interviewing him for hours on end was exhausting – and I am an experienced interviewer. He was so sensitive, and his views on many subjects were so different from my own, that I was walking on eggshells all the time, trying to keep the relationship going because I believed that ultimately he might help. Whilst he had some left-wing views on politics, the police and the establishment, on other issues he was paradoxically right-wing. He told me he had chosen Benedict Birnberg because he was a left-wing lawyer who would be prepared to challenge the establishment. On one occasion when I was with him he told me that he did not believe in God, that it was a nonsense to believe in a deity. But he said that after the killing of John Kilbride he looked up into the sky, shook his fist and said 'Take that, you bastard!' He was talking to God. He told me that he thought about it a lot afterwards, because it meant that he was acknowledging the existence of God.

His appearance was quite good at this stage and he looked healthy. A smoker – not, thankfully, as heavy as Myra Hindley – he smoked French untipped cigarettes, and also rolled his own. He made cynical, disparaging remarks about his good health, observing that at his age many people had cancer, but that he wasn't that lucky. Brady struck me as intelligent and cunning. Talking to him was like playing chess: he was always thinking three moves ahead. When I explained that he would not be allowed to commit suicide we had a long discussion about euthanasia, which was his way of making his condition sound more reasonable. Whenever I saw him he wore dark or tinted glasses, although he did sometimes take them off. I felt they were part of his illness, his need to be in control: he liked to be able to look into people's eyes without them looking into his – to see but not be seen.

After visiting him I went to the Home Office to ask permission for him to visit Saddleworth Moor. I spent two hours there, explaining my case for a visit to senior officials who promised to give it full consideration.

Three days later – and a fortnight before Pauline Reade's body was found – Brady was on the telephone to me from Park Lane. He said he had written me a letter, but had ripped it up and was phoning instead. He said there was nobody in the room where he was phoning from, but he was convinced that the call was being monitored. That was another of his paranoias: he was always sure his conversations were being eavesdropped upon by the nameless, faceless authorities he believed were ranked against him.

He wanted to talk about Myra Hindley's open letter to him, which she had sent via the BBC and in which she appealed to him to help. There had been a lot of publicity surrounding it. She had asked me about it, and whilst I wasn't hopeful that a plea from her would sway him I told her that I did not think it would do any harm. She was anxious at this stage to clear up as much as possible. Brady said that if he received the letter personally, he would return it to her unopened. He challenged her motives for sending it, again implying that self-interest was the only true one. He told me that

181

the letter might temporarily affect the matters we had been talking about, and added that he had no further thoughts about them.

It was in this conversation that he first coined a phrase that I would hear him use often in the coming weeks: the 'human week'. This was the term for the condition he was imposing before he would visit Saddleworth Moor. He wanted, he told me, one full week of 'normal' life, eating food that he chose himself, having a drink of alcohol, preferably Drambuie, now and again, watching television programmes of his own choice, and videos of old films, like *Gone with the Wind*, that he wanted to see. He explained he felt deprived of these things, and that after twenty years in custody it was not a lot to ask. Given his 'human week', he said, he would go with me to the Moor and co-operate fully.

He said he was 100 per cent certain that Hindley could have taken me to the right spots on the Moor, and that she was not helping me fully. He did not know why she had failed to show me the graves, except that she perhaps got cold feet when she was on the Moor. 'She knows what I know and I know what she knows,' he said, 'It's been hanging over her for years.' In his opinion she was trying to present herself in the most favourable possible light. He referred to the escape attempt she had made from Holloway Prison fourteen years earlier, and commented that she had only attempted it because she knew she had no chance of release.

As usual his conversation rambled on, and he began to cover details of his proposed visit to Saddleworth. Once again he stressed that he thought a helicopter was better than a convoy of vehicles. He said he would sign a document that would bind him to helping, as long as I promised him his 'human week'. He then asked me if I had talked to the Home Office about the visit: I refused to discuss confidential matters over the phone with him. By this time the Home Office had given approval for the visit, but of course both they and I were not prepared to grant him any conditions.

I told him that we needed to talk face to face, but he did not want me to go to the hospital immediately in case the press interpreted it as a response from him to Myra Hindley's plea. Again he demanded total secrecy about the contact that existed between us. I agreed that, as the press were no doubt watching the hospital, I would leave the visit for a week or two.

So I was astonished when, three days later, he rang me again, in a fury because he thought I had arranged to visit him that day. He was confused and angry. I explained there had been a misunderstanding, and went through the reasons he had given me for not visiting too soon. I wanted to placate him: I was optimistic that he could lead me directly to the graves, and I had the authority to take him up to the Moor. All that stood in my way was his willingness. I felt he was slowly coming round – the conditions he was imposing were lessening.

When I visited him two days later he immediately asked me about the 'human week', and I told him again that it was not possible. I had discussed it with the hospital authorities, and they had said they could never agree to it. But he argued that I could take him out of hospital into secure police accommodation, and give him his week before the visit to the Moor. He blamed the Home Office for not allowing it, although I had never discussed it with them.

I explained that if he was segregated from the other patients at the hospital the news would soon get out to the press, who would assume he was being given privileges prior to a visit to the Moor. He threatened to write to the parents of Pauline Reade and Keith Bennett, to tell them that he was not being allowed to help because the Home Office would not meet his small request. It was another form of blackmail. I replied that the public would regard his conditions as petty, and the publicity would rebound on him: refusing to help find the bodies of two missing children because he could not choose his own menus and watch a video or two would look pretty silly in print. He thought about it in silence for a few moments.

We talked for nearly three hours. He said that he was not asking for cordon bleu cookery – he just wanted things like macaroni cheese, which he said was a great favourite of his. He has the opportunity to do some of his own cooking at the hospital, and television and videos are available for the patients, so I knew that he was being unreasonable. We were going round and round in circles, he was getting more and more demanding, and I was getting nowhere. When I left, he said he wanted to see his doctor.

I felt frustrated, but I did not want to give up with him. I was aware of the contrast with my dealings with Myra Hindley, who asked for nothing apart from counselling by the Reverend Peter Timms. In the meantime, I was liaising with the hospital authorities about his possible visit. I felt that we had to be organized, ready to take advantage of any change of mood he might have.

The next time I visited him he stipulated which of the hospital staff he wanted to accompany him to the Moor. Specifically he did not want his doctor, Dr Strickland, to be with him, but he was happy to have his social worker, Bob Fitzpatrick, and he named one of the nurses. He also said he would not go unless I was in sole charge. I asked him directly if this meant he was willing to come to the Moor, and he said he could not because the Home Office had not granted him his 'human week'. Paradoxically, he then asked about the numbers of police who would be around him, who would be in his group, how I intended to keep the media at bay, and whether there would be a pair of binoculars he could use, as he would need to view some objects on the Moor from a distance. Despite all this talk which presupposed he was agreeing to the visit, he still came back to his demand for a 'human week', a 'last week of pleasure' as he described it.

Then he began to talk about his past life, about various places in Manchester and Glasgow. He and I are of the same generation, and I knew Gorton and the other areas of Manchester that he remembered. I did not give many personal details about myself to either him or Myra Hindley: I do not think it is a particularly good interviewing technique, and it can rebound on the interviewer. Brady never tried to ask me personal questions: he was always respectful to me and never called me by my first name. Often he would criticize

184

the Home Office, even though I was telling him that the decisions were being made by me – he seemed unwilling to accept that and tried to shift the blame elsewhere. He was always pleased to see me, and by this time he accepted that I kept my word and kept our conversations private.

He had established that I, too, was a dog lover, which obviously encouraged him to talk about them. He mentioned the dog he had had, and he knew I had a dog. In books and articles that have been written about him over the years there have been claims that when he was a child he tortured animals: I would be very surprised if that was true, as he seemed to care more about animals than he ever did about human beings.

Although he occasionally criticized the hospital authorities, this was just part of his general railing against any authority. He is well looked after at Park Lane, but not indulged. The staff always put his health and well-being first. I think at this stage they thought his sessions with me were helping him, giving him something to look forward to, a sense of purpose, although they never discussed his condition or his illness with me.

We talked, on this occasion and others, about how he felt in the countryside. He said he could sit on a stone until he felt he had become part of it. Sometimes he would feel an urgent need to go to Glasgow, to touch the stone of the tenement where he had lived when he was a child. It would be an overpowering urge – he would leave a note for Hindley, catch a train and go. After he had touched the stone he would return to Manchester straightaway. He told me how he loved the colour green – how important it was to him.

I was now dealing with him intensely, virtually splitting my time between him and the search of the Moor, from where I occasionally spoke to him by radiophone. In one of his strange, garbled telephone calls he said, 'A matter has entered my head this morning and been with me all day.' He said I would understand the conversation if I listened to 'the various tones'. I didn't have a clue what he meant, but we carried on talking. He asked me if we were talking about seven or eight days – again, I did not know what

185

this meant, except that it might be an allusion to his 'human week'. He said he had seven in his mind but I might have eight days in my mind. I pointed out that seven or eight days did not matter – there was going to be no 'human week'. He asked what 'police custody' meant, obviously referring to details of the visit to the Moor. Once again I was worried that he was talking too openly on the phone, so I said I would come and see him the following day. And that is how I came to be with Ian Brady on the day the body of Pauline Reade was found.

When I got to Park Lane Hospital, soon after noon, he said he wanted to clarify two things: the question of seven or eight days and the definition of police custody. I told him again the number of days was irrelevant – he could not have his 'human week'. We talked around the subject for a long time without getting anywhere. Then he asked what police custody meant.

I explained that when he visited the Moor the whole operation would be under my control, and I would be responsible for him. (He used this to go back to his 'human week', arguing that I obviously had the power to give it to him.) Then he asked if I could also take him to Whaley Bridge, and I said I could as long as the place had some significance to the inquiry. He said it did. He dictated to me some notes he had made, listing the conditions he wanted:

1. Define seven days, as in person.
2. Cigs, food, drink.
3. Video films.
4. Phone Mr Birnberg.
5. The visit to Saddleworth Moor should be during darkness.
6. Visit to Whaley Bridge.
7. See Hattersley in passing (then he went on to say that this was really not necessary).
8 Glasgow.

I asked him what he meant by the last one. He went silent for a while, and then said that he wanted to tell me something but was concerned about my jurisdiction. I assured him that for all matters, whether they had happened in England or Scotland, I would do the interviewing. He thought for a few moments longer and then told me to forget that point. Although he never spelled it out, I thought that he wanted to tell me about a crime he had committed in Glasgow, but that he was worried that after telling me he would have to see other police officers, which he did not seem to want.

The conditions he was imposing seemed to me to be more a trip down Memory Lane than a genuine desire to help, so I was feeling rather cynical about him at this point. He added another condition:

9. Handcuffs.

He insisted on wearing handcuffs because he thought it was 'proper'. I think he wanted to be seen handcuffed because in his own mind it was the image of him he wanted the public to see.

He also said that, although he appreciated the difficulty of his last request, this was it: he wanted to know if I could get full face and profile photographs of the eldest son of David Smith, together with details of his blood group. When I asked why he said he was not prepared to give me his reasons. I said that it was clear that he was talking about the boy's parentage, and he did not deny this. If the results of this request were 'negative' his hatred of Smith would remain, but if it was 'positive' he would have to 'seriously reconsider the situation'. He was obviously trying to establish whether he was the father of Maureen Smith's child: there are no grounds for thinking that he might be. He saw this as a way of getting at both Smith and Hindley at one go.

He went back to talking about the 'human week', and he said he needed some preparation for the ordeal of going on to the Moor. I told him that, if he was looking for a compromise, he should discuss variations in his diet with Dr Strickland. He said he also wanted to talk to Bob Fitzpatrick about the use of the video on his wing of the hospital. It sounded hopeful. He had moved first from the impossible demand to be allowed to commit suicide to the equally impossible but slightly less preposterous demand for a 'human week', and now he seemed to be shifting his position again.

At about this time in our conversation I got the message from Geoff Knupfer that they had found

187

something on the Moor, and that they were confident it was Pauline Reade. I told Brady there had been a significant development: he went silent, and I left him.

14

The discovery of Pauline Reade's body was a massive news story. Ian Brady responded to it by putting out a statement, through his solicitor, that he was willing to go to the Moor and do everything he could to assist the police. My heart sank when I heard it: it meant that the media were alerted to the possibility of a visit, and we would have the same problems we had had with Myra Hindley's first visit.

I rang Brady in the early evening of 2 July, the day after the body was found. He had left a message at police headquarters that he wanted to speak to me urgently. None of the team had had much rest – we had been on our feet for almost thirty-six hours, with only a couple of hours of snatched sleep – so I wasn't feeling inclined to play games with Mr Brady. I felt even less like it when he came on the line and told me he had nothing much to say.

He went on to gloat that we had been 'sitting on top of the body all the time', and said that he had plans to make things difficult for Joe Mounsey, the detective chief inspector from Lancashire Police who with others had found the original bodies, because Mounsey had had Pauline Reade's body under his nose twenty years ago and had not found it. This was typical Brady: on the one hand he was claiming that he wanted to help, and on the other he was trying to settle petty scores. (There could be no possible criticism of Chief Inspector Mounsey or the original search for not finding the body.)

He told me he had tried to stay awake after I had left him on the day that the body was found. He said he 'realized something was developing and wanted to cover events'. But because of his medication he had fallen asleep at 11p.m. and not woken until eight the next morning, when he knew 'the bubble had burst'.

He now wanted to go urgently to the Moor and show me the site of the other grave, so that the whole thing could be over as quickly as possible. He was no longer attaching any conditions to the visit, but just wanted to get on with it.

He rambled on about my telephoning him and using 'codewords' or 'trigger words' that would tell him the visit was on and that I was coming for him. We had never agreed any codewords, so I was not clear what he meant. Again, his inconsistency was typical: he had been talking openly over the phone about the visit, but now wanted to deal in codewords.

When I put the phone down, I considered the situation. I had permission from the Home Office to take him to the Moor, but I had made no plans. Normally the planning for such a visit had taken days. But I took a gamble: the journalists knew Brady wanted to go to the Moor, but they would assume I had to apply to the Home Office. They would not know that authority had already been given. They also knew we had worked for two days without a break, and they would not be expecting anything else dramatic to happen that week.

So at 7p.m. that evening I decided to take Brady to Saddleworth early the next day. Another factor I considered was that Brady might change his mind at any moment. I felt reasonably confident that he would be able to help, and I very much wanted to ease Mrs Johnson's sufferings, especially after having talked to her the previous evening.

I believed that the visit might be able to start secretly, but I realized it would only be a few hours before the media got wind of what was going on. Fortunately, we had the experience of Myra Hindley's two visits to fall back on. The policemen and women who had worked with me then were totally professional, and I knew they could handle the difficulties of another visit. I also knew that, however tired they might be, all the members of the Moors team felt like I did about Mrs Johnson, and would give everything they could to help her. In operational terms I was taking on a tremendous task at short notice and with no properly laid plans, so I tried as far as possible to use the same officers in the same key roles they had filled on the previous visits.

My plan was to bring Brady from Park Lane myself, because, unlike Hindley, he would only relate to me and would not travel with other officers. Throughout all my long talks with him he had always insisted that, if he went to the Moor, he could take me directly to the spots where the graves were. He had insisted that was all he would do – he said he did not want to be there when a site was excavated, and he did not want to talk about the killings. Whenever I tried to question him about the murders he would stop talking; I was only ever given information when he volunteered it.

I shared his confidence that he could take us to the right places. He had put a lot of planning into his murders and the disposal of the bodies – nothing had been left to chance. I was sure that in each case he had carefully chosen the grave sites, and that he would be able, even after more than twenty years, to go straight to them. If we could get the visit under way really early, I hoped he would have shown us the grave of Keith Bennett before the rest of the country was awake and before any journalists knew we were up there.

We worked through the night on the preparations. Despite the punishing work schedule of the past couple of days, we were all alert and excited. Just after 2a.m. I left police headquarters and drove to Liverpool, where I saw Brady at three.

He was less co-operative than Myra Hindley about wearing the clothing we provided, and I didn't want him to refuse to go for the sake of what he should wear. We had provided an anorak, over-trousers and foot-wear, but he would only concede to use the boots. He insisted on wearing his long woollen overcoat and dark glasses: somehow, in his tortured mind, he felt he was protected by them and would not be seen. In fact, of course, they drew attention to him. He did not want to be cautioned or questioned.

We set off at about 3.20 and as we came near Saddleworth I was told there were press cars about. Approaching Hoe Grain, we heard there was a car coming towards us. We had very little time, so I asked our driver to set us down at the side of the road and we quickly got out of sight. Brady recognized the place at which we had stopped, and said there had been a parapet wall at the side of the road when he had been there before. Although I had been there many times during the search I had never noticed it, but later we found the remains of a wall in the stream bed.

We set off across the Moor with Brady leading us. He was not handcuffed – our experience with Myra Hindley had taught us the impossibility of moving about safely in handcuffs – though I had some with me in case he insisted on wearing them. But there was never any danger of him escaping. We walked along Hoe Grain until we came to the junction with Shiny Brook; as we neared the junction he pointed to an exposed slope at the top of the right-hand bank and said, 'There's a spade in there.' I knew that after burying Keith Bennett he had also buried the spade.

He walked very purposefully at a good speed, occasionally taking great lurching steps forward when I had to catch his arm and steady him. He seemed to know exactly where he was going, but he hardly spoke. When we reached the top of Hoe Grain he turned right into Shiny Brook, which surprised me because, after the information Myra Hindley had given me, I was expecting him to turn left. But he was very definite; there was no hestitation.

We walked along the stream bed until we came to the area known as the sheep pens, where small dry-stone pens had been built years ago to help shepherds secure their sheep. The pens were no longer used, and their stones were mainly scattered, although it was still possible to see the shape of their walls.

Brady said they had been moved since he was last there, in 1965; he said they had been a few yards nearer to the stream. He was wrong, but we would not be able to prove that until later. He told us that he and Myra Hindley used to have target practice there, using a billy can as their target. They kept the can in the stream, pushed into the side under overhanging grass. He had no comprehension of the time that had passed, and seemed to think it would still be there.

We walked through the sheep pens to the junction of Shiny Brook with the next gully, Near Most Grain. Suddenly Brady looked up the steep stream bank and

191

said, 'There's the eagle's head.' I had never noticed it before, but the rock and vegetation formation on the skyline does look like an eagle's head. At this stage my excitement – and indeed everyone's – was mounting: he seemed so definite in his directions, and now he was recognizing landmarks. He wasn't worried about his own safety: the ground is rough and difficult and the slopes are steep, but he careered on, lunging from time to time and having to be held, but determined and sure.

He wanted to go up a very high rock formation above the eagle's head to get his bearings. Three or four of us went with extreme difficulty up to the top of the eagle's head – several times I thought he would fall. I was worried: it had occurred to me that he had talked of wanting to kill himself, that he had constantly referred to the 'human week' as his 'last' week of pleasure, and I wondered if he was considering throwing himself off. I had been aware of the risk before we started the visit, and I had instructed Sergeant Ron Peel to stay close to him at all times. Ron's sole job was to watch him very closely, throughout the day.

It was a difficult climb for someone who was not used to the terrain or any kind of outdoor activity. But we managed it to the top of the outcrop of rock, and he looked around him. Then he said he wanted to go back to the stream and continue towards the weir, a sluice which removes stones and shale from a stream which feeds a reservoir.

We went a short way and then he pointed to the right-hand bank, saying that that was the spot where he had had an argument with a shepherd who had threatened to shoot his dog. I was optimistic again: Hindley had told me that on the day of the row with the shepherd Brady had unwittingly pointed out to her the location of Keith Bennett's grave. He had uncharac-teristically become angry with the dog (something she had never seen happen before) when the dog had been sniffing around a dead lamb and digging in the area in which she believed he had buried Keith Bennett.

We carried on towards the weir. Brady said the area had changed – that quarrying had taken place and damaged the area. He said there had been a hut near the weir, and that there had been a railway line on the other side, which he presumed had been used for the quarrying.

His recollections were partly true: there had been a hut, and there had been a track which was used to take small trucks full of silt from the weir. But there had been no quarrying, and the area had not substantially changed. The Water Authority co-operated with us fully, and after the visit I went up there with several employees of theirs, including a retired one, who had worked in the area in the sixties, when Brady and Hindley had been regular visitors. These men, who had spent a lifetime working in the area, had no doubt that the place was more or less the same as it had been twenty-five years earlier.

We crossed the weir, and now Brady wanted to go to the top of a steep and dangerous bank. He was moving awkwardly, and I had to manhandle him to get him to the top. He said we were looking for a large rock, five feet tall, which he described as similar to those at Stonehenge. We searched the area, but by now he had lost the purpose he previously seemed to have and appeared lost.

He did not talk much. One of the few times I have seen him smile in all the many hours I have spent with him came when he first heard, and then saw, a sheep. We stopped from time to time for food. He had had hot drinks, but he refused to eat until we had finished, when he had a 'hot can'. Hot cans are tins of food, stews mainly, that can be bought in camping shops. When you puncture them with a skewer lime is released into water in an outer tin, and the chemical reaction heats the food in the inner tin. Brady had never seen one before, and he talked about it on several occasions afterwards.

We always carried flasks of hot water and disposable cups with coffee or drinking chocolate already in them, so he had plenty of hot drinks. He was impressed, he told me afterwards, that 'the lads treated [him] well'. They were very professional policemen, and they would never have jeopardized the success of the operation by letting their personal feelings show.

We walked a long way trying to find his large stone, 193

until we were looking down over a wide valley and two reservoirs. There is a group of rocks on the top of the moor, Grey Stone Rocks, which resembles those he had described, but he was not heading in the right direction. Eventually we took him to them, and he said they were what he was looking for. After that he said he wanted to find a gully with a sandy bottom. He described its appearance and location.

Then, without any prompting, he told me how he had buried the body of Keith Bennett. He described how Myra Hindley had been positioned behind the burial site to act as a lookout; he said she was there with the rifle. We looked at several possible gullies, retracing the route we had taken earlier in the morning. He told me at one point that he wanted to go back to the A635, to look at a marker by the side of the road.

We had managed to keep clear of the media until about 1p.m. I had been receiving information all morning about press activity, but by this time they not only knew he was there but had hired helicopters to try to find us. It was a beautiful warm dry day – Brady was sweating in his long black coat but he was very reluctant to part with it. Eventually he did let me take it, and put on an anorak.

Suddenly we were clouded in dust from helicopter rotor blades. We did our best to shield him from the photographers; he was critical of them, but he also said, 'I don't care.' And he honestly seemed to think they could not see him anyway, with his dark clothes and glasses. But perhaps the glasses were a good idea after all – the rest of us were suffering from dust in our eyes caused by the helicopter.

It was soon after this that, as we came down a steep bank, he took one of his huge lunging steps forward. It was not a bank anyone would normally climb, but he had insisted: if any of us had lost our footing we would have ended up in the stream bed. As he fell foward I had to hold him, and I took his full weight because there was no other officer close enough to help. As I caught him I felt a tendon in my right calf rupture: I was in pain, but not enough to hamper the rest of the visit.

I could see a photographer quite close to us,

concealed under some wooden shoring from two of my men, who were above him and no more than a few yards from him. I tried to radio to them, but they could not hear the radio because of the helicopter. This photographer, a freelance we nicknamed Rambo because he always wore a camouflage jacket, had actually walked and crawled miles across the Moor from the other side to get to his vantage point: our efforts had been concentrated on the other, much closer side. He was obviously very fit and determined, and got a reward for his effort: he took some very good photographs of Brady, and he was the only one who did. We discussed whether or not we should take the film from him, but I decided that he should keep it.

We had been on the Moor since early in the morning, and it was now 3p.m. – twelve hours since I had met up with Brady. The area was swarming with press, television and radio journalists, and I had to call in uniformed officers to supervise them. It was also clear that Brady had lost his bearings. We were all disappointed that he had not been able to lead us to Keith Bennett's grave – but we had been given a description that we had not had before, we had more information, and we were in a better situation to carry on with our own search. The fair conclusion was that the visit had been useful, even though it had not lived up to my original expectations – I had hoped the search of the Moor would have ended, successfully, on this day.

I made contact with headquarters, and arranged for a closed van to be brought on to the private road belonging to the Water Authority, and a four-wheel drive vehicle to come as far as the weir to pick us up. With a police car in front and one behind we drove back in the van to Park Lane Hospital. Brady told me that he wanted to look at the marker posts along the A635, as one of them was very significant. But I explained that, with the media attention, it was impossible to do anything else up there.

He seemed to be disappointed, but at the same time elated. The nurse from the hospital who had been with us all day and his social worker, Bob Fitzpatrick, felt that he had done everything he could to help us. At the time – and to this day – I was not entirely sure. It had

195

occurred to me that he might have been playing games with us. When he set off purposefully, perhaps he really did know where he was – and perhaps he later decided to play at being lost and confused so he would not have to show me the grave site. Perhaps he did what he had accused Myra Hindley of doing: intended to help but 'bottled out' when he got there. Or perhaps he was laughing up his sleeve all the time, just using the day to check up that we had not got close to the grave. His mind is so devious that it is impossible ever to know exactly what is going on inside it.

As soon as he got back to the hospital he issued a statement through his solicitor, criticizing me for bringing him off the Moor too early. He also said he had faced great difficulties because of the changes, especially the quarry blasting, that had taken place since the sixties. The following day a local shepherd gave an interview saying that the landscape of the Moor was constantly changing. But I established that no blasting had occurred since the 1890s, and the RAF photographs taken at the time of the original investigation showed very clearly that the sheep pens had not been moved. In fact, it was remarkable how similar the photographs taken in 1965 were to the ones taken in 1987. Local farmers and the Water Board workers confirmed what slight changes had taken place.

With hindsight, time seemed to have had a concertina effect in Brady's mind on the geography of the area, bringing Shiny Brook, Hoe Grain and the weir very much closer to each other. Perhaps I should have anticipated this, but he had seemed so confident about his knowledge of the Moor, which had been confirmed by his instant recognition of the place where the parapet wall had been, and the purposeful way he had started out.

He announced, through his solicitor, that he wanted to go back to the Moor. But that was out of the question: his visit had been carried out in perfect weather conditions and with plenty of time before the interference of the media for him to have pointed out the site, if he genuinely remembered it.

The following week we resumed our own search of the Moor, spending our first few days planning just where we were going to search, in the light of the information we now had. On the evening of 7 July I went to see Brady to talk about the changes he was claiming had taken place on the Moor. Until then, I had never had a detailed talk with Brady about the crimes. We had talked for hours all round the subject, but much of our conversation had centred around the visit. I had never been able to question him because he had resisted it, and I had gone along with that because I wanted his agreement to go to the Moor. Now that the visit was over, I decided to be more direct with him. I told him there was no point in developing the theme of blaming the changes on the Moor, because they had not happened.

He seemed puzzled when I told him how little it had changed. But he still appeared to be trying to be helpful, and we discussed in detail the description of the gully that he had given me. He talked about the possibility that he had taken a different route to Shiny Brook on that evening with Keith Bennett, but he eventually dismissed that idea. He was willing to talk more directly than he had ever done before, and I felt reassured that he was trying to help. He seemed determined to be the one who found Keith's body, almost on a tit-for-tat basis: she's given you Pauline Reade, I'm going to give you Keith Bennett.

He admitted that some of the things he had wanted to find on the Moor had no direct significance – the eagle rock, Grey Stones, the view of the reservoirs – but he had wanted to get his bearings from them because he had been confused. He went to his room and came back with some slides of the Moor that he had taken in the sixties. He also showed me some photographs of Scottish scenery, an area between Loch Long and Loch Lomond, which he said was significant though he would not tell me why.

This visit was the first of many that I made to Brady over the coming weeks – visits which punctuated days of hard work searching the Moor. The press did not know I was seeing him, although I never denied it. We spent a great deal of time in detailed discussion about the terrain, and he repeated at intervals his wish to go back to the Moor, but I told him that he would have to

197

have something new and very positive to offer before that could be considered.

The staff at Park Lane were very helpful, and allowed him to get telephone messages to me whenever he wanted to talk. I could not afford to ignore his calls: I knew he was mentally ill, but he was never raving. At worst he was confused, at best he was calm and controlled. It was normal to hear him sounding off about the Home Office, but on one occasion his vitriol turned into verbal violence, and he swore angrily – I rarely heard him swear. He had a very detailed knowledge of prison rules and regulations, and prisoners' rights. He blamed them, not me, for not allowing him a repeat visit.

Sometimes the details of what he was telling me about the location of the grave site would change, but he was being far more open than he had been before the visit. He even agreed to look at maps and aerial photographs: previously he had said he did not need them because it was 'all in my head'. We went over and over the same ground endlessly, talking for hours about where he and Myra Hindley had gone on to the Moor with Keith Bennett, where they had walked to, what they had seen.

I did not underestimate the fact that he had never talked to anyone about his crimes before, except perhaps a consultant psychiatrist many years earlier when he was first in prison. The police conducting the original inquiry had failed to get him to talk, and when he was approached in jail in the late 1960s by Detective Chief Superintendent Douglas Nimmo, then head of Manchester City Police CID, he had said nothing.

I received a letter from him in which he told me about other crimes he was claiming to have committed. He mentioned a body on wasteland behind Piccadilly Railway Station in Manchester; I visited him and asked if this was another victim of his, and he said it was. One evening, he said, he had left Myra Hindley parked in a car on a road which runs off London Road, directly under the Piccadilly railway complex. On wasteland behind the station he had had an argument with a man and had, in his own words, 'bricked him'. When I asked him why, he said something had just come over him. The attack was not premeditated, and from the way he spoke I gathered that he thought that for this reason it was not really murder.

Then he told me about another incident which he said happened in Glasgow, in the Salt Market area, by a canal. He said he saw an old woman whom he described as a tramp, with matted hair hanging down from a cap or bonnet. Her hair reminded him of the fetlocks of a Clydesdale horse which he had seen killed when he was a boy of eight or nine, after it had fallen and injured itself in the street. He told me that a man was treating the woman badly. He followed the man along the canal for some way and then stabbed him with a sheath knife. He said he was not sure that he had killed him, but that he had used 'full force' so he assumed that he had. He cleaned the knife blade by submerging it in nitric acid, which he said took all the chrome off the blade, leaving it with a dull, bluish tint. He told me the knife had been among his possessions which had been taken by the police after his arrest for the murder of Edward Evans, and that it had been returned to his family after the trial.

The next murder he told me about took place in Manchester, on the canal near the Rembrandt public house. He had been drinking heavily, he said, and had got into an argument with a woman. He didn't know what had caused his temper, but he picked her up and threw her bodily over the parapet wall into the canal. He heard a splash, and then he left. He did not know whether she had drowned.

I asked him about his request to see the road markers on the edge of the A635. We had not been able to look at them because of the press presence, but his interest made me ask about their significance. He went silent for a while, and then said one of the markers indicated where another body was buried – that of an eighteen-year-old youth. He said the youth was someone he knew. I questioned him about the location, but he replied that he had not been driving. When I asked if Myra Hindley had been the driver he told me he did not wish to implicate anyone else. I asked him to tell me, yes or no, whether it had been Myra Hindley, and he replied that if he was pushed he would have to say

199

no. There was a third party involved, but it was not David Smith. It was, he said, someone who had done him no harm, and he did not want to get them involved. I had the feeling at the time that he was trying to protect Myra Hindley, and that in fact she had been the driver.

Brady told me there had been another 'happening', involving the River Ouse, but he would give me no details. He also said there had been a 'significant incident' between Loch Long and Loch Lomond, but again he would not be drawn on it. He said it was difficult to know where to draw the line, but that the main thing was to clear up the search for Keith Bennett, which was distressing him. He had been in a lot of torment, he said, because he had been unable to fulfil his promise to help.

I told him that it would be very difficult for me to get authority to take him out of the hospital again unless he could give me more details of the new crimes he was claiming. I explained that if he could give me the identity of the eighteen-year-old it might be sufficient to consider releasing him for another search. I wanted any detail he could give me that I could corroborate. He would have to think very deeply about it, he replied and would let me know his decision.

So now I had four new murders to investigate, plus the hint of another two. I was not sure, from the very beginning, whether or not he was telling the truth. He had asked before, on several occasions, about my jurisdiction in Scotland, which suggested he had been thinking for a long time of telling me about at least one of the murders. I had also heard him express his deep love for animals many times, and he had talked about 'disposing' of anyone who was cruel to animals – the story of the old lady with hair like the horse's fetlocks seemed feasible in that light. I had a suspicion that he had only brought these extra murders in because I was telling him that to visit the Moor again he would have to come up with something new. But I certainly could not dismiss his claims.

15

Before we had a chance to investigate Brady's new claims, the BBC broadcast a report that he had written to them complaining that my senior officers were not allowing me to take him back to Saddleworth Moor. The first I knew about it was as I left the Moor after a hard day's searching, and was confronted by the rest of the media demanding my reaction.

Over the phone he tried to lay the blame for the leak to the BBC on me. The letter had obviously been part of a clumsy attempt to manipulate another visit, and to be even more devious he was implying that I had contacted the BBC.

It was fruitless to discuss it. I told him that we had reached a deadlock over the grave site of Keith Bennett: there was not a gully like the one he described at the place he described. I told him that we had failed to find the spade, despite borrowing sophisticated metal detectors from the armed forces. (I had even had an officer who had his own metal detector as a hobby up there searching, with no success.)

I tried a new tack: I asked him to describe the journey back to the car after burying Keith Bennett. He said that it was very dark, and that he and Myra Hindley had difficulty finding their bearings. They crossed an area of the Moor which he described as 'a moonscape, with craters'. At one point Hindley lost her shoe, but they went back to recover it. They had followed the lights of vehicles on the road – this was significant, as it is not possible to see the road from the Shiny Brook end of Hoe Grain.

I was again astonished by the areas of the Moor they had covered. My hobbies are rock climbing and fell walking, and I know how important it is to have the right footwear, with ankle support, if you are attempting to walk across a peaty, boggy moorland covered in springy tussocks of grass, holes and crevices. Yet they had traipsed across the Moor with a small boy, in their smart street shoes, and then in complete darkness they had walked back again.

When they came off the Moor, he said, they had to

walk up the road from the Yorkshire side to their car and he unwrapped the rifle, which was in a plastic mac, in case someone was near the car waiting for them.

I then explained to him the old wooden posts he remembered had been replaced with plastic road markers. He swore and shouted: 'What are they doing to me?' He seemed to believe it was part of some conspiracy against him, and did not appreciate that twenty years of weather and motorists would have taken their toll on the old markers.

He also got very upset when I told him that a public house he had referred to had been demolished. He was furious that a stone building could have been pulled down – he had a thing about stone. He reminisced about visiting the pub, and said there had been a large St Bernard dog living there.

Brady described the photographs he had taken of Myra Hindley at Shiny Brook as nothing more than an attempt to 'catch the prospectus [sic] of mists and atmosphere'. He started to talk about the psychological triggers that had led him to each of the murders, and how these had influenced the moment, and even the year, at which each had happened. But he refused to talk more because he was frightened that somebody might be listening in to our conversation.

When he telephoned the following day, saying the need to discover Keith Bennett's body was constantly on his mind, I was able to counter his accusations that I had leaked information to the BBC. I told him I had seen the letter they had received, that it was in his handwriting and that it was dated just a few days earlier. He seemed very disturbed and confused by this, referring to the letter as 'a touch on the Machiavellian' and explaining that he had sent it to achieve a purpose. It was this sort of behaviour that made me very suspicious of Brady's real resolve to help find the body of Keith Bennett.

He said he had seen Lord Longford earlier that day and told him that he did not want any appeals on his behalf, like the one Lord Longford had made on Myra Hindley's behalf shortly after Pauline Reade's body was found.

The following week I took the videos made on the Moor to show him. He was reluctant to see them at first, but eventually we watched them together. Then, for the first time, he told me that he was ashamed of what he had done. He said it very simply, his head down, not looking into my eyes. He said when he tried to recall the details of what had happened, 'blocks' came down in his mind. He was struggling to explain himself: he said he did not want to discuss how he had killed the children. He got very disturbed and agitated whenever the subject was mentioned, saying he was frightened of losing total control if the blocks were removed. But eventually he said that he was willing to be interviewed formally, although he was not sure that he wanted to talk about what had happened in Scotland.

On 3 August the inquest on Pauline Reade was opened. It was a matter of satisfying the Coroner about the identity of the body, so that it could be released for burial. The inquest was held in the Magistrates Court Building at Oldham, with one of the courtrooms used as a Coroner's court for the day to accommodate at least some of the press who were there. I gave evidence and so did Amos Reade.

The next day Brady telephoned me and I agreed that his solicitor should be present when he gave me a formal interview under caution. Our reasons were different: Brady said he did not want to be 'verballed', a criminal term for police attributing words to subjects which they dispute. I wanted Benedict Birnberg there because I did not want any suggestion that I had taken advantage of him. But Birnberg was in Greece on holiday, and Brady became very anxious and confused. He would ring me and say he didn't know why his solicitor was necessary for a visit to the Moor. I would have to explain again that I was not offering him a visit to the Moor in return for the interview. All I was saying was that if he did give me fresh details it might help the search if he went to Saddleworth again. Then, and only then, would I apply to the Home Office for authorization.

In yet another phone call, he told me that he was getting confused about the canal incident and the incident behind Piccadilly Station – he was wondering whether they were figments of his imagination. He asked me if I had made any inquiries about these other crimes, and I told him that I had not, because he had given me so few details. The truth was that some investigations had started, although we had only the sketchiest details to go on.

He told me how frustrated he was by the delay, and said he felt he needed to tell his part in the crimes as soon as possible. I suggested that a member of the hospital staff might be able to be present instead of his solicitor. We arranged that I would see him on 29 July with Bob Fitzpatrick; it would be a meeting about a meeting: I would not caution him, and we would simply discuss the formula for going ahead.

It was the first time Brady had agreed to see me with a third party other than Benedict Birnberg present. He said he wanted to get on with the matter, because his only real interest was to get up to the Moor. I tried, once again, to separate the formal interview from any possibility of going to the Moor: the two things seemed to be inextricably linked in his mind. He talked about his fears of a 'show trial'. He was afraid that if he confessed he would be put on trial as a public spectacle. I told him that if the authorities wanted to, they had enough evidence to charge him and put him on trial anyway. I explained that he could go ahead with the formal interview with Mr Fitzpatrick present, or he could wait for the return of Mr Birnberg. He thought about it and decided he preferred to wait for his solicitor.

He began to talk about the other 'happenings', the murders he said he had committed: the man on the wasteland behind Piccadilly Station, the woman he had thrown into the canal near the Rembrandt pub, the eighteen-year-old youth who had buried near the A635, an incident near Loch Long, and a man he had stabbed under some arches in Glasgow. The fact that he would talk about them in front of Bob Fitzpatrick seemed significant: Brady was prepared to let someone else share his secrets. He gave me more information but refused to answer questions. This was typical of Brady: he would tell me something, but the minute I asked a question he would go silent and look down. There would be long periods of silence – he said nothing unless he was prepared to say it.

In the case of the eighteen-year-old, he told me that they had approached Saddleworth Moor from the Yorkshire side. He and the youth had gone together on to the Moor, where Brady had shot him with a .38 revolver. In the Glasgow murder, he had previously given me the impression that he had followed the man along the canal bank, but this time he said it was through several side streets into Argyll Street, and from there into a park where Brady said he stabbed him several times with a knife. He was very firm that the knife still existed and it occurred to me that, from the way he was speaking, he might have asked his mother if she still had it, and that she had confirmed that she had. This was only my supposition – he did not say it. He would tell me when he was going to see his mother, but never gave me details of what they talked about. I knew he was pleased to be seeing her again, not having seen her for many years while he was in prison.

Then he talked of the 'happening' at Loch Long. He told me that the police who handled the original investigation in the sixties had assumed that he had committed a crime in this area, but they had gone to the wrong place, Loch Lomond, which is four miles away. He explained that when they went to Scotland he often got Hindley to pull into a petrol station even when they did not need petrol, so that he could enjoy the pleasure of 'hearing the Scottish voice'. On this occasion they had stopped the car by the roadside and he was viewing the landscape through powerful German binoculars. He saw a hiker with a rucksack and decided to speak to him, anticipating hearing a Scottish accent. Instead, the man had an English accent.

It was this, he said, that triggered the urge to kill him. He shot the hiker with a revolver. It was a difficult thing burying him, as he had no spade, but he had managed it by using the flat metal mess tins that the hiker was carrying. He was unable to bury the rucksack, so he took that back to the car and later threw it into a pine forest they passed.

I discussed with him again whether he wanted to

record all the matters he was telling me formally, with Mr Fitzpatrick there, but he replied that he was worried that when he started talking the blocks would come down at a crucial moment and he would be unable to go on. I said I believed he had gone a long way to removing the blocks already, and that he might not find the experience as difficult as he thought. What he really wanted to do, he said, was to go to the areas, find the bodies and then lay the matter to rest.

What happened next amazed me. Even though I was, by now, a seasoned hand at dealing with Brady, I did not expect this development. I received a phone call from Chris Kramer, a managing editor at BBC Television. He had a letter that Brady had sent to reporter Peter Gould, the BBC man to whom Brady had written before. In the letter Brady gave details of the five 'happenings'.

I could not believe it. The details were skimpier than the ones I had, but none the less he had outlined the other five murders. Brady was playing games again. After urging complete confidentiality on me, and even having the effrontery to accuse me of orchestrating leaks, here he was writing to the BBC again. It was staggering.

Although I was taken by surprise, when I had time to reflect I realized it was not out of character for him. But I had never allowed myself to be led around by anyone like this before, and I was annoyed. I was also, now, very seriously questioning his motives in telling me about the other 'happenings', and questioning how true these claims were.

Brady's correspondence with Peter Gould had sprung up after Mr Gould had written to him out of the blue, and Brady had replied. He trusted Gould, and described him to me as a journalist who did not rush to publish everything. But he was not so naïve as to believe that any journalist would hang on indefinitely to what was, in their terms a 'scoop'.

I asked Mr Kramer if, because of the sensitive point I was at with Brady, he could delay publication of the letter. He promised to hold on to it at least until Peter

Gould returned from his present foreign assignment. But naturally he said he did not want to lose the BBC's 'exclusive'. I gave him an undertaking that if I thought the news about the five 'happenings' was going to break anywhere else, I would alert him. I found his attitude very professional and responsible: I knew other journalists who would have put it on the news that day, whatever the consequences.

I went to see Brady and told him about the letter and its contents. He was nonplussed – at a loss to explain his own actions. He had not intended the letter to be a breach of the trust between him and me, he said, but he needed to put some pressure on the authorities, the Home Office in particular.

I told him forcefully that, as he had broken the confidence, he could not expect me to remain silent if the letter was published. Because of my now very serious doubts about his claims, I asked him again for more details of the 'happenings'. To investigate them, I needed the identity of the youth who had been buried on Saddleworth Moor. If I had his name I could easily check the records for someone of that age going missing. After thinking for a few moments, he said the murder had taken place after the killing of Pauline Reade: he thought it was in 1964, at around the time of Keith Bennett's murder. But he refused to give me the victim's name because he said there was a thread that would link it to the name of a third person whom he did not wish to involve. He said this person had done him a favour, murdering someone for him and disposing of the body in the River Ouse. The killing of the youth was a return favour. Nothing I said would persuade him to give me the name, although by this simple fact alone I could have confirmed the truth of one of his claims.

When I asked where the body was buried he said they had approached from the Holmfirth end of the A635, and had parked and walked on to the Moor not far from where he had gone with Keith Bennett. He said he had buried the body with a spade 'which was always in the Mini Traveller'. This made me think that the driver might have been Myra Hindley, as it was her car. He said he and the youth had gone about a quarter

207

of a mile into the Moor, and were shielded from the road by a rise in the land. Then he said he wished he had never told me about this murder, because he was so worried about involving the third person.

I asked him about the 'happening' on the wasteland behind Piccadilly Station. He seemed troubled when I asked for a description of the man, but said the victim was between twenty and thirty years old, wearing baggy trousers and looked like a workman. He could not remember what they had quarrelled about, but the man had bumped into Brady, who had been drinking heavily. In a frenzied attack Brady hit him with a brick or a lump of concrete, almost battering him to a pulp.

He could remember no details about the woman he threw into the canal, except that he believed he had been drinking heavily that night also. Again, he put her age at between twenty and thirty. As before he said he had no idea why he did it, but that something just 'came over me'.

The Glasgow murder, he said, happened under the railway arches in the Carlton area of the city. He told me again that when he saw the man hit the old woman he had been reminded of the execution of the Clydesdale horse. He had followed the man from the Saltmarket area through the streets to Argyll Street, and stabbed him several times in a frenzied attack. He could not remember how many times he had stabbed him. I asked about the knife, which he believed was at his mother's home. She had confirmed that she still had it, and he agreed that I could see her, as long as I did not arrive in a police car – that would upset her.

With the Loch Long incident he admitted that Myra Hindley was the driver. His story was that it happened after they had driven through a village called Arrochar. The hiker was in his twenties, with a heavily packed rucksack. After killing him Brady did not look in the rucksack for the man's identity. He claimed he shot the hiker once in the back of the head with .38 revolver, 'in such a way that it was a complete surprise, he had no warning'. It was identical to the shooting of the eighteen-year-old, he said.

The way he talked about these two killings was typical of Brady. He liked to give the impression he

208

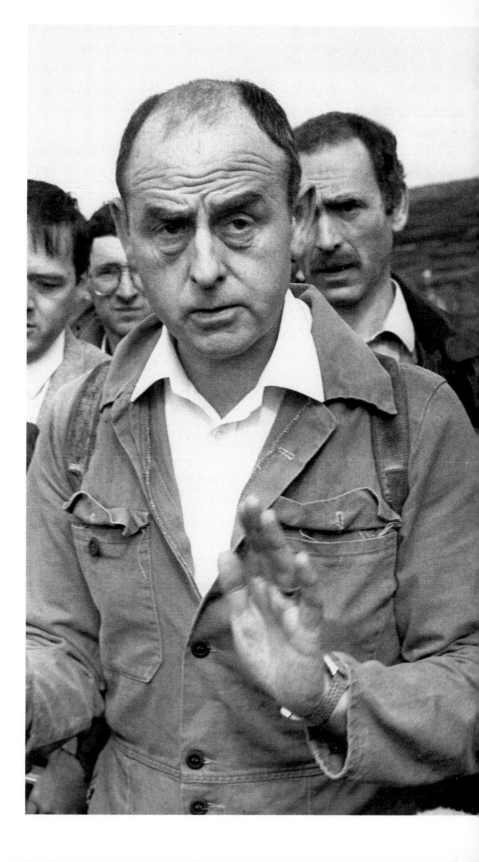

During that summer we were photographed constantly.
Left to right: Ged McGlynn, Steve Southward, PT, Pat Kelly, *unknown*, Geoff Knupfer, Martin Flaherty

In the early days of the reinvestigation and searches of the Moors, dogs were very much an integral part of the operation

The team line up. *Left to right* : D/Sgt Gordon Mutch, D/Inspector Geoff Knupfer, D/Con Pat Kelly, D/Sgt Steve Southward, PT, D/Sgt Martin Flaherty, D/Sgt Ron Peel, D/Con Alan Kibble, D/Con Ged McGlynn
(PHOTO: EXPRESS SYNDICATIONS)

The Rev. Peter Timms (*left*), former governor of Maidstone Prison, who supported Hindley throughout the confession with her solicitor, Michael Fisher

A recent photograph of David Smith who, as a young man, witnessed the murder of Edward Evans

The police helicopter transporting Hindley on her first visit to the Moors on 16 December 1986

The roped-off grave area where Pauline Reade's body was found

(*Above*) The funeral cortege and (*below*) burial of Pauline Reade, at Gorton, Manchester in August 1987

Greater Manchester Chief Constable James Anderton joined me to be briefed on progress in the search for Keith Bennett's body on Saddleworth Moor

Surrounded by hospital staff and police guards, Brady – in overcoat and dark glasses – attempted to identify key locations in our searches

I spent my last working day in the
police, 13 April 1988, on the Moors
with Winnie Johnson, mother of
Keith Bennett

Keith Bennett's family conduct their
own secret search for his body,
twenty-five years after his murder

could just 'blow people away',that his attitude to killing was cavalier, that it was easy and that the lives involved did not concern him. I believe this was an echo of those long forgotten conversations with David Smith, when he bragged about killing as though it was a natural and normal way of life for him.

But I still did not have anything very substantial upon which to base a murder investigation. We agreed that I would return to interview him formally about these five murders and those of Pauline Reade and Keith Bennett when his solicitor returned from holiday.

Meeting Ian Brady's mother was almost as distressing and moving as meeting the parents of her son's victims. She seemed a very sensitive person, very keen to help me. She remembered the knife, but was not sure where it was. She had moved house a number of times since the trial, she explained, and things had been mislaid. I felt she was being helpful, not evasive. After a good search she found an ornamental dagger which she thought was the right knife, but it wasn't. Both she and her home were very clean and tidy. She knew her son was anxious for me to find the knife, and she wanted to do her best to help. She said she would let me know if she found anything that might be useful.

She felt responsible for her son's behaviour, and was always trying to work out what had gone wrong. She felt it was her fault that so much damage and hurt had been inflicted on other people. She had obviously lived with a sense of guilt and distress for many years. I tried to reassure her that it was not of her making and that she should not reproach herself. But I do not think I was able to give her much comfort: she seemed to me to be a good woman on whom her son's guilt weighed very heavily.

But I was no further forward. I was now feeling very cynical about Ian Brady, and I was coming more and more to believe that he had deliberately misled me when I was on the Moor with him. This strong need to feel he is in control means that he likes to feel he knows something that others don't: it gives him a feeling of superiority. It would have given him a real high to have led me, the head of Greater Manchester CID, all around the grave site, enjoying the fact that I had not found it. As time went on and I was subjected to telephone call after telephone call, game after silly game using statements to the media as pawns, I came to feel even more doubtful about the value of his help. He had never been open with me like Myra Hindley had. She might not have told the whole truth about her motivation and the level of her involvement, but she had been frank about the details of the killings. So not surprisingly the next step in my investigation took me back on that familiar journey to Cookham Wood, to interview Hindley again.

16

When I saw Hindley on 4 August, one of the first things she said was how relieved she was that Pauline Reade's body had been found. Michael Fisher was there, and I had Geoff Knupfer with me. The purpose of the visit was to show her the videos of Saddleworth Moor which Ian Brady had already seen, and we spent more than an hour and a half going through them.

She was reluctant to identify any area positively – I think because she was afraid of misleading us. Both she and Brady had given similar descriptions of the site of Keith Bennett's grave, but neither had been able to pin down the location. Among the possible sites Hindley identified from the video were some well over a mile apart. It made life difficult for us, but I suppose in the end it meant that we searched as wide an area as possible, and any gully that remotely resembled the one they had described was painstakingly excavated.

I asked her about a picnic she and Brady had had on the Moor with the Waterhouse children, at Grey Stones rocks. She said she remembered the picnic, but was not sure that it was at the rocks. I also asked her what she had taken with her on the evening that she had followed Brady and Keith Bennett across the Moor to the spot where the boy was murdered. She confirmed what she had told me before, in her confession: she had binoculars with her. I asked her if she had taken a rifle, because Brady had talked about having a rifle with them on this journey. She said she had not, nor had she carried a spade.

Then I told her that I wanted to question her about the other five murders that Brady was claiming. She had mentioned on a previous occasion that she remembered parking and waiting for him one evening near Piccadilly Station. In the light of his claim that he had murdered a man on wasteland behind the station, this became important. She had taken Brady into the city centre after they left work, dropping him outside the Queen's Hotel. He said he was going to the cinema, and she had assumed that she would be going with him. But when they neared the city centre he told her he was going on his own, and he told her to pick him up at 11 p.m. She was angry. He had given her no good reason why he would not take her with him – merely told her categorically that she wasn't coming.

The arrangement for picking him up, she said, was that she would park and wait in Store Street, under a railway arch beneath the station. She went home and then went round to Maureen's, where she had a bath and put her hair in rollers with her sister's help. She realized that if she wasn't careful she was going to be late to pick Brady up, so she put on a headscarf over her rollers and drove off. She waited in the agreed parking place for some time, but he did not show up. Apparently he was never very punctual.

After some time she left the car and went up some steps on to the station approach. She looked around, knowing that he 'had a thing about railway stations'. She wasn't sure, but she thought she had even asked someone to go and look in the gents for him. When she returned to the car he was still not there. He eventually turned up at 1 a.m., drunk. She was furious, and for the first time in their relationship she dared to question him about where he had been. That made him in turn angry, and he told her it was nothing to do with her. The area where she had been waiting was, at that time, dimly lit and derelict – a lonely place for a woman to be on her own. That was why she was in such a temper, she explained.

I asked if she had noticed anything unusual about his clothes or his demeanour – anything that would suggest he had been involved in a violent struggle. She said she had not, but that her rage might have blinded her to those sort of details. We tried to establish the date of this evening: she said it was after the murder of Pauline Reade. And then she remembered that she had gone to Maureen's flat at Hattersley, which meant that it must have been after July 1965, when Maureen and David Smith moved there.

Hindley said that there were several occasions when she had waited for Brady at that same spot near the station, but that this was the one that stuck out in her memory because he had been so late, and because she had been waiting with her hair in rollers – she implied that she was embarrassed by this. It was also the first time she had questioned him. He had not answered her properly. She said he had an infuriating habit of going silent and not arguing back.

In order to provoke a reaction she drove too fast and erratically on the way back, but he continued to say nothing. So when she came to a clear stretch of road she checked that there were no vehicles behind or in front, and then slammed on her brakes. Brady nearly went through the windscreen. He reacted by punching her hard on the side of her head, nearly embedding one of her rollers in her scalp. Then he laughed, and started to talk to her. But he still would not tell her where he had been, and he would not respond to her accusations that he treated her 'just like a chauffeur. You arrange for me to pick you up and you're hours late.'

I asked if she could recall ever dropping Brady on Saddleworth Moor with a young man, someone he knew, having driven from the Yorkshire side of the Moor. She said the only person she had dropped on the Moor with Brady was David Smith, when they were going potshotting.

Then I inquired if she knew any of Brady's associates in Yorkshire. She said she only knew of Gilbert Dears, who had been in borstal with him, and another man called Douglas Wood, who lived in Hull. She had dropped neither of them on the Moor with Brady. Nor had he mentioned a road marker post to her. She wasn't even clear until I explained it to her what a marker post was.

I reminded her that we had talked earlier of holidays that she and Brady had shared in Scotland, and when I asked if she could remember going to the Loch Long area she said they often went there. She could not remember him leaving her and returning with a rucksack. I told her that he claimed to have thrown the rucksack into a pine forest, but she had absolutely no memory of this. She would certainly have known, and asked him about it, if it had happened. I tried to establish which of the two cars, the Traveller or the pick-up, they had been in when they visited Loch Long, but she said they had been several times, probably in both cars. They used to camp up there, sleeping in the car, but she did not remember the name of the village of Arrochar.

When I asked if Brady had ever left her to go off on his own in Scotland, she recalled a day in the St Andrews area, when they had visited a little fishing village to which he remembered going as a teenager. They walked to a rock formation called the Devil's Cauldron, where the sea rushed in and out of a hole in the rocks. He had left her while she went looking for an old church. I asked her if he had taken binoculars, and she said that he always carried them to view the countryside. I asked if he had a gun. She said he usually carried one, probably the .38 Smith and Wesson, although he could have had both the revolvers.

When they were on holiday he would often go walking on his own while she cooked a meal, or prepared the back of the van for them to sleep in. He might have done this at Loch Long, but there was no particular occasion that stuck in her mind. I asked if she could remember anything about the condition of his hands or his clothes when he returned from these walks, but she said there had never been anything out of the ordinary. He had never been dirty – which he would have been, had he buried a body with a mess tin. All in all Hindley could not give me any information that corroborated Brady's claim to have killed a hiker.

I asked her about the 'happening' in Glasgow, when Brady said he had stabbed the man who was harassing the old woman. She had been to Glasgow with him, but she had no memory of him ever telling her about being in a fight, or knifing a man, nor had she ever seen him cleaning a knife. I also asked about the woman he claimed to have thrown into a canal in Manchester, and again she said he had never mentioned it to her.

Hindley raised the subject of the letter that she had written to her friend May Hill, which May was supposed to take to the police in the event of anything happening to Hindley. The letter had been supposed to contain the names of three men whom she thought were at risk from Brady: she said she could not remember writing down three names, but if she had, one of them would have been her ex-fiancé, Ronald Sinclair. She remembered talking to May Hill, and giving her the letter, but she could not remember it containing names. Knowing how meticulous Hindley's mind is, and how well she does recall events of the time, I believe she would have remembered them had they been there.

We were obviously interested in these names, and in anyone Brady had known at the time, because we were trying to find the identity of the eighteen-year-old youth he said he had killed. We interviewed May Hill, but she could not remember, and we spent a lot of time tracing anyone who had known Brady and Hindley at the time, including his old borstal contacts.

I told Hindley that the inquiry was not yet completed: we were still searching Saddleworth Moor for Keith Bennett. I said I would probably need to interview her again. As usual she had been calm and helpful throughout the day, and again I believed that she was doing her best to clear the matter up.

Her answers had confirmed what I had suspected all along: there were no other murders. Although I could not rule them out just on the basis of what she had said, and a thorough investigation into them was already under way, I felt she would certainly have been able to tell us about the hiker 'happening', had it been true. On that occasion Brady admitted she was with him, driving the car. And the murder on Saddleworth Moor of the eighteen-year-old youth: although he had said she was not the driver, he had named one of her cars as being the vehicle involved. Yet she knew nothing about that, either.

I spoke to Brady again on 13 August, but only to tell him that his solicitor was still away on holiday. He seemed in good spirits, and was prepared to wait. It was the 20th when I finally went to the hospital to meet Benedict Birnberg before formally interviewing Brady. I made it clear to Mr Birnberg that at this stage I intended to interview his client on tape formally, whether or not Brady agreed, although I hoped he would be co-operative.

Brady came into the room wearing the tidy casual clothes he always wore: I never saw him wearing a tie, but he was always neatly dressed in trousers or jeans and sweaters in dark colours, and his black shoes were always well polished. I cautioned him and told him that I was there to interview him about the disappearances of Pauline Reade and Keith Bennett. He announced that he did not want to be questioned formally.

I told him that he had put out a public statement through his solicitor saying that he was willing to go to Saddleworth Moor to assist the police in their search for Keith Bennett's body, and that this statement implicated him in the murder of Keith Bennett. To help locate the grave, he must have been involved in the burial. He repeated that he did not wish to be formally interviewed. He was very controlled, precise, polite, distant. Although he had never been on friendly terms with me, he had been more helpful at our earlier meetings.

I reminded him that when he was on Saddleworth Moor he had tried to help find the grave, and he agreed he had. Did he still want to find the grave? He said he did. I talked about some of the details he had given me of the description of the area of the grave. Suddenly he announced that Myra Hindley 'knows the location of the grave on that slope'.

I asked him whether, when he was on the Moor, he

215

had known the location of the grave all along, and he answered this obliquely by saying that he had looked for it for twelve hours. I put it to him that he knew where it was but could not bring himself to point it out. He denied it, and said he had been determined to point it out and would have done so had he been able to. Was he witholding information? He said he was not.

When I asked him questions about the location of the grave, he answered happily enough. This was a formal interview, so he was clearly admitting on record his involvement in the murder of Keith Bennett. After a while he asked me if the tape recorder was still running, and I said it was. His solicitor objected: he said his client had wished to be interviewed informally. I pointed out that two children had been murdered, I believed Ian Brady was responsible, and I was duty bound to ask him about them. He had the right to stay silent.

Then I asked Brady about Pauline Reade. How had he disposed of the knife that had been used to cut her throat? Brady replied that he had offered on a number of occasions to show me where he had thrown the knife, and he was still willing to do that. When I inquired if he was admitting responsibility for the murder of Pauline Reade, he said 'no'. Was he responsible for the murder of Keith Bennett? He seemed hesitant about answering. I put the same two questions again: had he murdered Pauline Reade? 'No,' he said. Had he murdered Keith Bennett? He wanted to know whether I was asking if he had done it alone, or whether others had been involved. I told him that Myra Hindley admitted being involved in both murders, and then I asked if he was implying that there were others involved apart from her. He said he wasn't saying that.

At that moment refreshments were brought in. It was a bad moment, for he had started to open up a little bit. When we resumed he said he was not denying his part in the murder of Pauline Reade. He commented that we had had long conversations about it before, from which I should have known he was involved. But what I wanted was a positive admission on the tape, under caution.

The machine bothered him. He wanted to continue

informally, and kept referring to 'the box' being switched on. He was getting more and more agitated, and said, 'that box, it inhibits me.' I was quite happy: he had made admissions, in the presence of his solicitor and under caution, implicating himself in the murders. I had enough evidence to charge him, should that be necessary. I could see that I was not going to get anything more from him formally about the other murders he was claiming to have committed. I tried to persuade him, but he refused to say anything about them other than to tell me that he had 'thrown in the happenings in Scotland as a bonus'.

Benedict Birnberg raised the point that his client was worried about the possibility of a trial. I said I could give no guarantee that there would not be a trial. Brady was clearly aware that anything he said on the tape might be used in evidence, and he was constantly reminding himself that there was a tape recorder running and asking for it to be switched off. So we ended the formal interview there.

It had been fairly satisfactory. Perhaps, at the start of my whole investigation, I had hoped that Brady would confess fully one day to everything he had done, in the way Myra Hindley had. But as I became more involved with him, I realized that his mental condition would probably never allow that. So I was pleased to have achieved what I had: admissions on tape, with his solicitor present, to the murders of Pauline Reade and Keith Bennett. With the other evidence I had about these murders I was happy with the case against him.

He agreed to carry on talking informally, and did not object to Geoff Knupfer being there. But he was no longer under caution. I asked him about the 'happenings'. I tried to establish the date and exact location of the alleged murder behind Piccadilly Station. He said it was in 1964 or 1965, and that it had happened on a long, straight, dimly lit road. I asked him if he remembered asking Myra Hindley to wait for him under a bridge, and that she had been upset when he returned late. I told him he had hit her after a row, but he said he could not remember this. He had only hit her twice and he could not recall the first occasion.

He said he had hit her at the time of Pauline Reade's

217

murder, when he thought he had dropped to the depths of depravity. But as a consequence of something she said, he realized she had 'dropped even further'. When I asked him to tell me more he said it was something that was said to Pauline Reade before she was killed, but he would say nothing further. So I offered to give him a résumé of Myra Hindley's account of the killing of Pauline Reade. He made comments: he said the sun was shining and it was daylight until late, so there was no need to flash lights when picking her up. (Myra Hindley had said that he was behind her car on his motorbike, and he had flashed his lights when a suitable victim was spotted.)

Brady said Hindley picked up Pauline Reade by asking the girl to help carry a pile of records to the van, which she said was parked in Cornwall Street. He was at least an hour behind them going up to the Moor. I asked if Hindley had set out to pick up anybody or somebody specific, and he said it could have been anybody. She took Pauline Reade to Hollin Brow Knoll on her own, he said, and that was where they met.

I told him Hindley had said he was introduced as her boyfriend, and that Pauline had been told she was there to help look for a lost glove – he agreed with this. But he did not agree with Hindley's version that she had left him with Pauline while she went to move the van. He said all three of them went on to the Knoll. Hindley had said, I explained, that she was in the car when Pauline Reade was killed, and I asked if this was true. He said it was 'in general terms'. He said she was there when the body was buried, and that was when he had hit her. I asked again if she was there when Pauline was killed, and this time he said yes.

I moved on to the abduction of Keith Bennett. He said Hindley had been on her own when she picked the boy up, and that she had then driven to the Ardwick area to meet him in a street coincidentally called Bennett Street. He said he could not remember what they said to the boy, but that they went to Saddleworth Moor. He said Hindley had a spade and a rifle, wrapped in a plastic mac or a piece of plastic. The boy walked with him on to the Moor.

Again, his version of events was at variance to

Hindley's. But my instincts tell me that he is not telling the truth about how they picked the boy up, or about Pauline's murder: if he had sent Hindley out to pick up a victim from anywhere, how would he have known where to wait for her? Bennett Street was a very convenient place from where she had picked up Keith. But why did he choose it? How did he get there? Similarly, it would have been difficult for Hindley to keep Pauline Reade occupied for an hour until he arrived at the Knoll. Hindley's versions are more detailed, and I think they have the rring of truth about them.

We looked at aerial photographs of the Moor, and once again Brady tried to describe where Keith Bennett had been buried. I told him again that there was no gully in the area where he thought the grave was. I asked him if there was a photograph of the grave among their many snapshots – he had photographed other graves.

He talked about the collection of their photographs in a tartan-covered album which had been an exhibit at the trial. He had tried to keep Hindley out of the case, he said, and in her five days of freedom between his arrest and hers he had passed instructions to her to destroy certain things. He said again – he had mentioned it on other occasions – that if she had been able to get into the house she would have destroyed the left luggage ticket, but a policeman was posted outside. He said the tape should have been destroyed with the things that Myra Hindley found at Millwards, and I gathered he meant the tape of Lesley Ann Downey. I asked him if he had taken any photographs of Keith Bennett. He did not answer directly, but said that everything was destroyed, including the negatives.

'Thank Christ the police didn't get to them,' he said.

We then talked about the killing of the eighteen-year-old. He said he had tied a white handkerchief to one of the road marker posts to show him where the grave was. I told him that it would be easy to substantiate this story if he gave me the identity of the youth, but again he said he could not. Was the person he did not want to implicate David Smith? He said it was not. He contradicted what he had told me on a previous occasion by saying that the spade was not in the car but was buried or hidden up there on the Moor.

I pointed out that he had made a public statement about the matter in his letter to the BBC, and that he had told me that he knew the identity of the victim. He replied by saying there was nothing in writing about the identity. He said he had done all he could, and once more said the letter to the BBC was sent 'to push the authorities'. Had the murders actually occurred, or were they something he had made up in order to 'push the authorities' into giving him another visit to the Moor? He replied by asking me if I had made any inquiries in Glasgow.

I brought him back to the murder of the eighteen-year-old, and asked if there was anything more he could tell me about it. He said, again, 'The thread is there.' It was significant, he told me, that the car was being driven from the direction of Bradford and Leeds. I asked if it was anything to do with Gilbert Dears, but he said that Dears was just a reliable friend of his – it was not a tit-for-tat arrangement made with Dears. The person involved with him was still alive, and had settled down and had a family.

Then we talked about the death of the woman in the canal in Manchester. I asked if he had been in the Rembrandt pub; he said what he could remember were the bridges on the canal and the pub. He couldn't give me any further information about the victim, except that she was female. He said he did not believe he had injured her in any way: he had just thrown her into the water. It happened during the time of his relationship with Myra Hindley, but he could not remember which car she had at the time. He asked me if a woman had been found in the canal, and I told him that there had, although I did not know if it had any connection with him. I would need more information to confirm that. Brady said he was trying to give me a 'glimpse of how he acted and thought'. It was another reference to the careless attitude to human life that he had at the time.

We moved on to the incident in Glasgow. I asked if Myra Hindley was with him on that trip. He said she was in Scotland with him, but that she wasn't with him at the time of the attack. They were on holiday in the

Mini Traveller, which would mean that it was 1965. We went over the details of that 'happening' mainly for the benefit of Mr Birnberg, and I explained that Brady's mother did not have the sheath knife.

The Loch Long incident had also occurred while they had the Traveller, he said. We again went over the details for his solicitor. Brady said he knew exactly where he had buried his victim because there was a pinnacle, a natural rock twenty to thirty feet high, from which he could get his bearings. After our experience with him on Saddleworth Moor I was not convinced: it sounded like more evidence of his obsession with rock.

I told him that Hindley could not remember the rucksack, and I asked if he could tell me anything that would help identify the hiker. To the surprise of both Mr Birnberg and myself, Brady completely changed the subject. 'The second time I hit Hindley was on the Knoll. She wanted the pendant,' he said.

I asked if the pendant he had mentioned belonged to Pauline Reade. Brady replied: 'She said, "you won't need that where you're going." And that's when I hit her.'

We went back to the Loch Long 'happening', but all he could add was that the gun he had used for this killing was the same one that the police had found at Wardlebrook Avenue when he was arrested.

His solicitor asked Brady about an interview he had given to Fred Harrison, in which he had apparently claimed to have committed his first murder when he was only eight years old. He said it had been more of an accident than a murder. He had been swinging on a very heavy swing in Hutchinson Square in the Gorbals when a boy younger than him had come behind him. He had heard a heavy thud as the swing hit the boy, and then he had run out of the park. He did not know whether the boy was dead, but he had assumed he was. It sounds like the sort of accident that is common in children's playgrounds; the idea that the boy died may have sprung from Brady's obsession with death.

I asked him about four half-crowns found on Pauline Reade's body, which he said he had forgotten about. When I asked what happened to the pendant he said he had buried it, probably the day after the murder, at a

221

place in Oldham. He said the bloodstained clothing and the knife he had used had been burned.

17

Pauline Reade was finally laid to rest at Gorton cemetery on Friday, 7 August 1987. It was a very moving occasion. I and all the officers from the team were there, and our wreath was one of many in memory of the lovely, happy teenage girl whose body had lain on Saddleworth Moor for twenty-four years. Pauline's mother Joan was there, supported by nurses from the psychiatric hospital where she was being treated. Her husband Amos and son Paul was next to her throughout the requiem mass at the Monastery of St Francis in Gorton, where Pauline had worshipped as a child – and where Myra Hindley had converted to Roman Catholicism. They later steadied her as she sprinkled soil on the coffin of her daughter as it lay in the grave at Gorton Cemetery.

No words could ever express the sympathy we all felt for Mrs Reade. As the father of two daughters myself, I know how much I have enjoyed watching them grow up – and I know how close they both are to their mother. Joan Reade had been deprived of the companionship and love of her daughter, and of the grandchildren she would no doubt have had. But perhaps the worst thing she has had to cope with has been the uncertainty, never knowing what had happened to Pauline. For years she had left the back door of her home open every night, so that if her daughter returned she would be able to get in. Now, at least, the uncertainty was over. For that we were able to give thanks.

As we saw Mrs Reade that day, sad and unsure of herself, none of us could have known that witnessing her daughter being buried was the first step on her road to recovery. Within a few months of the funeral Mrs Reade was well enough to leave hospital. Today she is very much better and is living at home with her husband Amos.

To those politicians and journalists who criticized the Moors search, who talked scathingly about searching for a needle in a haystack and complained about the cost of the search, to them I would like to say: look at Mrs Reade. We could never bring her daughter back to life. But we ended nearly a quarter of a century of uncertainty that had finally broken down her mental health. I believe the Moors inquiry team have many things to be proud of: not the least is their contribution to Joan Reade's recovery.

Relatives of other victims of Brady and Hindley were at the service and the burial. As the cortege drove from the church to the cemetery, the road was lined with hundreds of people, most of them from Gorton. The cemetery was crowded. It is difficult for me to remember all the people who came up to speak to me on that day, to congratulate the Moors team on our work. One conversation I remember vividly was with John Kilbride's father, and his grown-up sons. They were friendly, and very pleased for Mrs Reade's sake that the search had been successful. But the sadness of the occasion only heightened their vehement hatred of Brady and Hindley. With tears in their eyes, they told me what they would do to the Moors Murderers if they were ever released. I knew they were not making idle threats.

On 24 August I called off the search for the body of Keith Bennett on Saddleworth Moor. It was a sad moment for all the members of the Moors team: we were unusually quiet as we drove back to police headquarters at the end of the day. The thought of another mother, Mrs Winnie Johnson, was in everyone's minds. We would have liked more than anything to have given her the same comfort that Mrs Reade had derived from the finding of Pauline's body,

But it was not possible. We had systematically searched all the areas that our review of the case had made us feel were likely, and those that even vaguely matched Ian Brady's and Myra Hindley's descriptions of the grave site, but with no success.

I saw Winnie Johnson at her home that morning, and

223

explained that I would be calling the search off. I wanted her to hear it first from me and not from a journalist. I explained how, with the information I had, I could no longer justify continuing the search, but I gave her a promise that if I received any more information, I would search again. She was desperately upset and sobbed all the time I was with her.

Mrs Johnson will never rest until her son's body is found, or until we have evidence that it never can be found.

The following day I saw Myra Hindley again, at Cookham Wood. Michael Fisher was there, and Geoff Knupfer was with me. She said she had heard on the radio that the search had been called off and expressed regret that we had not been able to find the body. I said I had come to see her to finalize matters, and to go over what she could remember once more, in case there were any details that we had overlooked.

Once more we talked through the possible locations for Keith Bennett's grave. I spent a lot of time questioning her and cross-questioning her about the journey they had made, and the other trips to the Moor when they were picnicking with the Waterhouse children or going there for target practice. I asked her about the footwear they wore, and she told me, as she had before, that they wore ordinary shoes, and she hadn't worn high heels.

We went over the question of whether or not she carried a spade and a rifle when she followed Brady when he took Keith Bennett on to the Moor. She said again that she only carried binoculars, and asked if Brady had said that she carried a spade and gun. He had, but I also wanted to know because, if the spade was already on the Moor, he must have known exactly where he was going. He did know where he was going, she said because when he reached a certain spot with the child he motioned to her to wait. But when I asked if she had seen the body buried, or had seen Ian Brady dig the grave, she answered categorically that she had not.

Had the envelope that she had burned at Millwards contained negatives of photographs? She said she didn't know but had destroyed it quickly because she was frightened and in a hurry. To the best of her knowledge, she said, it contained plans for bank robberies.

She described Keith Bennett's last journey, when he crossed the Moor with Brady, as a 'long, long walk'. She said Brady had told her he wanted to get as far away from the road as possible. But you do not have to go as far as they did to be really secluded and sheltered from the road, and the further they went the more they were running the risk of the child asking where he was going and why. But Hindley had told me that the children never objected, they went, in her own words, like 'lambs to the slaughter'.

Pauline Reade, although she was older than the others who were taken to the Moor, must have felt very safe, climbing into a car with another girl, on her own. Even though Myra Hindley was a few years older, they knew each other.

We discussed whether Ian Brady could possibly have moved to another area on the Moor with Keith Bennett, after he had motioned to her to stay where she was. But she said she did not believe it possible. She said 'he and the boy both went in and only Ian came out'.

Both Myra Hindley and her solicitor Michael Fisher were anxious to know whether Ian Brady was giving a different version of events. I explained that he had only talked about it informally, but that he had said her role had been different to the one she had claimed.

I asked her what she thought about his version of the abducting of Keith Bennett – when he said that she had picked up the boy and he had waited in Bennett Street. She said it was untrue, he had been in the back of the vehicle, and had signalled her to stop, and again she denied that she carried the rifle and spade. Even though she was young and fit at the time, she did not think it would have been possible to carry them so far. I also put to her that Ian Brady said that she was positioned at the front of the gully, where she could see him and the child, and that she moved to the back later. She said this was not true: when they went into the gully she could no longer see them.

I asked her about Pauline Reade's locket and chain.

225

Though it was thought she was wearing the locket when she went missing, it was not found with the body. She said she knew nothing about burying the locket and chain and forcibly denied ever seeing the locket, or having it in her possession.

The missing locket is a puzzle. Although Myra Hindley had told me in her confession about the half crowns, she had not mentioned the locket. If they took it, it would have made sense for her to tell me because she must have realized there would be a list of Pauline's clothes and jewellery. Perhaps Brady had taken it and not told her and was now using it as a way of hitting at her. He had introduced it: I had not been questioning him about it. On this point, I did not know which of the two of them to believe.

Myra Hindley also stuck to her original story that Ian Brady was right behind her, on his motorbike, when she picked up Pauline Reade and took her up to Hollin Brow Knoll.

Michael Fisher then asked me flatly if Brady agreed with his client that she had not taken part in the killing or sexual assault of Pauline Reade. I told them that he agreed she had not, but that he had said she was on the Moor when the girl was killed, not in the car as she said. She denied it.

I told her I had come to the end of the formal interview, and she said she could not put into words how she felt about Keith Bennett's body not being found, although she realized the police had done their utmost. She was upset for Mrs Johnson, whose letter to her had initially triggered her help. She claimed she could identify with so much that Mrs Johnson must be feeling, and would like to go back to the Moor one more time – though she hated being there, and had nightmares for weeks after each visit – to have one last attempt at finding the grave. I told her this was unlikely unless some new information came forward, but that I had recorded her willingness to help.

She said she wanted to talk about the other crimes that Brady claimed to have been involved in. He had been very attached to the foster family who brought him up, the Sloans, and called his stepfather Pa or Da, and his stepmother Ma. When his stepfather died,

Brady returned to Glasgow for a week. She wondered whether he might have committed the killing there as a reaction to the death of the man he loved. I pointed out that Brady had specifically said that she was in Scotland with him – though not with him at the time of the incident.

Michael Fisher asked me four questions, all to do with Brady's version of events. The first one was about the rumours that the victims had been tortured before their deaths. Had Brady confirmed these rumours? I said no, he had not, and no other source of information confirmed them either (the bodies had shown no signs of physical torture). I told Mr Fisher that the only full account of the deaths that I had came from his client.

The second question concerned the death of Edward Evans. Fisher wanted to know if Brady had told me any more about that. I said that in general terms Brady's account was close to that of Myra Hindley's. The third question was about the same killing: had Brady agreed about the level of David Smith's involvement? I said that he had.

The final question was whether Brady had implicated Myra Hindley in any of the 'happenings'. He had not.

I then told her that the interview was ended and that I would be sending a report to the Director of Public Prosecutions. She did not, on this occasion, say anything about the possibility of a trial, but she knew that once the matter was in the hands of the DPP a decision would be made.

It was at this meeting that I mentioned hypnosis for the first time. For some years there has been controversy both in this country and elsewhere over the use of hypnosis by the police, and I know the arguments from both sides. But I felt in this case it could be useful.

The point of putting Myra Hindley under hypnosis would not be to get evidence to be used in court or as part of a case: it would simply be to try and trigger in her mind some small forgotten detail of the location where Ian Brady buried Keith Bennett. If the DPP decided to prosecute her I already had enough evidence in her confession.

I was aware that Greater Manchester Police had used hypnosis in the case of a girl who had been brutally raped and savagely beaten. She had been so badly injured that we treated the case at the same level as a murder investigation. There was very little information to go on, but one witness who had been in the same road as the girl when she disappeared had been hypnotized. Under hypnosis he had been able to give detectives considerably more details than when under normal interrogation.

But I did not know whether it would be effective after a time lag of nearly a quarter of a century, so I consulted the psychologist, Dr Una Maguire, who had helped us with the rape case. She told me that there should be no problem going back that far, as long as the subject was receptive. She said she used hypnosis with adults who had problems stemming back to their childhood, and they were able to recall details from many years ago quite clearly.

By this stage, I had done everything possible to prompt Myra Hindley's memory. I had been over the same ground with her time and time again, and we were getting nowhere. I was sure she was doing her best to help: she wanted the body to be found, whatever her reasons. I felt her memory might hold a clue that would unlock everything: after all, we had only found the body of Pauline Reade after she had remembered an inconsequential detail.

She had not thought about hypnosis until I mentioned it, and I told her that I did not expect her to commit herself to it straightaway, but that she should think about it and discuss it with her solicitor. She said she would let me know her decision.

Although the search itself had been called off, the investigation was still going on. On 29 September Ian Brady fired off another letter of complaint via his solicitor to me, this time claiming that he had not been properly fed on the day that he had been taken to visit the Moor, and that I had called off the search too early on that day. I replied to his solicitor that he had been given Irish stew and bread at the conclusion of the search, and that he had refused earlier offers of food, but had had plenty of drinks. I was, by now, resigned to playing games with him: it was the only way to tease any information out of him.

I went to see him on 16 October, at his request. He was claiming that he 'now knew where we had gone wrong'. But when I got there we again went over many of our previous conversations. He started to heap vitriolic criticism on Detective Chief Inspector Mounsey for not finding Pauline Reade's body during the original investigation – another of his familiar themes. I think Brady's obsession with Joe Mounsey stemmed from the fact that he had never got the better of Mounsey, and even after all these years that irked him.

To test his memory of the geography of the Moor I asked him how close he thought the graves of Pauline Reade and Lesley Ann Downey were to each other, and he said twenty to thirty paces. In fact, they were seventy paces apart, which was further evidence of the concertina effect of time on his memory.

It was not a cordial interview. At one point he threatened to approach the Chief Constable of West Yorkshire (in whose area the grave site of Keith Bennett lies) to arrange a visit to the Moor through him. When I pointed out that West Yorkshire would refer the request to me, he ignored me and went on to say that he would send a detailed map to Keith Bennett's family. But when I asked if he had any criticisms to make of the way I had handled the inquiry he said no, and that he would only involve the Bennett family as a last resort.

He began to suggest that the body might be buried in a completely different area of the Moor. I warned him that he should not invent information in the hope of getting another visit to the Moor.

We talked about a railway sleeper, which he said he had left on the opposite side of the A635 to the side where Pauline Reade and Lesley Ann Downey were buried. He said they had used the sleeper for target practice, but that it was also 'a marker to other matters'. He could not remember seeing any video of the Moor:

either his mental condition or the medication he takes seems to play tricks with his memory. I promised to show it to him again.

I was reaching the point where I felt it may have been necessary to take him back to the Moor. I did not believe a lot of what he told me, but he was confused about certain features of the Moor, and another visit might clear up this confusion. It was, I felt, one of the two things left to me: the other being to subject Myra Hindley to hypnosis. (The difference between them was that if Myra Hindley knew anything else, she was not deliberately concealing it, it was simply buried in her memory, whereas with Brady, I really did not know whether he knew more or not.)

More telephone calls and visits to the hospital followed. Sometimes he seemed quite lucid, at others he rambled. He was paranoid about being taped, and on one occasion he insisted that I search the room we were using: he even looked inside a wardrobe for wires and microphones. The room was in a disused ward at the hospital, and in order to show him the video tapes an electric cable had been fed through a window: he maintained this was evidence that the place was bugged.

Our conversation invariably ranged over the same ground, but occasionally he would add interesting comments. When I questioned him about his assertion that he knew where the police had gone wrong, he said: 'Some things are too important for generals, and likewise some things are too important for the police."

I was angry with him, and asked him if this obscure statement meant that he knew where Keith Bennett was buried, and was refusing to tell me. He answered obliquely, by referring to the original investigation, and how the police had been close to the body of Pauline Reade and had not found it. Did that mean we were near to Keith's body in the Shiny Brook area? He said yes, and that if he was taken back to the Moor and given a shovel he would find it – which was obviously preposterous.

But he discussed the location where he said they had buried Pauline Reade's pendant, on a country road near Oldham. On the day after her murder they had gone to the Odeon Cinema in Oldham. One of the films showing was *The Lost Patrol*, the record of a trumpet solo of the theme music was in the hit parade at the time. He said that whenever either of them whistled it, the other knew what they were thinking about. Brady challenged Myra Hindley's published letter to Mrs Ann West saying that she was trying to play down her role in the murders. He said the opposite was true. He referred to the remark she had made when he claimed she took the locket off Pauline Reade: 'You won't need that where you're going.'

He said Hindley had also asked him to murder her ex-fiancé, Ron Sinclair. He had followed Sinclair to work early one morning, from his house in Gorton to a bus stop on Hyde Road, near Belle Vue. There he boarded the same bus and followed him to some lock-up garages where Sinclair worked. He had not taken his plans any further, he said, but Myra Hindley had told him to remove Sinclair's false teeth before killing him, to degrade him. According to Brady, this showed how vindictive she was, far more vindictive than he. Although he killed people they were never aware of what was going to happen, and he could not behave in the way that she wanted him to.

He, too had written to Mrs West, naïvely thinking that asking her not to publish the letter would guarantee that it remained private.

He talked about the other five crimes he had committed. He said they were 'realistic' in his mind, and he was concerned that other people had been 'stitched up' for them (convicted of crimes of which they were innocent). He said this might apply to the one behind Piccadilly Station, the woman in the canal and the knifing in Glasgow. I told him that investigations had not revealed any crimes, either unsolved or for which someone else had been convicted.

He continued to try to prove the point by saying that the knife he used in Glasgow had been wrapped in a handkerchief to prevent blood getting on the inside of his pocket. As they had arranged to travel back to Manchester the next day he had been unable to see any newspapers. He cleaned the knife in Manchester, saying there was nothing imaginary about that. The

Scottish police, he believed, were just not interested. I was able to reassure him on that point. I had met them and discussed it with them several times.

We had, by this time, made detailed and searching inquiries into all his claims, but had found nothing that fitted the details he had given of these crimes. Because of this, it was increasingly important that he gave me the name of the eighteen-year-old youth buried near the A635. But Brady could not do that 'because of threads' leading back to someone he did not want to involve.

Although I tried to explain that this was the one piece of information that would put some credibility into his story, he refused to give it to me. 'It is a question of images. I can keep the images in my mind,' he said, he could see the blood and could feel the knife. The blood was real enough. 'There's an old principle: never go down with them. Always keep standing up on your feet. But *he* went down, and I went walking on after that.'

But when I repeatedly told him that my inquiries had not just covered undetected crimes, but any crimes committed in Glasgow at that period, he became agitated and annoyed, and continued to accuse the police of a cover-up.

Certain themes recur in conversation with Ian Brady, and one that he would come back to was the tape of Lesley Ann Downey, which he maintained should have been in the evelope that was destroyed by Myra Hindley at Millwards. He was very proud of his professionalism as a criminal, and what he was trying to say was that he was thorough; he looked at all the angles, and had meant that tape to have been des-troyed. He was trying to suggest that it was not his fault that it was not destroyed, yet there was no doubt that he put it into the suitcase that went to the left luggage office.

If it had been destroyed, he said it would have changed the whole 'concept of the thing'. – i.e. the trial. In the five days after he was arrested he tried to keep Myra Hindley out of things, yet he suggested that she had told the police where the suitcase was – knowing full well from the trial that the police discovered the suitcase without any help from her.

The main refrain was that he wanted to return to the Moor, and he was talking by the end of October of being 'in a race against the snow'. He knew that I had applied to the Home Office for authority for the visit. But he would threaten me with the media, with letters to Mrs West to get her to put pressure on me through the media, and with 'frog-hopping Yorkshire Police', a phrase I had never heard before, but gathered meant that he would go over my head to Yorkshire Police. He also threatened to deal directly with Glasgow Police over the Scottish murders. I told him threats would not help, and publicity would be positively detrimental to his chances.

There were times in my dealings with Brady when he wanted to talk and talk and talk, but it was in these garbled ramblings that I was able to get some background to the killings from him. Sometimes he would bring our phone conversations to an abrupt end, other times he would want to talk on and on.

There were bizarre offshoots within our conversations. He discussed buying BP shares. He told me he was going to sue a journalist who had said that he had plans to assassinate Sir John Mills. He became very distressed and angry when he talked about some letters which had been stolen from a girl student in Scotland, with whom he had been corresponding, and he said extracts from the letters that had been published were fabrications. He also talked about David Smith's oldest son. He was pleased that a newspaper had published a photograph of Smith's family, and he had been able to see the boy.

I felt that, despite what he said about Myra Hindley being more vindictive than he was, these veiled references to the fatherhood of David Smith's son were his way of getting at Smith, the ultimate insult to the man who had betrayed him. He was also getting at Myra Hindley, both by insulting the memory of her sister Maureen and insinuating that her own relationship with him had not been strong.

He told me he was worried about making the visit to the Moor in the autumn, because autumn and winter were a bad time for him – Edward Evans, John Kilbride

233

and Lesley Ann Downey had died when the evenings were long and dark. He claimed to be refusing visits from his mother so that he could be in a constant state of readiness should he be allowed to visit the Moor.

I kept him informed in a very general way of my dealings with the Home Office as I tried to arrange the visit. But he had no patience, and he could not resist writing letters both to Mrs West and to Peter Gould, the BBC journalist. In the end I had to see Mrs West myself, and ask her to keep confidential the contents of his letters, as they would hamper our efforts to find Keith Bennett's body. I appealed to her, as the mother of one of the victims, to help another mother. She wanted to visit Brady, but both I and the hospital vetoed that move. But she did promise that she would keep the letters confidential. Peter Gould was, once again, very responsible and agreed to hold publication of the letter Brady had sent to him, at least for a while.

I was worried. I was trying to get Brady back to the Moor, but his own quest for publicity was going to drive a bus through all my plans.

18

I was surprised – and pleased – when Myra Hindley agreed to hypnosis. I felt she might have been reluctant to lose total control of herelf, even though I had made it clear to her that my only interest would be to find out more about the burial of Keith Bennett. The fact she agreed demonstrates that she really was committed to finding his body. I discussed the implications of hypnosis with the office of the Director of Public Prosecutions, because I did not want to do anything to jeopardize the evidence that I had obtained against Brady and Hindley. They told me there would be no legal objections to hypnosis in this case, and the Home Office Prison Department also said they could see no problems.

On 12 November I travelled to London to put two proposals to the Home Office: for another visit by Ian Brady to Saddleworth Moor, and for Myra Hindley to be hypnotized. I thought that the difficult part would be persuading them to release Brady for a day, and I was quietly confident that the hypnosis was a foregone conclusion. Myra Hindley was willing, nobody could see any legal objections, there would be no security risks as with a visit to the Moor, and there would be no opposition from the public. What's more, I felt that of the two proposals it was the one more likely to bring success.

I was questioned for two hours by senior officials from the Prison Department and the Police Department, one of whom expressed great surprise that the DPP's office had accepted its use in this case. Despite the DPP's decision there was a lengthy debate about the effects on any possible criminal trial, and I was also told that both the British Medical Association and the Royal College of Surgeons were opposed to the use of hypnosis. At another meeting, which I was not invited to attend, the question was discussed by senior officials and the Home Secretary.

The result was that I was given the go-ahead to take Ian Brady to Saddleworth Moor again, but I was informed that no decision had been made about the hypnosis. A couple of weeks later I was told unequivocally that the Home Secretary had decided against allowing it. I was, to say the least, disappointed.

After months of living with his obsession about returning to Saddleworth Moor, when Brady's chance finally came he refused. On 8 December I arrived at Park Lane at 5a.m., only to be told by the staff that he was saying he no longer wanted to go to the Moor. For security reasons he had not been told that he would be going until that morning.

I went to his room to see him and he was still in bed, refusing to get up. We talked for a long time. He said it was too late in the year to go, the weather would be bad, there would not be enough hours of daylight. He wasn't abusive, just annoyed, and as usual blaming the Home Office for everything. I told him that the weather forecast was good, and that with our climate good weather could not be guaranteed even in the summer.

I suspected the real reason was that he was afraid he could not find the grave. It was worrying him, so he was finding other excuses. He asked if he could speak to his social worker, Bob Fitzpatrick, who had been asked to accompany him again to the Moor, and after seeing him for a couple of minutes Brady finally agreed to the visit.

I was now very concerned about security. I had hoped to travel to the Moor in darkness, and get a few hours of searching in before the press knew we were there. But because of Brady's reluctance more than two hours had now elapsed since my arrival at Park Lane, and traffic would already be busy on the A635. There had been a change of shift for the hospital staff, and although I would not impugn their integrity, I knew that a casual remark by one of them could result in the secrecy of the visit being blown. But in spite of all this I decided to go ahead, and at 7.20 we left the hospital. It was a close run thing. We arrived at Saddleworth at quarter to nine, and transferred Brady into a Land Rover to take him down the Water Authority's private road just minutes before the first journalists arrived.

It was an exhausting day: the weather was fine, but it was chilly. Brady seemed physically and mentally stronger than on his first visit, and despite the bad start, was very co-operative. He accepted that the terrain had not been altered, and that any changes had occurred in his head. He also acknowledged that the distances between landmarks had been telescoped in his memory, and he said that the visit helped to put them back in their proper perspective. He concentrated on the Shiny Brook location, and worked on establishing whether they had walked on to the Moor down Hoe Grain or Near Most Grain. After a break for lunch we worked on until the light started to fail at four o'clock. From lunchtime onwards we were plagued by journalists, but they were kept at bay by our back-up team. Brady was back at Park Lane by 5.40.

In the final analysis, however, we were no further forward after this visit. The area Brady said the grave was in did not contain a gully that answered his description of the grave site, but he was convinced it was the right location and insisted we should search there. In fact it was an area that we had already searched very thoroughly – to no avail. I was astonished when a few days later he told me he wanted to go to Saddleworth Moor again – just him and me he said. I told him his visits were over: he had had two full days up there, and there would definitely be no more. But there were more phone calls and meetings with him, including one at which I took another formal statement. Nothing he told me added anything to the information we already had. He was very worried about the possibility of being called to give evidence at the full inquest on Pauline Reade which was scheduled for 29 January, and he asked me to explain the procedure and formalities of a coroner's court.

On one occasion Brady asked if it would be possible for him to meet Myra Hindley and discuss the location of the grave, but I said it was out of the question. I do not know whether he really wanted to see her to further the search for Keith Bennett, or whether it was just for old time's sake. Despite the fact that he was at times very critical of her, and despite the fact she had not hesitated to outline his crimes, I felt they both still had a lingering regard for each other. Neither seemed to want to hurt the other. Although they were both vindictive towards David Smith, they were each careful never to criticize the other.

When the inquest on Pauline was adjourned to a later date, Brady contacted me in a very agitated state. He believed that it had been adjourned because the *News of the World* was threatening to take out a private prosecution against him and Myra Hindley for the murders of Pauline Reade and Keith Bennett, and I had to reassure him that the two things were unconnected.

A lot of time and effort had been put into investigating Brady's claims about the five 'happenings', even though from the beginning I was dubious about them. He had, I believe, only been able to commit the murders of small children with the help of Myra Hindley, yet here he was claiming to have mindlessly killed grown men. It didn't add up.

His claim to have killed a man on wasteland behind

Manchester Piccadilly Station was typically vague, with no date and no description of the man except that he was between twenty and thirty years and wearing workmen's clothing. There had been a murder in that area on 30 August 1965, when the body of fifty-five year old William Cullen had been found on open ground in St Andrews Street. He had severe head injuries, probably inflicted with a piece of concrete found near his body. I remembered the case: as a young uniformed bobby working in that area I had been involved in routine inquiries at the time.

This murder would have fitted reasonably well with Brady's claims, and at the time of the investigation into it the murderer was not traced. However, it was an obvious killing for Brady to claim: two months after it was committed he was in police custody and was interviewed about a number of unsolved crimes, including the murder of William Cullen. The case had been given a lot of local publicity at the time, so he had probably known about it even before the police questioned him.

What he did not know when he claimed the crime twenty-two years later was that in 1984, out of the blue, the Cullen case was solved. A man came forward to the police to say he had witnessed the killing, and that the murderer was a close member of his family, currently a patient in a secure mental hospital. The police interviewed both men and made sufficient inquiries to satisfy them and the DPP, that this was the truth. No prosecution ensued, because of the man's condition.

I discussed the case with the detectives who had reopened it in 1984, and I was convinced they had been dealing with the right man. Nothing Brady said persuaded me that he really knew anything about the murder other than what he had read in the papers or picked up from the police officers interviewing him in 1965. I felt that anyone involved in a murder would have known and remembered more about it.

Investigations into another of Brady's claimed killings had also produced some results. He said that he had thrown a woman into the Rochdale Canal in Sackville Street, near the Rembrandt public house, that he had heard a splash and presumed her dead. He had put her age as between twenty and thirty. We found that in 1961 the body of a drowned fifty-one-year-old woman had been found in the canal at nearby Princess Street. There was a slight injury to her head, which could have been caused by an attack; alternatively she could have hit it as she fell into the canal. The coroner recorded an open verdict, but there was some evidence that pointed towards her death being suicide – she believed she had a terminal illness, and had tried to commit suicide once before.

Brady had said that this 'happening' had occurred while he was involved in the relationship with Myra Hindley, but he did not actually go out with her until two months after this body was found. Again the story was covered in the local papers, so he could have read about it. It might also have been talked about at work, because the woman lived in an area where some of the members of Millward's staff lived. Had he been able to give me more detailed information about the encounter with this woman I would have taken his claim more seriously.

It occurred to me that if he had heard about the case, he would have been fascinated by it. Brady is interested in death in any form, and he may have realized that this could have been a perfect murder. Whether he had dwelt on it, and over the years worked himself into the story in his own imagination, I don't know. But the conclusion had to be that there was insufficient evidence to support Brady's claim.

The murder victim he claimed at Loch Long, in Scotland, was an English hiker, again in his twenties whom he shot with the Smith and Wesson pistol and buried using mess tins since he had no spade. He could put no date on the murder, but records show the pistol was bought in July 1964 by Myra Hindley.

Strathclyde Police made extensive inquiries, and there were no undetected murders in that area between then and Brady's arrest. The only record they have of a missing person is of a German tourist who disappeared in the Loch Lomond area in the summer of 1961, before Brady was involved with Hindley and before they went on their driving holidays to Scotland. The tourist was not dressed as a hiker, he did not have a rucksack, and he had a German accent – which, since Brady has a fondness for all things Germanic, would probably have been as musical to his ears as 'the Scottish tongue'.

Burying someone with an aluminium mess tin would be a very difficult task, if not impossible. It would have guaranteed that when he returned to the car his hands and clothes would have been dirty – yet Hindley has no memory of this, nor of a rucksack being thrown into a forest.

Strathclyde Police also investigated his claim to have knifed a man to death in Glasgow after seeing him harassing an old woman. Again, he said the incident occurred during his relationship with Myra Hindley. The police can find no record of any undetected murder or attack that fits his description even remotely. It is always possible that it was a minor attack, that the man's clothes protected him, and that it was never reported to the police. But we have no ground to believe it was a murder.

The fifth murder he claimed was that of the eighteen-year-old youth, whom he said he buried on Saddleworth Moor after shooting him in the back of the head. He claimed he knew the youth, but that because of the involvment of another person he would not reveal the identity. Despite numerous appeals and questions he never changed his position on this, although he ruled out Myra Hindley and David Smith as the other person.

We had searched the area of the Moor where he said the youth was buried, but he was so vague about the location that we did not spend too much time on it. The other person involved was a friend, he said – but he had very few friends. We traced many of his associates and interviewed them. They were mostly men who had been in borstal with him when they were young, and he had never kept in touch with any of them; they did not admit being involved in any crimes with him. He did not have close friends at work, although we traced many of his colleagues from Millwards. It was difficult to believe what he had told us – that he had had such a close friendship that he and the other party agreed to kill someone for each other on a quid pro quo basis. He claimed that the friend had now settled down, which suggests Brady is still in touch with him, or had had some contact with him. Yet again we could find no record of anyone fitting the description writing to him or visiting him while he was in prison or hospital.

We found no record of a body in the River Ouse – where he claimed his friend had dumped it – that could have any possible connection to Brady, and there was no record of an eighteen-year-old going missing. I think he regretted saying that he knew who the victim was, because it meant I could always accuse him of withholding vital information – whereas with the other four 'happenings' he could claim he was telling me all he knew. It seems unlikely that he was trying to protect someone: he tried to protect Myra Hindley at their trial, but that may have been because she knew so much. I don't believe protecting other people is a natural part of his character. Although he claimed to be concerned about the parents of Pauline Reade and Keith Bennett, he obviously felt no concern for the parents of this eighteen-year-old youth – if they exist.

Myra Hindley was questioned at length about all the five extra murders, and could not help. He was not trying to implicate her in any of them, and she had confessed to the others, so it was likely she was telling the truth about these: she had nothing to lose. I believe that, had she known anything about them, she would have told me.

So we are left with five claims, each supported by only the sketchiest of details. The only one that I felt we could not completely dismiss was the claim to have killed the eighteen-year-old, but there was no corroborative evidence at all. Had Brady been claiming only this one I might have given it more credence, but, included as it is with four other claims that are without any facts to support them, it becomes very suspect. We had reached the point where no further action could be justified.

I decided there were two possible explanations for Brady making up these claims. The first is his mental condition: they could be the product of his distorted memory, in which fact and imagination seem to interweave. Or he could have simply manufactured them maliciously, in a bid to arrange visits for himself to Saddleworth Moor and Scotland, two places which held specially potent memories for him.

In the final analysis, Ian Brady remains an enigma. I cannot be sure how much help he ever intended to give us, or how much he would have been able to contribute. But I know that the sum of everything he told me amounted to very little. He provided no practical help, and the only information he gave about the killings was incidental: he never offered me his complete version, which is what I needed to make a full and fair appraisal of Myra Hindley's version.

He never talked at all about the deaths of John Kilbride and Lesley Ann Downey; if he did the blocks would come down, he said, and he did not know what would happen. I tried many times to persuade him to talk about the killings, but he would not. I do not know if he ever will, but I think not. He told me that once, during his time in prison, he had told everything to a consultant psychiatrist. If he did, it certainly has not made it easier for him to face up to what he has done. He talked to me perhaps more than he has talked to anyone else about the crimes, but he was not frank and never pretended to be.

In a very quiet moment he told me that he was ashamed, and that was why he could not go through it with me. He knew he would be describing horrendous details, and he was concerned how others, including me, would feel about him. I tried to explain that I already knew what he had done, and that my attitude would not change, but he still felt he could not cope with it. I offered to go through the facts as I knew them from Myra Hindley, and he got very alarmed and agitated whenever I suggested that approach.

Never did he come out with anything clean – any information I gleaned was released in passing. He gave me the impression that he is frightened of talking about it all, that he does not know how he will cope, and that he thinks it will destroy him. When he said that Myra Hindley might have been unable to bring herself to

242

show us the grave site, it was really something he had thought about in connection with himself: he imagined that he might not be able to go through with it. I shall never know whether or not that is what happened.

It is part of the paradox of Brady that he cares a lot what people think of him, and he is ashamed about certain aspects of his life. I questioned him once about the trips he made into Manchester without Myra Hindley, and asked him if he was picking up men. He did not reply, so I asked him straight out if he was bisexual. He nodded, but kept his head down and his eyes averted as though he was deeply ashamed to admit it.

He never talked to me about the fact that he was illegitimate. But, interestingly, the very last letter he wrote to me, after my retirement, was signed Ian Stewart-Brady. Stewart was his mother's maiden name, and his name at birth. On previous letters he had simply signed his name as I. Brady.

He is always very worried that he will be held up to ridicule. After his first visit to the Moor he was concerned that I would criticize him to the media for not coming up with anything, for not fulfilling his claims. After all the criticism he has had from the press since his arrest it was remarkable that he should care so much, but he did. He was gratified when I said at the press conference that I felt he had done his best.

Yet despite this craving for approval, perhaps the most significant aspect of his personality is his craving to be in control, his need to feel that he knows something that others do not know, that he is at all times one up on whoever he is dealing with. Sometimes his attempts to fulfil this need were naïve and clumsy – like threatening to go over my head to the police chiefs in Glasgow or Yorkshire, or trying to play off Mrs Ann West against me. But ultimately, because of this highly developed trait, I could never dismiss the possibility that he was concealing information about the site of Keith Bennett's grave.

I was aware of, and went along with, his enjoyment of having me – as he believed – on a hook. It gave him great satisfaction to feel that he could ring up the head of Greater Manchester CID and have me running backwards and forwards at his beck and call. He never realized that I knew all about his game and was playing it for my own ends.

He is obsessive, perhaps most notably in his constant diatribes about the Home Office. Out of a faceless government department he has created a windmill to spend the rest of his life tilting at, and that is how he sees himself: he is taking on the Home Office. He blames them for keeping him in prison when he should have been in hospital – in fact he blames them for everything that goes wrong and only just stops short of blaming them for the weather. His tortuous thinking is illustrated by the fact that in his prison years, he stopped his mother visiting him as part of his protest against the Home Office.

His fear of going back to prison may have been partly behind his reluctance to confess. He is much happier in Park Lane Hospital than he was in prison, where he said he always had to have eyes in the back of his head in case another prisoner attacked him. He tried to extract a promise from me that if he confessed he would not find himself back in the prison system – in his convoluted mind 'they' at the Home Office had sent him to Park Lane to soften him up for a confession, and as soon as he had made it he would be sent back. I could not give him a promise, although it was obvious throughout my dealings with him that he has a serious mental condition and that hospital is the right place for him.

Park Lane is spacious, well equipped and well designed. He has his own room, with its own toilet and washing facilities. Patients can have television sets in their rooms, and there are sitting areas and games rooms. The doors are barred, but there is freedom within certain areas of the hospital. But perhaps the most impressive thing is the very high calibre of the staff working there: I found them all very helpful, very professional, and ultimately concerned for the welfare of their patient, although at the same time trying to do everything they could to help my inquiry.

Brady does not mix much with the other patients. He was very upset when newspaper reports said that he attended social functions to which the staff brought their families, including small children. He said, 'I never went out of my room', and then launched into one of his familiar tirades about the 'gutter press'.

But I got the feeling that he, like Myra Hindley, has an ambivalent attitude to publicity: while affecting to despise it, he actually enjoys it. He would prefer the newspapers to print nice things about him, but anything is better than being ignored. He quietly revels in his notoriety.

Brady rarely talked about his private life, but he did tell me once that he was grateful to the Sloan family for bringing him up. He seemed to have a deep and lasting affection for them, although he never told me whether he has had any contact with them since his trial. He was always upset if he read about cruelty to animals, and he did not like the articles and books which claimed he had been cruel to a cat when he was a child. 'I prefer animals to people,' he would say.

When he was fourteen, he told me, he had a deep spiritual experience that was connected to the colour green. He found it hard to explain, but after that green always had a great significance for him. He talked about going to the country with the Sloans when he was young, and how it gave him an enormous feeling of elation to be in a large expanse of green. But he was not in the countryside when he had this spiritual experience. He also talked a lot about his love of 'natural substances', stone and rock, and his need to travel to Scotland to touch the stone of the Gorbals tenement building where he had lived when he was young.

He said that eveything he had done was in Dostoevsky's *Crime and Punishment*. 'That's me, that's what I am all about,' he said. *Crime and Punishment* is the story of a student who tries to commit the perfect murder, and rationalizes it to himself. Brady was obviously very impressed by the book, and explained that they (which I took to mean himself and Myra Hindley, and possibly also David Smith) would talk about 'just getting rid of somebody'. He was very annoyed that a book found among his possessions was said in court to be his. It was an abridged version of *Justine* by the Marquis de Sade. Brady said it belonged

245

to David Smith – he would never read an abridged version.

The life he had led before his arrest had been unreal in many aspects. He had often carried guns, and had always had a strong feeling of his own superiority to others. He and Myra Hindley drank heavily on occasions – and halfway down the second bottle of wine it is easy to believe that you rule the world. He talked often about drinking: in his memory it gave him great pleasure. When they drove about in the Mini they had virtually a small bar with them.

He remembered one occasion when he threw a bottle out of the car as they were driving along, and he was very concerned that their licence number had been taken. It was a rash, out-of-character action for him – he was normally careful not to draw attention to himself. He recalled another time in Scotland, when a policeman stopped them to check on the car. Brady said he was quaking: he had both the guns with him. If necessary, he said, he would have used them.

Getting into Ian Brady was, I found, like getting a crowbar into a crack. Dealing with him was like walking on very thin glass. He is sensitive, prickly, and thinking three moves ahead all the time.

PART FOUR

THE END OF THE INQUIRY

19

When I broke the news to Myra Hindley that there would be no criminal prosecution, she took it calmly and quietly. She was relieved, she said, but I sensed she was also slightly disappointed. Unlike Brady, who was terrified of the prospect of another trial, I think she secretly hankered after the opportunity to put her case in public.

As far as she was concerned, a trial could not damage her. Her public image was that of the brassy blonde monster in the official photograph taken at the time of her arrest, and the popular press regularly referred to her as 'evil Myra'. She had stated at the time of her confession that she did not want even to be considered for parole in 1990, knowing when she did so that public opinion would have prevented her being paroled anyway, as it had done before. So what was there to lose?

Yet there was plenty to gain. Ian Brady was not seriously disputing the events as she had outlined them in her confession; he was not going to challenge her version of the role she had played. At a trial she would plead guilty and appear very contrite. She would present herself as very much the second-in-command, and the public would become aware that she had played no part in the actual killing of the victims. Instead of the hard-faced, unrelenting figure she had cut at the first trial, they would see a softer, gentler, educated, middle-aged woman who would explain how she had become involved with the killing madness of Brady.

Even if they did not swallow her story hook line and sinker, she was sure that at the end of a trial she would emerge with a better public image – and that maybe, in ten years or so, she would be considered sufficently rehabilitated for release. She knew that it was public opinion, fuelled by the picture painted of her by the tabloids, that was keeping her behind bars. No government would risk unpopularity over an issue so unimportant (politically speaking) as the release of Myra

Hindley: if she was ever to achieve it, it would be when she had swung public opinion either to be in her favour or to be indifferent to her.

She did not say that she was disappointed not to go to trial, and I am sure that on one level she felt some relief. It would have been an ordeal. But I sensed that it was an ordeal she would not have minded facing.

I believe the Director of Public Prosecutions made the right decision. A trial would have been enormously expensive, and ultimately it would have achieved nothing: both Brady and Hindley are imprisoned on life sentences, which means that they can, literally, be detained for ever. The fact that most lifers get parole after serving an average of eleven years is irrelevant: the sentence is reviewed, but the option is there to keep the prisoner in jail indefinitely. So a trial could not have imposed any extra punishment. And to have played into her hands by giving her the chance to perform her confession role in public would, I think, have been a mistake.

Once the decision not to prosecute had been taken, I applied again to the Home Office for permission to subject Hindley to hypnosis. Even if they had had reservations about the use of evidence gained under hypnosis being used at the trial, surely now that there was to be no trial there would be no further objections.

But again my request was turned down. I could not understand it. I am not qualified to give an expert appraisal of the medical arguments for and against hypnosis, but I know about its use in criminal cases and I believe that it might have helped unlock some significant detail buried in Hindley's memory. I was not pinning great hopes on it, but I felt that the technique should have been tried. At least then I would have been able to comfort Mrs Winnie Johnson with the knowledge that everything possible had been done in the search for her son.

The Home Secretary, Douglas Hurd, was opposed to its use in criminal cases – mainly. I believe, on the grounds that it is known to be possible to tell lies under hypnosis, and also that leading questions can be asked and can prompt the answers the questioner is seeking. I accept this, but I believe hypnosis has a proven record as a means of obtaining information. I understand the difficulties if witnesses are to be cross-examined in court about statements they had made under hypnosis, and I would be concerned if defendants were convicted solely on the strength of evidence gained under hypnosis. The Home Office have also expressed concern about the long-term effects of hypnosis on the subject – yet other medical opinion contradicts their views.

Had the Moors case been less celebrated, I would not have had to seek permission from the Home Office before using hypnosis. It has been successfully used in a number of major cases since then: West Mercia Police, for instance, used it when they were hunting for the killer of newspaper boy Stuart Gough. There had been twenty-nine other attacks on boys in the area, and under hypnosis one of them was able to give the police a detailed description of his attacker's car. He described some special microphones it contained, said that the radio was on but not playing, and that although it was a coupé it had window handles in the rear. From this the police were able to identify it as a Colt Sapporo, and by checking vehicle records they traced Victor Miller, who subsequently confessed to the murder.

Dr Una Maguire, who had assisted us with our rape investigation, carried out the hypnosis for West Mercia Police. Another celebrated case in which she was able to help the police was the brutal murder of seventy-eight-year-old rose grower Hilda Murrell, whose death was alleged to have involved British Intelligence. Although the murderer was never found, Dr Maguire was able to obtain a good description of him from a woman who had driven behind the car in which Miss Murrell was taken to her death.

Dr Maguire's services are in great demand. She is the principal psychologist for sexual and physical abuse cases in the Metropolitan Borough of Wigan, and a former Professor of Psychology at the University of Minnesota. But apart from her track record and academic achievements, she has other qualities which

250

recommended her to me, and which convinced me, within minutes of meeting her, that she would be the right person to hypnotize Myra Hindley. Una is a gentle, sympathetic, intelligent woman; I was confident that she would be able to get on with her intended subject, and that her intellectual status would also appeal to Hindley.

Una and I have talked many times about the way the hypnosis would have been conducted, and the likelihood of success. 'Ninety-eight out of every hundred people are receptive to hypnosis,' she said, 'and given that Hindley was anxious to help, I feel sure it would have been possible to work with her. It would have taken about an hour altogether, and in that time I could have taken her back mentally to the evening when she and Brady took Keith Bennett up to Saddleworth, and we could have re-created the whole journey across the Moor. We could have ascertained exactly where the car was parked, and where they entered the Moor.

'Very often people cannot remember the details of traumatic events: they block them out. Hypnosis can release these memories. And even if the event is not traumatic, hypnosis can help bring to the surface trivial and seemingly unimportant details. Deep relaxation enables people to re-live the whole experience. It is an information-gathering tool, a help to memory.

'I have never been involved in a case where the sole witness has been subjected to hypnosis – there have always been several witnesses, so that any information gained by hypnosis is an added bonus, not something that will be relied upon in the witness box.

'It is unfortunate that hypnosis has been given the status of a music-hall act, and that the impression that people have of it is of subjects being told what to do by the person who has hypnotized them. When it is used in police investigations it is used under scrupulous conditions, and there is no possible suggestion that ideas are implanted into witnesses' minds. The sessions are always witnessed, and are videoed.'

Una shares my belief that it is cruel and unnecessary of the Home Secretary to turn down what is almost certainly Mrs Johnson's last hope of finding her son's body. Douglas Hurd has not given me a reason for refusing to allow hypnosis, and the reasons he has given Mrs Johnson are not, in my view, defensible. The factors that worry the Home Office do not apply in this case: Myra Hindley is not a witness; there are no criminal proceedings to be taken and therefore no legal difficulties: and her prison doctor did not raise any objections, so there are no medical arguments.

Puzzled and disappointed by the decision, I telephoned a senior Home Office official. Again I was not given any reason, other than that the Home Secretary had considered all the factors and was not convinced it would be successful. I pointed out that I felt this was not the real reason – nor was it a satisfactory reason. In my opinion the real reason was fear that it would be successful, and thereby give credibility to a practice the Home Office did not support.

Whatever his reasons, the Home Secretary has made his decision. The outcome is that Mrs Johnson and her family are now wandering about Saddleworth Moor every weekend, digging haphazardly in a touching and hopeless search for the body of her son Keith.

When in August 1987 I told Mrs Winnie Johnson that I was calling off the organized search of the Moor, she was very upset. Repeatedly she said that it was not fair. She explained that she was not blaming me or the Moors team: she simply felt that life had given her a raw deal.

But although I stopped the systematic search, we still went back on to the Moor throughout that autumn, whenever we felt that there was an area we had not explored fully. But I was only giving part of my time to the Moors inquiry by this stage; there were other pressing matters for me to deal with.

The date for the inquest on Pauline Reade was postponed from January until 12 April 1988, to enable the coroner to be fully prepared. The day before, I went to see Mrs Johnson's family doctor to ask him two things: should Mrs Johnson be told the details of her son's death, as she was asking to be, and was she fit enough to go up to the Moor with me to see the extent of the search we had carried out? He told me that in his opinion she could face both of these things.

The inquest was very well attended by the media, and Pauline's father and brother were in court to hear the jury return a verdict of unlawful killing. The coroner commended the Moors team for our work, and that evening we had a small celebration. We felt that we had at least brought peace of mind to the Reade family, which had made our back-breaking work on the Moor worthwhile.

I knew that I would not be able to return to Saddleworth, and yet I also knew that Winnie Johnson would never give up her campaign to have the search continued. She was saying that she would go up there and dig herself, as she subsequently has. I knew how distressing this would be for her, and also how hopeless, given the enormity of the task. That is why on the day after Pauline Reade's inquest, I took her and one of her sons to the Moor.

At this stage I was in some pain myself, because the digging had reactivated an old neck injury. Two specialists had told me to rest, but I did not feel able to take any time off until I could leave Mrs Johnson as well informed as was possible in her sad circumstances.

The press knew we were there that day, but they honoured an appeal from me that we should be left alone for as long as possible. We went by Land Rover down the Water Authority's private road, as close as we could get to the Shiny Brook area. Then we walked the rest of the way, and I pointed out to Mrs Johnson the areas that we had searched. She seemed overwhelmed by the size and openness of the land around us, and by the amount of work we had done.

Fortunately, the weather was good. When we reached the approximate area where Keith had been buried, she sat on her own for a while. As we left the Moor she told me she was satisfied that everything possible had been done, and that she would not be coming back to dig herself; later, however she changed her mind about that.

I then took Mrs Johnson back to police headquarters and discussed with her how Keith had been taken on to the Moor, and how he had been killed. She had told me several times before that she would never rest until she knew what had happened to her son: I hoped that by telling her I would be able to bring her some peace. I chose my words very carefully, pointing out to her that Keith's death had not been as horrendous as Pauline's. Her son was still with her, comforting her. She was upset, but not surprised, and she told me she was grateful for being told.

I explained that there was nothing more I could do, and she understood. She knows, as I do, that hypnotizing Myra Hindley would be the only remote chance of getting the information we need – even if all it did was to confirm that we had been searching in the right place and that the body is no longer there.

For me, the Moors Murders inquiry was over. And although I did not realize it immediately, so was my police career. I went on sick leave the next day, to try to rest my damaged neck. My injury had originally been caused in 1973 when I was a detective sergeant, on my way in the early hours of the morning to a reported safe-blowing. (Today criminals do not bother blowing safes – they just wave shotguns about and get terrified people to hand over their valuables.) As our car was waiting to turn right another vehicle hit us from behind and both I and the driver suffered whiplash injury.

The doctor who treated me at the time told me I would never really be free of this injury. Over the years I had certainly suffered with my neck, but I had never been in severe pain until those hours I spent on the Moor with a Shillington hoe.

When we finished searching, many of us in the team had injuries – bad backs, sprained shoulders and other similar problems. I had strained the calf muscles in my right leg when I had caught hold of Brady to stop him falling, and I was in pain from my neck. I thought that if I rested, it would improve. But after a fortnight's holiday in September 1987 my neck was no better, although my leg injury quickly responded to physiotherapy.

According to the specialists I saw, my neck muscles

had been in spasm since the earlier injury, and I had disturbed them with my work on the Moor. They diagnosed my condition as cervical spondylitis with nerve root damage. The effect was that I was in constant pain, and the ache from my neck stretched down my right arm into my fingers; it was acute enough to stop me sleeping at night. The combination of pain and lack of sleep meant that I was very tired and found it impossible to deal with the demands of my job.

I tried resting again, and this time the injury improved. But when I went back to work it was aggravated once more. I saw the police surgeon, who explained that I would have extreme difficulty returning to the twenty-four-hours-a-day seven-days-a-week commitment of my job. Reluctantly I had to accept his advice that I was not fit to go back to it.

So on 31 July 1988 I left Greater Manchester Police. It was a sad day for me. I was forty-eight years old, and had hoped to have many more years of service ahead of me. I had enjoyed my time in the police immensely, and the force had treated me very fairly. I will always remember the kindness of my colleagues, the Chief Constable and the members of the Police Authority. Before leaving, I was called before the Police Authority where the chairman, Steve Murphy, who had supported me throughout the search on the Moors, presented me with a certificate of commendation of outstanding service – a rare honour. The certificate cited my 'dedication, courage and determination throughout twenty-seven years Police Service, with particular regard to his work as Head of the CID and Discipline and Complaints Departments, and his tenacity in continuing the Moors Murders Inquiry, and the respect and admiration he has earned not only from his fellow officers but also from members of the public generally'.

Two days before I finally left my desk for ever, all the members of the Moors team were presented with certificates by the Chief Constable, commending us for bringing a difficult inquiry to a successful conclusion. Part of the citation read: 'The search of Saddleworth Moor for the bodies of the victims of murders which occurred almost twenty-five years ago was conducted in the most difficult circumstances with regard to the terrain and the media coverage. The patience and tenacity with which members of the team conducted the enquiry was of the highest order.'

And I was surprised and honoured when, six months after leaving the force, I heard I was to be presented with the Queen's Police Medal for distinguished service, the highest professional honour I could receive.

I was very sad to leave the job that was such a large and important part of my life, but in the end I had to accept that I, too, was another victim of the Moors Murders case. The compensation is that, having left the force, I am now free to give this account of the case and also to explain other things that happened inside Greater Manchester Police while I was there – most notably, the Stalker Affair.

PART FIVE

COMPLAINTS AND DISCIPLINE

20

I do not believe my background was the key to my success with Myra Hindley and Ian Brady, but it certainly helped. To be able to talk about the Gorton they remembered, to know the shops and churches and pubs, to be familiar with the back streets around Piccadilly, must have made it easier for them to grow to accept me.

Despite the fact that Gorton was a poor area I certainly did not feel my childhood was deprived or depressed, and compared to many of my peer group I came from a relatively well-off family. In those days men had their hair trimmed once a fortnight, so my father's barber's shop was a thriving business. Our accommodation above the shop seemed comfortable enough – we had our own bathroom. My brother John, eight years older than me, was a gifted sportsman: he played football and cricket for Manchester boys, ran for Lancashire, and was on the books of Manchester United football club. I followed him to the local Church of England primary school, and then, after passing my eleven-plus, to Ducie Avenue Technical School; but I'm afraid I was a disappointment to the schools. They saw the name Topping and thought they had another brilliant sportsman – but my interest lay more in the countryside than on the sports field, and eventually developed into a passion for fell walking and rock climbing.

At the age of nine I was alone with my mother when my father collapsed and died one Monday evening. His death had a profound effect on all the family, but it completely changed my brother's life. For a time John gave up all his sporting activity, which Dad had encouraged so much, and he never played football seriously again. Tragically, many of the youths with whom he played regularly at United were on the plane that crashed at Munich.

My mother tried to run the shop for a time, with a manager at first and then with my brother. But John wanted to join the police, and he was now married. So the business was sold and my mother bought a terraced house in which she lived until her death in 1984.

I did not like school, and foolishly spent as much time as I could avoiding academic work. I left as soon as I could, at fifteen, with no qualifications to my name. I have regretted it ever since, but at the time I could see no advantages in education – anyway, when I left school it was as much a necessity as a choice. My mother was in poor health, which meant she had to give up her job as a cleaner, so there was little money in the house.

My first job was in the building industry, but I soon moved to work for Scott's, a retail company in the Ardwick area of Manchester. The owner, Gordon Scott, had a son a few years younger than me, and he took me under his wing. He had very high standards, and I learned from him the value of hard work; he broadened my outlook and improved my education. This awakened my interest in learning, which has stayed with me to this day.

At nineteen I joined the police, influenced by my older brother. I had always wanted an outdoor job and my first choice was the Royal Marines, but that would have left my mother on her own.

It was through my brother, too, that I met Barbara, whose family lived near John and his wife. She and I had actually been in the same class at infants' school, but we obviously hadn't made a great impression on each other because neither of us could remember it! We married when we were both twenty-one. Gordon Scott asked me to return to work for him and offered me a much better salary; that proposition, coupled with the fact that I shared some of the discontent that was rife in the service at the time, persuaded me to go back as sales manager.

But I was unsettled: even though I had not been in the force for long, in my mind I was still a policeman. So after a break of two years I was back in uniform again. I was welcomed back, and I was happy. I was not particularly ambitious – apart from a strong day-to-day ambition to be a good policeman and to do my job well – so I was not constantly eyeing the promotion ladder. I liked driving, and I passed both the standard and advanced police driving courses, after which I was posted to road patrol duties.

One day I was sent for by the Chief Constable, John McKay, and interviewed about my future in the force. He wanted to know why I had not taken my promotion examinations. It had frankly never occurred to me, though I had always achieved high marks on the training courses I had attended. He asked me to state when I would take the examination, and explained that he was writing my answer on my personal file. Having opted for the first opportunity, I came near the top of the list of successful candidates. By this time our first daughter, Susan, had been born, in March 1964, and Barbara was expecting our second, Pamela, who was born in March 1967, two months after I qualified for promotion to the rank of sergeant.

For six months I worked in the Force Information Room. But by now I had decided on the career I really wanted: to be a detective. One chief superintendent told me I would never make it: he said I was not 'Hail, fellow, well met' enough for the job. But thankfully that old definition of what CID work is about was dying out, and Detective Chief Inspector Tom Butcher gave me the chance I had been longing for. I became an aide to CID.

I started my CID career at Whitworth Street Police Station in the centre of Manchester, which was responsible for the inner city districts of Ardwick, Levenshulme, Longsight, Gorton and West Gorton. It was a marvellous time in my working life. I can honestly say that I have enjoyed every aspect of my career as a policeman, but those early days, and the later period I spent as a detective sergeant, were perhaps the best. I met many friends to whom I am still close. Detectives usually work in pairs, and care goes into choosing who should be partnered with whom. My partner was John Simons, now a detective superintendent and we have remained the best of friends ever since.

Although it was rewarding, it was hard work and hours were long – we were not paid overtime in those days. Detectives at the end of a hard day often drink together to unwind: my family saw very little of me at this time, which I regret – I missed much of my daughters' early years. But Barbara was always very understanding, and shouldered all the burdens of family and home. I knew many good CID officers who returned to uniform because of the strain on their families, but Barbara never complained; in fact it was her encouragement that made me realize I could go higher up the ladder.

I learned a lot about crime and its detection in those years. Manchester is a tough city – there is always plenty going on that should not be going on. I was involved with all aspects of crime, from simple theft through to murder. In the sixties there was a new but burgeoning drugs problem, mostly with cannabis and 'purple heart' pills being sold in the city centre clubs. Belle Vue was in my area, and there were many woundings in and around the dance halls on Friday and Saturday nights. The lager lout is nothing new: the local beer, Chester's bitter, was referred to as 'lunatic soup' because of the effect a few pints could have on some of our customers.

By 1969 John Simons and I were both feeling disenchanted with the hours we were working, and hankered after being our own bosses. We both gave in our notice and bought a lorry with the idea of going into the haulage business.

But one evening I arrived home to find Barbara in great pain. She was taken to hospital, where it was discovered that she was seriously ill, with blood clotting in her lungs. The cause, they eventually discovered, was the birth control pill. Susan and Pamela were very small, and without the help of our neighbours, Gert and John Turner, I don't know what I would have done. My boss, Detective Chief Inspector Geoff Rimmer, sent me home from work to look after my family. His consideration and compassion greatly impressed me, and when later I achieved high rank myself I did not forget his example.

Barbara's illness also made me take stock of my life. I knew that if we went into business on our own, John and I would end up working all the hours God sends to make a go of it. And I realized just how much I had been missing in my family life, anyway. I decided that

261

from then on my career was important – but not more important than my family. I withdrew my notice.

For the next twelve months I worked at Willett Street Station, between Oldham Road and Rochdale Road. It was an old Victorian building in an interesting area. The crumbling lodging houses had a floating population – some were hard-working citizens, but there were too many who supplemented their dole with crime.

In 1970 I was promoted to sergeant in the central CID administration department of Manchester and Salford Police. I had no experience of administration, and would not have thought I was particularly suited to it. But it was a tremendously broadening experience, in which I had to deal with many of the problems of a big force. I was there for only eight months but I learned about what is involved in running a force – the sort of detail you do not think about when you are away from headquarters.

My next move was as a detective sergeant, to Mill Street Station, in the Bradford area, where I remained from 1971 until 1973. In many ways detective sergeant is the best rank in the CID. You are fully operational, not too bogged down by administration, but often able to choose your own work. It was a very good time for me, working on a well-run section with excellent staff. It was very busy – my colleagues and I dealt with stabbing, rape, serious indecency and murder. Crime rates were rising, and there had been no corresponding increase in manpower – but we were a dedicated team, with a good detection rate, and our workloads were kept manageable by the long hours we worked.

In 1973 I became a uniformed inspector. I had not been in uniform since 1967, and, like most CID men, would have preferred to stay out of it. At a promotion board I was asked by Assistant Chief Constable Peter Collins 'How would you feel if you were promoted to inspector and posted to Hall Lane Police Station?' Hall Lane, in Wythenshawe, was about as far away from my home in Denton as was possible inside the force area, but I gave the pat answer: 'I'd be delighted.'

But when it did happen, and a few weeks later I was sent to Hall Lane, I was shattered. I would willingly have given up the rank to go back to detective work – a very silly, narrow-minded view, I realize with hindsight. But I forced myself to settle in and start to enjoy my new responsibilities – only to be posted back into CID after twelve weeks, as a detective inspector at headquarters, dealing with central CID administrative matters.

At HQ I had to deal with various bodies outside my own force – the Home Office, the DPP and the Criminal Injuries Compensation Board – as well as coping with the financing of the department. It was a hectic time: we were preparing for the formulation of Greater Manchester Police, a much bigger force than Manchester and Salford Police, with a manpower level increased from approximately two thousand officers to seven thousand.

The head of CID at the time was Charles Horan; he worked out a blueprint for the formation of the centralized CID, incorporating superbly detailed systems for recording crime, its management and progression. But over the coming years crime increased beyond all expectations; it troubled me that so much time was spent writing up the crimes, and not enough time was spent detecting criminals. We ended up with immaculate reports, but fewer crimes solved! If the number of staff is static and the crime rate is rising, and more time is spent writing up reports detection practically grinds to a halt. And that is almost what happened in Manchester.

At the end of 1973 I attended an inspectors' course, first for four weeks at Crewe and then for four months at Bramshill, the Central Police College, in Hampshire. It was a good course, although I think it was far too long for the subjects covered (the structure of courses at Bramshill has since been changed). I am still not sure that the police have got higher policy training right: I think it should be more service-orientated. We should be anticipating problems rather than reacting to them. I was brought up in a small business, and I think the small business precept of value for money is a good one. The police have only recently become aware of the need to budget stringently and put resources to their best use; that course could have been adequately fitted into half the time.

Before I went to Bramshill I was concerned because I knew that quite a number of the officers on the course would be graduates, and almost all of them would be better educated than me. I feared I would be out of my depth, although I had done well on all my previous police courses and had continually broadened my education. At the end of the course, out of 140 participants only 29 were given A grades, and I was one of them; my confidence received an enormous boost.

By the time I returned to the force, the amalgamation had taken place and Greater Manchester Police had been born. Our task at headquarters was to get the systems set up for the largest centralized CID operation in Britain apart from the Metropolitan Police. It was a demanding job, and as ever we were working long hours. So when I received a phone call from my tutor at Bramshill to say that they were working on the nominations for Bramshill scholarships, and to ask if I would consider putting my name forward, I did not know what to do.

Bramshill scholars are policemen who go to university for three years, sponsored by the college and their own force. The possibility of being offered a scholarship represented a tremendous opportunity. I looked at my situation clinically and tried to assess the next three years: I was an inspector, I was well respected, I had a vital job to do in the amalgamation. I felt that when I came back in three years' time the force might have changed out of all recognition, and in the end I decided not to put my name forward. It was the right decision, because in those three years I was promoted from inspector to superintendent. But I do have some personal regrets – university would have been a great experience.

I worked for a short time in the commercial fraud squad, and then went back to the CID administration department as chief inspector. Eventually I took on the responsibility of a superintendent, covering for one who was at Bramshill and who was subsequently moved to another department. It was expected that I would get the promotion to go with the work I was doing, but the new Deputy Chief Constable, James

Brownlow, did not believe in men being promoted within the department in which they were working. The policy has a lot to recommend it; but it was strange, after spending ten months doing the job, to find myself training the superintendent who would take over from me.

I left headquarters to take up an appointment as a detective chief inspector on the D division of the force, a busy inner city division. For most of the time I was working from Didsbury Police Station, a great place to be based: the station was well-run and the staff were capable and experienced. I was the most senior officer at the station, king of my own castle for the first time. In management terms it had few of the problems I had been dealing with daily at headquarters, but it brought me back to dealing with crime again, which I enjoyed. The work was varied, and the workload was manageable. Some of the local areas had a high and difficult crime load, and there were a number of major criminals living thereabouts.

Then came the Royal Commission on Criminal Procedure. I was selected by Charles Horan, the head of CID, to be secretary to the Manchester working party that would report to the Commission. Our task was to research controversial areas of police work: powers of arrest, rights to search and so on. The 'sus' laws – the power of the police to stop people on suspicion that they had been involved in a felony – were under a lot of scrutiny, and there had been a great deal of criticism of them.

I was disappointed to leave Didsbury but soon became absorbed in my new task. I saw it as a unique opportunity to get the system right for the future, because the police were experiencing difficulties in dealing with certain aspects of crime. They did not have the right powers, and in other areas were being accused of misusing the powers they did have.

Unfortunately, the Royal Commission report resulted in the Police and Criminal Evidence Act, which I believe is a disaster. We are now completely out of balance – the police have lost too much ground. The procedures involved, combined with the right of silence, mean that the criminals now have a great advantage. The Act has imposed many bureaucratic demands on police forces, without allowing them any extra resources to cope with these demands. The right of silence, which means that a suspect can say nothing without his refusal to speak being construed as an indication of guilt, needs to be reviewed.

I was only with the working party for a few weeks. I set it up, analysed what we would be doing, and was about to set about the research when I was called before another promotion board. John Stalker, who was a superintendent in the Discipline and Complaints Department, responsible mainly for administration and report reading, left in February 1978 to become head of CID in Warwickshire, a very small force. My background spanned both investigation and administration, so I was considered qualified for the position. I passed the promotion board and spent three days with John, learning about the department, before he left.

John and I had known each other throughout our police service, and it was a smooth handover. I was an acting superintendent for a few months, and the rank was confirmed later that year. There was plenty to do. Complaints by members of the public against the police are always investigated by senior officers. This task used to be limited to superintendents, but the Police and Criminal Evidence Act has widened the net to include chief inspectors, which spreads the load, but still means that a senior officer is often taken away from his normal duties. Many of the complaints are, unfortunately, petty.

And of course the professional criminals and their lawyers know how to play the system: as soon as they are charged they often allege malpractice to obtain a confession, or ill treatment by the arresting officers. When their case comes up in court it sounds good to say they have made a complaint against the police. When the case is over, the complaint is often dropped. The solicitors who stoop to this practice are well known to the staff of the Discipline and Complaints Department.

Of course there are very many respectable and responsible members of the legal profession, but misuse of the system is a dangerous practice and could affect the attitude of investigating officers dealing with genuine complaints. To avoid this situation, attitudes are monitored and a great deal of care is taken in selecting officers to investigate complaints, particularly serious ones.

I know that many people feel that there should be an entirely independent body investigating complaints against the police, and in a perfect world we would all agree. But I don't think the people who put this idea forward appreciate the size of the job, the enormity of the organization that would have to be set up to cope with it, and the vast costs involved. My department dealt with the complaints against just one police force: across the country the number of complaints each year runs into many thousands.

The major aspect of my job was to read the reports prepared by the senior officers investigating the complaints and to put a balanced view on them for the Deputy Chief Constable, who is the overall head of Discipline and Complaints in a police force. I also had to write to the complainants. There was a mountain of paperwork in front of me every day, and it was difficult to find the time to do much investigating myself until Superintendent Philip Arnfield joined the department. Then we split the work between us, and I was then able to take a more active part in investigation. I needed all the time I could get, because at the end of 1978 I was faced with a problem that would dominate my police work for the next four years.

21

Complaints from the public about the police some well founded, some not – are a normal, everyday occurence; but complaints about policemen by other policemen are a different matter. They do not happen often: most day-to-day differences between individual officers are settled well below the official structure of the Discipline and Complaints Department. So when I was alerted by other detectives that some members of the CID at Platt Lane Police Station, in the Chorlton area of the city, were possibly helping criminals and sharing in the proceeds of crime, I took the allegations very seriously.

I had to monitor events discreetly for a few months. A small number of people were interviewed and evidence began to accumulate, but it was impossible to go any further; one key witness, in particular, could not be traced. The situation obviously needed a full investigation, so after consultation with my senior officers we decided that I would set up a small squad of detectives, and that I would be taken off other duties for the six to eight weeks we thought would be needed. That was in September 1979; it was 1983 before investigation of the case was completed, culminating in two long and difficult trials.

It would have been possible for the inquiry to have been handled by another force, which would have guaranteed impartiality. But the case involved dealing with inner city informants and criminals, and an outside team would have found it difficult to trace them and understand all the ramifications. On balance, it seemed that a successful investigation – whether it ended in prosecution or exoneration – was more likely if it was conducted internally. It is easier to opt for an external team. You throw the inquiry on to the resources of another force, who have to provide valuable manpower; and you can never be accused of it not being independent. But there are times when it is right to and I believe this was one of them. A totally independent inquiry team for all allegations against the police would be the ideal, but it would be enormously expensive and would need a very high standard of investigator when dealing with inquiries like this one. It has been said on many occasions that you don't get vicars coming forward to give evidence about corrupt policemen; you are inevitably dealing with criminals, which requires experience and careful handling.

The allegations centred around a house in Caldervale Avenue, Chorlton-cum-Hardy, the home of a woman who was alleged to deal in stolen property. A detective sergeant and three detective constables were said to have been in the house when stolen property was brought in, and it was alleged that they set up break-ins and shared in the proceeds.

I chose, as I was later to do in the Moors inquiry, to work with a small hand-picked team – Detective Inspector David Booth, Detective Inspector Norman Collinson, Detective Inspector Chris Baythorpe and Detective Sergeant Rob Murray. Later Detective Inspector John Simmons, Detective Inspector Joe Joyce and Detective Sergeant Ron Gaffey joined the team to allow some of them to take leave and deal with other urgent commitments.

I could not recall an investigation like it before in Greater Manchester Police: nobody in the force, apart from my senior officers, was aware of our duties. This was why it was important that all the members of the team were of the highest integrity – it was essential that they should not discuss the case with anyone else, even their friends. Investigating another policeman is perhaps the most difficult job any police officer has to do. You feel isolated because you cannot discuss what you are doing with your colleagues, and this affects your social life as well as your working one. In choosing these men I had to be sure they had the strength of character to cope with the added pressures of this kind of investigation. Time was to prove that they understood my terms of reference – simple ones which should be followed in any police investigation: show no bias or favour to either side. The team was totally dedicated. As with the Moors team, they were given the opportunity to speak their minds and told that they could leave at any time without prejudice.

Inevitably what we were working on became known, because the detectives at the centre of the allegations were suspended from duty. But the details remained confidential, and we found resentment from some CID officers who would have liked the whole thing swept under the carpet. 'When are you going to come back and do some proper police work?' was a question the team were constantly asked, usually by officers senior to themselves who would not have been capable of the sensitive kind of investigation involved. Remarks were made by those who did not know the facts, suggesting that we were involved in a witchhunt – this was just

269

not true, for we would have been delighted to have found the allegations completely unfounded.

Early in 1980 we were not making any positive progress, and I was just about to close the inquiry when we had a lucky break. A key witness whom we had been unable to trace was arrested for something else entirely, and we were able to interview him. He confirmed what we had suspected and opened up many avenues of investigation.

At this stage I faced a difficult personal decision. I was given the command of a CID division, a posting that I wanted more than anything else at this point in my career. I knew that if I took over the responsibility of the post I would probably have had to close down the inquiry – which would have pleased some of my colleagues. One or two senior policemen had been urging me to wrap it up; even though they did not support corruption, they would have preferred to see the inquiry ending with the officers concerned being warned off, and no scandal for the force. But I did not believe this option was open to me, nor was it the proper course to take.

It was important to me for my investigation to stand scrutiny by anyone. At this stage there was not enough evidence against the officers concerned to go to court nor yet to exonerate them, and I could see there was a protracted investigation ahead. I spent a lonely weekend thinking it through. Barbara could see I was troubled, and I explained all the difficulties of the situation to her. As always, I had her full understanding and support. I don't know how I would have reacted if Barbara had ever said she opposed what I believed my duties demanded of me. I would certainly have respected her opinions and feelings – but luckily she has never put any pressure at all on me, even when she was under pressure herself – and there was plenty of that during this inquiry, and later the Moors inquiry. Although it was a terribly difficult decision, despite the possible effects on my career I knew at the end of that weekend that I had to carry on with the corruption investigation. I however on paper remained posted to command a CID division.

I had interviewed three of the officers named in the

allegations in the first few weeks of the inquiry, when they were suspended from duty. The fourth was not suspended until 1980. Interviewing them was not a problem: it was in their interests to be treated the same way as any other suspect. I knew one of them quite well, and I did wonder whether I could manage to be impartial. But he was not a close friend, and I did not at first know how involved he would be. I also realized that, because of the way policemen change postings, it was almost inevitable that I or any other senior officer would have had some contact with some of them before.

As a result of this investigation, further possible corrupt behaviour was uncovered concerning a detective chief inspector. It was believed he was involved with a criminal and had intervened on his behalf when his premises were being searched.

I submitted a report of over eight hundred pages plus supporting statements of evidence to the Director of Public Prosecutions at the end of 1980, and the team disbanded to go back to normal duties. I was transferred and became deputy to a chief superintendent who was heading a computer project, looking at the use and introduction of computers to the Command and Control of the Force and the Criminal Records Office. But I was only there for a few weeks. At the end of January 1981 the DPP decided there was substance in the corruption allegations, so the team had to reassemble. The committal hearing was held at the end of 1981, and we were hoping that the trials would take place early in 1982. In fact they were not held until a year later, mainly because of defence demands.

When it finally came to court, the first trial lasted for nine weeks. I was in the witness box for a week; although it was not a new experience for me, it was strange giving evidence in a trial with police officers in the dock. The jury went out on 10 March 1983 and returned their verdicts on the following Monday: it was unusual for Manchester Crown Courts to be open over the weekend, and city centre public houses, which would normally have been closed, stayed open to provide refreshment for the police, public and press.

The scene inside the court building was one that I and my colleagues had never witnessed before: large groups of people standing around in near silence in an otherwise deserted building, anxiously waiting for the return of the jury. There was an eerie feeling about the place.

The jury returned a guilty verdict on one of the policemen, and on the civilian who was charged with them. The police officer was sentenced to four years' imprisonment, and the civilian to two years. The others were found not guilty. Disciplinary proceedings followed. The detective sergeant was retired on medical grounds. The two detective constables later appeared before a disciplinary tribunal: one was dismissed and one was required to resign the service. I am pleased to hear that they have all now rebuilt their lives outside the police service. The trial of the detective chief inspector followed immediately, and he was found guilty and sentenced to a total of four years' imprisonment.

When I returned to the Discipline and Complaints Department I was promoted to chief superintendent in charge of the department. My immediate boss was Ralph Lees, the Assistant Chief Constable who had special responsibilities for discipline and complaints. I had never worked with him before, and we came from different police backgrounds: his was predominantly uniform, mine was predominantly CID. But whatever misgivings I may have had disappeared immediately; I have never worked for a better boss.

He is one of the strongest men I have ever met, but many do not appreciate this because he is quiet and polite – unlike some senior officers, who exert their authority by being loud and aggressive. He is fair, but I never found him frightened to face any problem. It was refreshing to work with someone who was open and honest with me. He never asked me to deal with anything in a way that caused me trouble with my conscience: he would not sweep things under the carpet to avoid scandal.

He and I did not always agree. But we always

respected each other's position, and knew that the other was arriving at his opinions for good reasons. I worked closely with several chief officers after moving to headquarters in 1970, but none impressed me more in overall ability than Ralph Lees.

During the investigation of the corruption case I was able to take a close look at the workings of the CID, and I saw how bogged down in paperwork detectives were getting. I was not the only one feeling disquiet – there were rumblings from all ranks in the CID. Manchester had always had a good detection rate against crime, but the system, coupled with both the rise in crime and the reduction in overtime caused by budget cuts, meant that our figures were sliding. The judge at the corruption trial, while praising the work of the investigation team, had also criticized CID procedures. So a working party was set up to look at ways of cutting down on non-productive writing and bringing in a fully automated reporting and management system. Many officers, including me, contributed to the review by the working party, whose recommendations were acted upon in January 1985.

In the autumn of 1984 Ralph Lees took on the responsibility for crime, and asked me if I would return to the CID. I did not even have to think about that decision – CID work was always my first love. In January 1985 I went as deputy to Detective Chief Superintendent Ken Foster, who was the head of the CID, but it was soon decided to split the department into two: I was given command of operations, while he took charge of policy and administration. Ken retired soon afterwards, because he was not completely happy with the changes that were being introduced.

For me, being head of CID operations was the fulfilment of an ambition. But any feelings of satisfaction and self-congratulation I might have had were tempered by my realization that it was going to be a difficult time. A lot of changes had already been implemented, but more were clearly needed. The Serious Crimes Squad, for instance, was fragmented, with contingents in different areas of the force. I wanted to centralize them, recognizing that, although murder was still a major priority, the growth in armed

273

robberies and organized crime needed more attention. My proposal was opposed by three of the four detective chief superintendents in the force, but I had the support of Ralph Lees, and the centralization was implemented. It proved to be a success story, and those who had had misgivings quickly put their support behind the changes.

Other types of crime were growing, too. We had seen a huge mushrooming in the number of 'bogus officials' crimes, in which men or women knocked on old people's doors claiming to be from the council, the Gas Board, the Electricity Board, the Water Board – any official cover that would get them into the house so that they could steal property. Statistically, the crimes might not look important: the amounts stolen were not usually very large. But these are the lowest form of criminals, and if challenged by the victims they often resort to violence. Even if they don't, the intrusion into the home and the loss of money and valuables is distressing enough to cause some pensioners simply to fade away and die: I had seen it happen.

There was also a need to enlarge the Drug Squad. I was determined to try to tackle this increasing problem from the top, by targeting the big suppliers in the city. The squad desperately needed new vehicles and better communications. Again, with the support of Ralph Lees I was able to double the size of the squad quickly. But as there was no extra money available to fund this growth, it had to be found from other departments. Crime Prevention and Juvenile Liaison were areas that, historically, were part of the CID, but with changing approaches to these areas of police work there was no real reason for them to stay so. Efforts were also made to take as much clerical and administrative work as possible away from detectives, and give it to civilian clerks and administrators.

With the help of Ralph Lees I also created a dedicated surveillance unit and increased the staff and changed the direction of the work of the Criminal Intelligence Unit, because I felt that these were areas of CID work that had to be improved in order for us to be successful in our battle against professional and violent criminals. Budget provisions were made and a working party set up to implement the use of computer equipment in the investigation of major crimes, mainly murders.

My sole aim was to get as many detectives as possible operational. The Home Office was stressing the need for forces to become more efficient, and that was what I intended. But change does not bring popularity, and there were some officers who resented what I was doing. I did not worry about it: you cannot afford to court popularity, only respect. And I was also being supported by detectives who had realized that change was long overdue, as well as by Ralph Lees and the Chief Constable, Jim Anderton.

When Ken Foster retired, Chief Superintendent John Thorburn took his job as head of CID Policy and Administration. We had known each other since we were detective constables, and at first I welcomed his appointment. We were aware of each other's strengths and weaknesses, and he supported the changes that were being made in the CID. Unfortunately, it seemed to me that John would have liked control of the operational side of the CID. He would have liked to change seats, putting me in charge of Policy and Administration and himself in charge of Operations. I preferred things the way they were.

While John Thorburn was away in Northern Ireland working on the inquiry into the Royal Ulster Constabulary with John Stalker, I took over his job as head of Policy and Administration as well as my own. I was soon to reopen the Moors inquiry, and I was already heading another important inquiry into the affairs of a Manchester businessman called Kevin Taylor. It was events surrounding this latter inquiry that would eventually lead to the suspension of John Stalker, the Deputy Chief Constable of Greater Manchester Police.

PART SIX

THE STALKER AFFAIR

22

After his resignation as Deputy Chief Constable of Greater Manchester Police, John Stalker appeared on the *Wogan* show. Terry Wogan asked him if he thought someone had been 'out to get him', Stalker replied: 'I look at the facts. If you ask me as a policeman, I'm not sure. If you ask me as a man, I am.'

With those words he endorsed the conspiracy theory that had been rampant throughout the British press since 29 May 1986, when John Stalker was removed from the Northern Ireland inquiry and instructed to stay at home. Headlines had screamed: 'Police boss is gagged', 'How Stalker was stopped in his tracks', 'Top cop probe is a set-up' and 'The hounding of Stalker'.

He then wrote a book on that theme, tying in his suspension from the force with what was happening in Northern Ireland. In that book and in newspaper articles I have been criticized for my part in the Stalker Affair, and if I do not comment on what he has said about me it might be construed that I accept his version of events. I do not.

John Stalker's suspension had nothing to do with his role in Northern Ireland. It was a decision based entirely on information and events that occurred in Manchester. I was the person who initiated the 'Stalker Affair' – and at no time did I have any detailed knowledge of what was going on in Northern Ireland.

In May 1984 two months after he was promoted from Assistant Chief Constable to Deputy Chief Constable of Greater Manchester Police, Stalker was asked if he would head an investigation into the conduct of the Royal Ulster Constabulary, in particular the circumstances which allegedly led to police fabricating cover stories in three incidents in which six men had been shot dead. He set up a team of senior Manchester detectives, and in June 1984 they went out to Northern Ireland to start their difficult and sensitive job. Although I knew some of them well, the nature of their investigation and the difficulties they were facing were never discussed with me. Just as I always expected complete integrity from the teams I formed to work with me on difficult inquiries, so John Stalker was given the highest loyalty and professionalism by his men.

There are problems in trying to explain what happened in Manchester, because I am restricted by an ongoing legal matter the current prosecution of Kevin Taylor, a man who, in John Stalker's own words, he 'regarded as a friend'. Because of this constraint, I cannot go into the detail I would wish to about the Stalker Affair.

Even if the matter was not *sub judice,* I would not risk compromising any current investigations that might end before the courts; in this I differ from John Stalker, who was willing in his book to discuss the details of his Northern Ireland inquiry – before the inquiry had concluded. He excused this by saying that he was not including anything that had not been said before by other commentators. But I believe there is a difference between journalistic leaks and statements from an ex-senior police officer who had been the head of the inquiry. By discussing the details, he confirmed what had previously only been informed speculation.

In 1984 I was a chief superintendent in charge of what was known as the Y department, which investigated complaints against police officers. I had been in the department in a senior rank for over six years, and before that I had been a detective chief inspector on an inner city division. The criticism was later levelled at me that I was inexperienced, and over-reacted to information I received; in fact I had a proven track record for dealing with all levels of corruption in the police, having headed a major inquiry into it in the largest provincial force in the country. John Stalker infers that a more experienced officer would have been more circumspect about the information that came to light about him: I doubt if there were many senior policemen in the whole of Britain with greater relevant experience than I had.

In May that year, at roughly the same time that John Stalker was being approached to take on the Northern Ireland inquiry, I was told, in my capacity as head of the Y department, that a police informant was claiming that the Deputy Chief Constable was corruptly associated with a number of people who were involved in organized crime in Manchester. The news came from an inspector who had been dealing with the informant.

My instinct was to disbelieve it: allegations like this are not uncommon, and I certainly did not give credence to an unconfirmed report from a police informant. My relationship with John Stalker had always been good. We had never had any differences, and I respected him as a colleague. We were not close friends, but we always had a friendly word for each other when we met. As I had done many times with other allegations about other officers, I decided to monitor the situation and establish what substance there might be in these serious charges.

It must be remembered that his appointment to head the Northern Ireland inquiry was kept confidential for security reasons, and was not known about until the inquiry team had begun their work in June 1984. The public did not hear of his role until much later, which would prove to be a crucial factor in countering some of the allegation he subsequently made.

The informant who had made the allegations about Stalker was one David Bertelstein, also known as David Burton, who died of natural causes in Preston Prison in March the following year. He was a criminal who had been passing information to the police for some years. I knew of him, and I knew that the material he passed on varied considerably: he had given us some very valuable information, but on other occasions he had given suspect information. I was experienced at dealing with informants, and I was naturally suspicious of them and their motivation, but on the other hand I knew that it would be wrong to ignore what Bertelstein was saying.

Stalker describes Bertelstein as an 'RUC informant', suggesting that he had some allegiance to Royal Ulster Constabulary officers. I cannot comment on whether Bertelstein ever passed information to the RUC or not, but the crucial fact is the date on which Bertelstein gave information about John Stalker. It was not, as Stalker suggests, in February 1985, when he had reached a critical point in his Northern Ireland inquiry;

it was in early May 1984, before anyone knew that Stalker was going to Northern Ireland. I personally interviewed Bertelstein on 22 June 1984, when he reiterated his accusations against Stalker at a time when the Northern Ireland inquiry was still cloaked in great secrecy. There is no possibility, therefore, that at this stage David Bertelstein was being prompted to lodge his allegations as part of a conspiracy to get Stalker out of Northern Ireland. Even if the news of Stalker's appointment had leaked out it was far too soon to guess what stance he would take. There was no possible Northern Ireland motive for wanting to smear him.

But I was concerned at the time that it might be a malicious accusation made for some other reason. Criminals often have scores to settle with senior policemen, sometimes stretching back years to when they were junior officers. To institute a major inquiry on the basis of accusations like these was not warranted. Corruption must never be overlooked, but there is a delicate balance between destroying the morale of officers and the force by over-reacting, and ignoring valid information.

Then, totally independently of anything Bertelstein had said, I received more information about John Stalker's connections. A senior detective superintendent, now retired, came to see me. While playing golf he had met a respectable Manchester businessman who had told him that John Stalker was connected with a man called Kevin Taylor, who associated regularly with people believed to be involved in serious organized crime in Manchester.

The superintendent was a very experienced detective, and he was obviously deeply concerned about what he had heard. He didn't know me well. We were not friends. He came to see me officially in my capacity as head of the Discipline and Complaints Department. If he had thought it was nonsense he could have dismissed it – but he was worried enough to report it to me.

I listened to what he had to say and then asked him to commit it to paper. Quickly and discreetly I confirmed that Kevin Taylor was a businessman with no criminal convictions, but that from time to time he was indeed believed to associate with a group of people whom the police suspected of controlling organized crime in Manchester. The group were nick-named the Quality Street Gang, and were often referred to as the QSG – a nickname derived from a TV commercial for Quality Street chocolates.

I also discovered that Taylor's connection with John Stalker was real enough: Taylor had been a guest of Stalker's at senior officers' mess functions at Greater Manchester Police. That was a matter of record. Further inquiries, which for legal reasons I cannot go into, had given me more information about Taylor and his associates; this, together with the information from the police informant and the superintendent, was enough to make me realize I had to report the matter to my senior officers. I had already talked informally to my boss, Ralph Lees; on 17 July I submitted a report to him.

I remain convinced that I took the right course of action. What else could I have done? I knew that Stalker was the Deputy Chief Constable and that he had responsibility for discipline and complaints. I could have gone to see him – but that would have been grossly unfair to him. It would have put both of us in an invidious position should it have later been felt that a proper inquiry into the matter had to be launched. If I presented him with that sort of allegation it could have attracted criticism later, even if the allegation was unfounded. It would have been an improper way of reacting – and it was in his interests, as well as in those of the force and the public, that the correct procedure was followed. So I applied the system just as I would had it been a detective constable who was being accused. There should be no difference: allegations of corruption are the same whoever they are against. I would not have gone to a constable with the allega-tions; no more would I go to the Deputy Chief Constable. I was not being vindictive. If allegations of corruption were made against me, I would like them to be investigated properly and fully, so that when I was exonerated there could be no room for doubt; I assumed John Stalker would feel the same way.

Apart from the allegations against John Stalker, my report also covered other discoveries I had made about serious crime in Manchester, which I knew needed more attention than it was getting. As a result, I was appointed to head a select team of experienced detectives to investigate it. I was told by my senior officers that I was to report any further information concerning Stalker that came to my notice, but that I was not to make direct inquiries about him.

The team started work at the beginning of 1985, and we made extensive investigations into various areas of criminal activity in the city, as well as the activities of Kevin Taylor and the use of his yacht *Diogenes*. Matters relating to John Stalker were reported by me: one concerned a holiday that Stalker had been on with Taylor, who had paid the air fares.

I had no knowledge then about the details of Stalker's work in Northern Ireland. I learn from reading his book that he believes the searching of Kevin Taylor's home was timed to correlate with a significant stage of his inquiry: this is simply not true. I had given this part of the inquiry to Detective Inspector Tony Stephenson, a devoutly religious man known by all his colleagues to be of the highest integrity. There were no instructions from above to search Taylor's home; the decision to apply for authority to search was a normal development of our inquiry – Inspector Stephenson merely approached me when he felt this was the next step to be taken.

The search revealed a photograph album containing pictures of Stalker and his wife as guests at a party at Taylor's home. It confirmed what I had been told about the reputations of a number of the other guests. In his book Stalker scoffs at the idea that some of the people who were later discussed with him by Colin Sampson could be members of a criminal 'group'. He refers to the fact that they have only very minor criminal convictions, which he uses to dismiss any suggestion that they could be involved in serious crime. But good professional criminals often have no, or very few, convictions; the man with the long criminal record is the habitually unsuccessful criminal, as experienced detectives like Mr Stalker know. It is naïve to think that

283

all criminals have criminal records.

The photographs had been seen not only by the inquiry team but by other officers assisting them because, several premises had been searched at the same time that day. I realized, therefore, that the pictures might now be discussed openly around the force, and there was even a risk that what they showed would get to the ears of the press.

The point had been reached when, for the sake of everyone concerned, an inquiry had to be held. It was obviously not my decision to launch it, but I believe it was the right decision. I believe the point had been passed when John Stalker could have simply been approached and asked to explain things: in any case that route really only applies in very minor cases, and this was not, in my view, a minor complaint. I was not pre-judging Stalker: I simply felt that the weight of information we now had before us demanded a thorough and fair investigation.

The Chief Constable, James Anderton, had obviously been kept informed. If the news had ever got out that, on the strength of the information that was before him, he had not ordered an inquiry, he would have been accused of a cover-up – of not treating his Deputy Chief Constable in the same way that a lower-ranking policeman would have been treated. There would have been an enormous scandal. If he had not acted properly, and this had been found out, I believe he would have had to resign.

Those who say he did not act properly can only be arguing that it should have been swept under the carpet. This is why I have found it hard to understand the role of the media, who sided so heavily with the idea that the whole thing was a put-up job inspired by Mr Stalker's work in Northern Ireland. But they would have been baying for James Anderton's blood had he handled it any differently.

From what I know of him, I feel a second reason for James Anderton acting the way he did was because he believed that it was right. He was not merely trying to protect his own position. I'm sure he considered the matter very deeply and took the decision to order an inquiry because that was the fairest and most honourable thing to do – fair to John Stalker, as well as to himself and the reputation of the force.

Mr Anderton is a man of tremendous personal strength and conviction. I worked closely enough to him, as head of Discipline and Complaints and then as head of the CID, to have formed my own opinion of him, and it is a very high opinion. His religious convictions are well known, but he does not preach them at those around him. He has a very strong personality, but also has the facility of making people feel at ease in his company. He is well read and can talk fluently on most subjects. Professionally he has tremendous judgement, common sense and honesty. He thrives on hard work, frequently starting his working day before 7a.m. and not finishing until after 10p.m. He is personally capable of doing any task that any police officer of any rank ever has to undertake: he leans on nobody. Thanks to him, I believe the efficiency of the Manchester force stands above any other in the country. He is the supreme police officer: I do not think there is anyone in Britain at the present moment who can measure up to him.

His comments have often been outspoken, and have attracted a great deal of publicity. But he has spoken from the depths of his own convictions; others would have kept quiet in order to further their own careers. He has, I think, sacrificed his own career for the sake of saying what he believes. Even those who do not agree with him have to admire his strength of character in doing that. It was this same strength that led him to make the decision to ask for an inquiry into John Stalker. Obviously he consulted high-level Home Office officials, and they agreed with him.

It is a normal, well-established police practice that when an officer is being investigated he is removed from any sensitive inquiry he may be engaged upon. This protects the integrity of that inquiry; otherwise, those whom he was investigating would have a weapon to use against him and the findings of his inquiry.

It would not have been right to allow John Stalker to continue in his role as Deputy Chief Constable with responsibility for discipline and complaints, or as head of a very difficult and sensitive inquiry. There was nothing sinister in his removal from duty, despite the way he has presented the sequence of events in his book. No one in Manchester wanted anything but the Northern Ireland inquiry to be concluded in a thorough and proper way. It is nonsense to suggest that I and others wanted to hinder Stalker's work there. But it was clear at this stage that the work on that inquiry would have to be completed by someone else.

I believe he understood that. He has had to decide to take officers off duty himself. He knows that officers have to be suspended, often before there is any hard evidence against them, because a proper investigation often cannot be carried out while they remain on duty. It is always a difficult decision, but a necessary one.

The Deputy Chief Constable operationally runs the force. How can anyone conduct an inquiry into him if he is still on duty? Initially John Stalker was on extended leave for a month, before the decision to suspend him, which shows that a lot of thought went into the handling of the affair. It was realized, I'm sure, that there would be an outcry about his removal from the Northern Ireland Inquiry, although I don't think anyone expected quite the media attention that resulted.

If there had been any desire in high places to subvert the Northern Ireland inquiry, there would have been far easier ways to achieve it. If that was the motive it was a very public way of doing it – and a very ineffective way too: the only person removed from the inquiry was John Stalker. The rest of his team – the ones making the discoveries that were causing some people in Northern Ireland headaches – were still working. I don't know every member of that team personally, but those whom I do know are strong individuals who would never have countenanced any cover-up, and would know how to expose any attempt at one.

The inquiry was, in the end, concluded in the same way as if Stalker had stayed in place. It was acknowledged that there was evidence of malpractice, although in the final analysis the Director of Public Prosecutions for Northern Ireland and the Attorney

General decided it was not in the public interest to institute criminal proceedings. Stalker himself could not have achieved any more.

It was naïve of the media to believe that, because John Stalker was no longer there, the whole inquiry was compromised. But they seemed to buy the conspiracy theory hook line and sinker, and every other issue was ignored. From the moment Stalker decided to talk to the reporters who had gathered outside his home they embraced his version of events, despite assurances that his extended leave and subsequent suspension had nothing to do with Northern Ireland.

He said that he faced three options: to remain silent inside his house, to go away with his family (which he said was impossible, as he lives on a smallholding) or to face the cameras. Whilst all of us had enormous sympathy with him and his family because of the constant press attention they were suffering, I do not believe most senior police officers would have chosen to air their views publicly whilst an inquiry was in progress.

But it would appear that John Stalker was no stranger to using journalists for his own ends. After he had resigned from the police force, the editor of the *Manchester Evening News*, Michael Unger, who had championed him throughout, published diaries chronicling his involvement with Stalker. To the amazement of senior policemen in Manchester, Stalker, the diaries revealed, had first telephoned Unger – and taken him into his confidence about the Northern Ireland inquiry – in May 1985, a year before he was taken off the inquiry. According to Unger who was himself surprised, Stalker phoned him and saw him several times during that year, giving him a lot of information about what was happening in what should have been a top-secret inquiry. The members of the inquiry team who were still with it at the time the Unger diaries were published were so incensed that they wrote an open letter to Sir John Hermon, head of the RUC, disassociating themselves from this unethical behaviour.

The publicity following Stalker's removal from duty was so enormous that it placed a great deal of pressure

287

on Colin Sampson, the Chief Constable of West Yorkshire Police, who had been called in to conduct the inquiry into his activities and to take over the Northern Ireland inquiry. The Manchester Police Authority also suffered in the same way. An inquiry of this kind cannot be hurried if it is to be done properly: regrettably for all concerned, particularly John Stalker in my opinion, Sampson was under too much pressure and rushed the inquiry. He also brought into the inquiry the question of misuse of police vehicles, which I do not believe was wise; it clouded more important issues. Nor did the Police Authority take their time, or solicit enough advice. They ignored Sampson's recommendation that 'the evidence supports, indeed demands, that it be ventilated before an independent tribunal', and returned Stalker to duty.

On the day that they were making their decision on the report, Stalker was leaning heavily on them to give him a hearing. I found that strange: the Authority were deciding whether he was to be the subject of a tribunal or whether he was to be reinstated, and they were being guided by an independent report. I did not feel that was the time or place for him to be presenting his case: the report was not a prosecution document that required balancing with a defence – it was impartial.

The Authority was newly formed and inexperienced. I suspect that if they faced the same problem today they would deliberate more on it, and would probably come to a different decision. Returning Stalker to duty, without totally exonerating him, seemed to me a very unsatisfactory conclusion. His knuckles were publicly rapped; he was told by the Police Authority that he should be 'more circumspect in his political and criminal associations in future in view of his high office'.

What I found hard to understand then – and still do now – is that he accepted this. The Deputy Chief Constable, in charge of discipline and complaints, needs to be whiter than white. He should have demanded a full hearing at a tribunal in order to clear his name completely. Instead, he was shouting for an early resolution to the affair, turning to anyone for support of his reinstatement.

He said he did this for the sake of his family, and I can sympathize greatly with their predicament. But many other police officers have been put under pressure while inquiries into their behaviour have been carried out, and their families have had to shoulder the burden quietly. At his rank, Stalker should have set an example by coping with quiet dignity while everything was properly and openly resolved. He should have done what other officers are expected to do: sit quietly, despite the strain they are under.

During the time that John Stalker was being investigated, the police were at pains not to name Kevin Taylor. Taylor named himself to the press: he came forward and declared that he was the businessman whose association with Stalker was causing all the problems. Afterwards, he bleated about the effect on his business. I believe the press would probably have found out about him anyway. But he invited the publicity, even after we advised his solicitor against him going public.

In his book John Stalker describes a meeting with me when he returned to duty; that account does not tally with my memory of the hour and forty minutes I spent in his office on 26 September 1986. But he was careful in what he said, and was at pains not to accuse me directly of anything.

He claims that he told me I had presented an over-inflated story to the Chief Constable, who had acted on it to the extreme detriment of the force, me, himself and his family. The Sampson report, he said, was 'Being analysed by journalists line by line'. According to him it contained a number of inaccuracies, but he did not know whether this was due to the incompetence of the investigators and report writers, or whether Sampson had been deliberately misled by officers who supplied him and his team with information during the course of their inquiries. He said that some readers of the report were under the impression that I had exaggerated information to bring about the formal inquiry against him.

289

The strength of my response clearly shocked him. I told him that with the benefit of hindsight I would take exactly the same action if I was faced with the same situation again. He seemed quite taken aback at these words, which were intended to show my contempt for what he had just said.

He said he had been told deliberate lies by an officer – but he stressed it was not me, nor was he making any allegations against me. But during the period of his suspension he had been approached by many serving CID officers who criticized my management of the CID. He said he had also spent a couple of hours talking in a lay-by with a serving detective chief inspector. He then detailed the criticism he had received. I was unapproachable as a person and unwilling to listen to my subordinates about matters affecting the CID. They objected to the manner in which I selected officers for promotion or posting. I was thought to lack experience as a senior detective in the management of major incidents, particularly murder inquiries. And many of the departments in the CID, they alleged, had a strong masonic influence which I engineered. Stalker refused to identify the detective chief inspector, but he had told me enough about the man's background for me to feel confident that I knew who it was.

There were also others who were unhappy about the major changes that had taken place in the CID in the past eighteen months – changes introduced by me for the efficiency of the department.

On the accusation of unapproachability it was well known that I – for perhaps the first time in decades – had sought the views of constables and sergeants throughout the CID, as well as colleagues from the uniformed branch, about the way in which crime should be investigated and how detectives should best use their working day. This revolutionary approach had resulted in cutting down paperwork, and meant that we responded to patterns of crime rather than attempting to investigate each crime singly, which was difficult with the workloads that detectives faced. Three pilot schemes had been set up to test this new way of working, the ideas for which had come from the detectives and uniformed officers on the ground.

On the matter of the way I selected officers for promotions and postings, I pointed out that I never selected alone but always in conference with my Area Commanders and the Chief Superintendent in charge of Policy and Administration. Although I had the authority to make the decision on my own, I chose not to.

The point about my lack of experience on murder inquiries came as no surprise – it had been used in the press campaign to damage me. But to hear John Stalker repeating it did surprise me, considering that I have had as much experience at the sharp end of policing as he has. It is a fact that as a superintendent I did not act as an investigating officer on a murder inquiry. The policy in Greater Manchester is for murders to be headed by a senior investigating officer, a detective chief superintendent, usually the area commander, and for him to have as his deputy the CID commander of the division in which the murder was committed, usually a detective superintendent, who becomes the investigating officer. Because of the way my postings had gone, and because of the corruption inquiry that had taken up so much of my time, I had never been in that role. But I had worked on many murder investigations up to that rank, and of course I had overall responsibility for all murder inquiries in my current post as head of CID operations. In the final analysis the policy, conduct and direction of all murder inquiries was mine. And in any case murder, though it is a top-priority inquiry, is not the most technically difficult of offences to investigate. Those who had fed this criticism of my lack of experience – and I know who they are – would be lost if they had to take on a protracted and complicated fraud or corruption inquiry.

Then I went on to refute the comments made about freemasonry. I asked John Stalker to name the departments in the CID in which I was supposed to have engineered a masonic influence and the individual officers concerned. He did not give me a positive answer. I strongly rejected this allegation, and told him I had always appointed people on their individual merits, as the record confirms.

I am indeed a freemason, and have been for twenty-five years. It has never given me any of the benefits sometimes associated with freemasonry, nor have I passed any on. Freemasonry is often criticized for being the preserve of white Protestant males from middle- or upper-class backgrounds, and for the unhealthy favours it is claimed its members enjoy. In my experience it welcomes and enjoys the membership of all races, all religions and all social backgrounds. If all men practised the principles of freemasonry the world would be a far more peaceful and contented place. It has given me many hours of enjoyment, and socially it has brought me and my family a circle of friends outside the police. But I would cease being a mason tomorrow if it demanded that I perform favours for anyone. In my twenty-seven years in the police, only one individual ever let it be known to me that he was a mason in the hope that it would help him. What happened was quite the reverse of what he had expected. My judgement was influenced by the realization that he was the sort of person who thought he could gain favour. In the event he was sadly disappointed.

The degree of my masonic 'bias' can be measured by the fact that the major serious corruption inquiry I carried out culminated in a detective chief inspector, who was a freemason, being prosecuted and sentenced to four years imprisonment; and a detective constable – someone whom Stalker knows and who was also a mason – was dismissed from the service. There are other examples on record of freemasons being admonished and moved by me because they were not performing their duties properly, or were misbehaving. I judge police officers purely on their merits, not on their colour, creed or membership of any group. When promotions were being discussed, if I knew one of the candidates as a friend or through a masonic connection I would declare my interest and allow the others considering the matter to make the decision. Other senior officers would do the same: it is a simple matter of integrity.

In his book Stalker said he told me that, now he was free of the Northern Ireland inquiry, he would be looking more closely at the management of the CID and would be making his own inquiries into the matters that had been brought to his attention during his suspension. At this point his version of the meeting and mine tally: he did say that, but because of his manner I did not answer, but my contempt showed on my face. When he asked me if I resented this I told him firmly that I did – but not because I had anything to hide. He said he wanted to assure me that he felt no personal animosity towards me. I found this statement paradoxical, given what had gone before.

He then asked me, without any preamble, whether I had made it known that three very senior retired detectives were corrupt and had associated with criminals in the city area of Manchester. I had never heard these allegations before, so couldn't understand why he expected me to have passed them on. I told him so, strongly. He backed off, and said that a journalist had told him – the man had not named me personally, but the position I held in the force made it clear he was referring to me – that I had passed on this information.

I told Stalker plainly that if I had been aware of evidence of impropriety by officers of any rank I would have reported the matter formally, and would not have resorted to gossiping, which is what he was trying to lay at my door. I told him I had the highest regard for each of the officers he named: they were men of tremendous professional ability and integrity. Not surprisingly, he refused to name the journalist.

In his book he says that at the end of the meeting – without any reason – I offered to let him search me for recording equipment. Yet again, it is not as he explains it. Would anyone leaving an interview they had covertly wanted to record offer themselves to be searched at its conclusion? If the gesture were to have any meaning it should have been made at the beginning of the interview. What actually happened is that, early in the interview, he asked me if I had a concealed tape recorder. I assured him that I did not. He asked me again, and at this point I stood up, held open my jacket and asked him if he wanted to search me. He said no. I asked if he was recording the interview. He denied this, and pointed to a dictating machine on his desk which was clearly not switched on, as though that was

293

all the proof necessary.

He made an effort to end the interview on friendly terms. We shook hands, and he said it was for the benefit of the force that we should be able to work together. I agreed with him. I had made it clear during the interview that the criticisms that he had presented – and he took pains always to say that the allegations came from someone else – were sufficiently strong for me to feel that I should pass them on. I told him I would be writing a report to the Chief Constable, who could then decide whether he wished to have them investigated. And that's what I did: I submitted a written report of the meeting, including the criticism of me, to Jim Anderton.

John Stalker has been critical in his book of my timing of the search of Saddleworth Moor. He mentions his own 'long and intimate personal knowledge of the case', which means that when he was a junior policeman he was one of hundreds from five different forces who worked on it. He was in no way involved in directing operations or in the management of the case.

He says that he was not kept informed about Myra Hindley's visit to the Moor, and that he denied, to a journalist, the possibility of her making a visit, dismissing it as 'another bizarre press story about the Moors Murders'. But he did know she was going to visit Saddleworth: on the Friday before her visit all the chief officers, the Assistant Chief Constable and the Deputy Chief Constable, were told, in strictest confidence, that the visit would take place shortly. I was not sure until the visit was actually successfully underway that I would be going through with it that day. A couple of times during that night I nearly aborted it, for different reasons. I was not required to inform anyone, minute by minute, what I was doing: the timing was down to me entirely. Once the visit was definitely on, Stalker was informed before he got to his office that morning that Myra Hindley was on her way to Saddleworth Moor. And as far as the journalist who called him the evening before was concerned, Stalker would have had to deny it even had he known the schedule.

He criticizes the timing of the search of the Moor, saying 'I do not believe the search of the Moors should have been reopened in the manner it was. To begin with, it was the wrong time of year.' I would have thought a senior detective would have appreciated that my timing was a ploy to influence Brady and Hindley towards confessing. It was vital to have started the search at the onset of winter, and I was anticipating calling it off soon after I began it, knowing that it would play on the minds of both Brady and Hindley during the months that they were waiting for me to resume it.

In earlier chapters I have gone into the reasoning behind my opening the search in great detail. I expected criticism from the press and public; I am surprised that a man with Stalker's knowledge of investigation joined in. Had I not opened the search when I did, Myra Hindley would not have confessed, Pauline Reade's body might not have been found, and Mrs Johnson would not have known what happened to her son Keith.

As for the accusations that were levelled at me that the Moors Murders case was only reopened to divert attention from the Stalker affair, they are completely without foundation. As I have already explained, the case was reopened at the instigation of the Director of Public Prosecutions and the Home Office, and the search of the Moor was begun when, after discussion with Geoff Knupfer and Gordon Mutch, I decided that was our next step forward. There was no chain of command from above, no sinister motivation.

John Stalker's friend Kevin Taylor is at present awaiting trial on a charge of conspiracy to defraud, having been sent for trial after a six-week committal. For that reason it is impossible to deal with him or his connections here. But before he was charged he instituted some unusual proceedings against the police. He applied in the Chancery Division of the High Court for an order that James Anderton and the Greater Manchester Police Authority should disclose the confidential documents they had produced when they had applied for warrants to search his home and business premises. He argued in a statement to the court that the police inquiries into him had caused 'mental distress and suffering', and that the pressure on his wife and family had been horrific. He said he felt he was being persecuted.

The court decided that the documents should not be released to Taylor, as they were covered by 'public interest immunity'. In other words, it was not in the public interest to hand them over (our investigation into Taylor was still going on). But even before this ruling was made, Taylor's wife Beryl, acting as a director of one of his companies, obtained summonses against me, James Anderton and Detective Inspector Tony Stephenson, alleging conspiracy to pervert the cause of justice by obtaining the search warrants by 'laying false and improper evidence on oath before Manchester City Magistrates Court whereby the said court issued the search warrants'.

We applied to the High Court to have the summonses quashed, and they were. The judge said that obtaining the issue of the summonses was 'oppressive and an abuse of the court'. He also said that the main aim of the action against us was to try to find out the exact stage our investigation had reached, and whether it would result in criminal proceedings.

In his book John Stalker talks about these summonses and remarks that 'for the moment they are not being proceeded with', which mischievously implies that they may be. Yet they have been quashed, and he knew that – yet he omitted to say it, or to quote from the High Court judgment that so resoundingly rejected them. He must appreciate, as an ex-senior policeman, that complicated investigations into business affairs do take a long time. The investigation into Kevin Taylor was not inordinate, and it has resulted in him being charged with criminal offences.

It is regrettable that the last part of this book has had to concern itself answering unnecessary accusations levelled at my colleagues and me by a man who was himself once a colleague. It leaves a bad taste. And it may also leave readers wondering, since our accounts of events are so different, just whom to believe.

All I wish, by responding to the claims he has made, is to redress the balance for myself, for other colleagues who have been named in his book, for Greater

Manchester Police, and for James Anderton. John Stalker has very cleverly run together the timetable of events in Northern Ireland and Manchester to support the conspiracy theory that he, and those journalists who espoused his cause, believe was at the bottom of his removal from duty.

My timetable of events is much simpler: it concerns Manchester only. That is the only sequence of events of which I was aware. It was not until I read John Stalker's book that I knew anything of the ins and outs of the Northern Ireland inquiry. It was the happenings in Manchester, and Manchester alone, that influenced his removal from the inquiry and his eventual suspension from duty. The truth is very often simple: too simple, perhaps, to be palatable for some.

INDEX

299